Male and Female

MALE AND FEMALE

Christian Approaches to Sexuality

edited by
RUTH TIFFANY BARNHOUSE
and URBAN T. HOLMES, III

with a Foreword by John Maury Allin

A Crossroad Book
THE SEABURY PRESS • NEW YORK

Third Printing

The Seabury Press
815 Second Avenue
New York, N.Y. 10017

Printed in the United States of America

LIBRARY OF CONGRESS CATALOGING IN PUBLICATION DATA
Main entry under title: Male and female.

   Bibliography: p.
   1. Sex (Theology)—Addresses, essays, lectures. 2. Sex—Addresses, essays, lectures. 3. Marriage—Addresses, essays, lectures. 4. Women—Addresses, essays, lectures. 5. Homosexuality—Addresses, essays, lectures. I. Barnhouse, Ruth Tiffany,
1923-
II. Holmes, Urban Tigner, 1930-
BT708.M34   261.8′34′1   75-42380   ISBN 0-8164-2118-8

contents

v

foreword

Two major doctrines of religious faith are the doctrine of God and the doctrine of Man. The key theme between the doctrine of the being of God and the doctrine of the nature of Man is relationship. Human nature, like religious faith, can only be understood in terms of relationships, the relationship between the divine being and human beings and the relationships between and among human beings.

Both the universe, in which humanity lives and moves and experiences being and the nature of being, and living and moving within humanity contain vast unexplored realms yet to be understood. Observing, collecting, and measuring data adds to human knowledge and extends exploration. The benefits of understanding are acquired, however, only when the results are correct relationships within one's own nature, between two individuals, among groups of human beings, within the nature of humanity, and within the structure of the universe. While human capabilities may now be sufficient to carry on both exploration of the unknowns of outer space and the inner recesses of human nature simultaneously, the lesson of human history indicates with increasing clarity that the priority of endeavor must be in the development of righteous human relations and interrelations. Previous theories and conclusions concerning human motivation and social drives require renewed analysis.

One component of human nature too long neglected is human sexuality. As a result of ignorance and superstition, naïve encounters, pseudosophisticated pronouncements, and religious prejudices shrouding human sexuality, relationships have been prevented, imperiled, or destroyed.

The Christian Church professes belief in the holiness of God and the potential wholeness within God's creation. Accordingly, the Church's mission is to the wholeness of humanity called into righteous relationship with the holy God.

This book is one effort by the Church to increase the understanding of human sexuality for the sake of better relations. No claim of presenting a complete or comprehensive report is made by the contributors. Rather, all join in an invitation to human beings of both sexes to seek together for a clearer understanding of male and female within the relationship of the God who made them.

John Maury Allin

preface

One of the most interesting things about the current debate over the ordination of women is that, quite unexpectedly, it has raised many new issues concerning the theology of priesthood. This debate has also stirred up questions about human sexuality which at first did not seem to have any connection with the question of women priests. As the editors prepared the outline for this book, recruited authors, and then sifted through the contributions, we became increasingly aware that the possibility of a female presence at the altar has aroused much feeling and stimulated much reflection, which raises deep questions about our understanding of what it means to be human.

All this has confirmed our mutual conviction that the priestly role is highly symbolic. Furthermore, far from being a more or less isolated physiological system for serving the purposes of reproduction or instinctual physical pleasure, sex itself is inextricably woven into the fabric of human personality and affects nearly everything we do. Therefore, the at first surprising fact that the great controversy over the ordination of women has attracted attention which far exceeds any merely theological discussion can be better understood once we realize the depths and complexities that the issue touches in each of us.

The essays in this book, in various ways and from various points of view, discuss masculinity and femininity. It is important to remember that these terms are abstractions, and they refer to qualities that are not the exclusive property of males or females. For example, many men are "nurturing" and "caring," qualities typically associated with women. Some of the authors in this book discuss this androgynous quality of the human psyche at length. It is important, however, to realize that this way of thinking is not related to bisexuality, a term the editors reserve to denote those persons who engage, or would seriously like to engage, in specifically sexual acts with persons of either sex. Now that the old familiar cultural patterns of sexual stereotyping are breaking up, it becomes very important to try to understand the proper relation between masculinity and femininity as qualities of consciousness on the one hand, and specifically male and female behavior, including sexual acts, on the other. Many of the essays address themselves to this question; although, as you will see, there is no unanimity with respect to the answers.

Some recent authors have suggested that people cannot fully understand their relation to themselves or to their world without understanding their own sexuality. Human beings are a seamless unity, not a collection of physical, emotional, mental, and spiritual parts sealed off from one another in watertight compartments. Each quality has some definite effect on every other quality. To the extent that theology begins with the study of humanity—as some theologians say "from below"—and particularly of human consciousness, it must therefore be related to our evolving sense of our own sexuality. In other words, theology continuously changes, and a barometer of this is the role played by our understanding of masculinity and femininity. This is why the editors are convinced that it is inappropriate to rely on the theological understandings of human sexuality of five hundred, a thousand, or two thousand years ago to make decisions for the Church today. At the same time, if the idea of evolution of thought and consciousness is understood, this is not any reason to berate past Church divines for their myopic vision in this area.

The editors hope this book will contribute to the resolution of today's questions with today's theology. We are not unmindful of the past, as will be clear from the essays in the historical section as well as references in other sections. We believe that Christians who ignore tradition do so at their own peril. But we also believe that the lessons of the past must be reworked in contemporary terms before they can be useful in dealing with the problems of the present. This demands a careful weighing of the history of Christian thought as it relates to judgments concerning sexuality.

Before choosing contributors to this book we first decided what subjects most needed discussion and then attempted to find the most competent person in the field. There was also a conscious attempt to find a balance of men and women, clergy and laity, Church people and non-Church people. The perfect balance is no doubt impossible, but we believe that we have achieved a good range of responsible informed viewpoints.

As the manuscripts came in, we were surprised, considering the wide variety of authors, to find that the same conclusions recurred in slightly varying forms. It seems to us that this happened because one can only understand sexuality in our time by coming to grips with the issues of symbolic reality. By this we mean that at the center of human awareness of the world, when that awareness has conscious coherence, lie certain essential symbols that root us in the mystery of being, thereby providing motivation and direction for our quest of the future. Among the most powerful of these symbols is human sexuality.

Readers who are looking for anthropological or theological arguments for or against the ordination of women will find little in this book. However, the earlier companion volume *To Be A Priest* addresses that issue more directly. As it happens, both of the editors also favor women's ordination, but not for the reasons most widely publicized. We do not believe that it is a feminist issue. Rather, we are convinced that ordination of women to priesthood would lead to a much deeper and more balanced—possibly also more risky—understanding of both the nature of God and humanity's relation to God.

It should be clear from the foregoing that the decision to have a man and a woman as coeditors of this book was not taken on merely political grounds, but rather to reflect the kind of integral cooperation between masculine and feminine toward which our culture must move. In addition, we believe that both the theological and psychological perspectives are essential to this enterprise, and it happens that each editor is generally familiar with the discipline of the other.

Two questions might occur to a reader scrutinizing the table of contents. The first would be why there is not more on the subject of pornography. Certainly Dr. Cooper's essay, "A Homeopathy of Sex," is related to this subject, but there is no systematic discussion of it. We think that while pornography is an important issue, it is usually discussed in inadequate terms. To limit consideration of pornography to the question of whether and to what extent the nude human body and its sexual functions may be depicted either visually or literarily is to miss the point. This merely smacks of latter-day puritanism and its obverse, the "playboy philosophy." In our opinion the real issue in pornography is whether the connection between body and soul has been severed. To put it another way: Has sex been dealt with as though it is separate from relationship between persons? If so, the occasion is indeed pornographic. Perhaps the original meaning of the word "pornography"—writing about prostitutes—clarifies what we mean: the reduction of one of the central and integrating symbols of our experience to a mere commodity for the release of tension.

The second question would be why we have devoted so many essays to homosexuality. In today's culture we are being confronted with the fact that the old ways of dealing with homosexuality, by branding it as a peculiarly sinful perversion, will not work. They are inaccurate, naïve, and positively harmful, not only to homosexuals but also to society in general. It is the judgment of the editors that

this is an issue which is just beginning to encroach upon the consciousness of the Church. We must therefore prepare ourselves for
some of the decisions which will have to be made in this area. Since
we believe that contemporary understandings of theology and sexuality are inseparable, we cannot just wait for the American Psychiatric Association, homosexuals themselves, or any other primarily secular group to tell us what to do. The question must be responsibly
engaged by the Church. It is being claimed in many quarters that
homosexuality is a perfectly normal alternate life style. Others vigor-
ously deny this. Both points of view are represented in this book.

It should be clear that different answers to this fundamental question will result in very different standards of behavior. For instance,
if it is normal, then sex education for children in adolescence will
necessarily offer them a choice as to which sexual behavior they
prefer. If it is not normal, how do we learn to take a fully charitable
Christian view toward behavior which, while not ideal, is nevertheless not the "fault" of the people who engage in it? In either case,
should people's sexual orientation be a factor in deciding on their
suitability for ordination to priesthood? These obvious questions do
not begin to reveal the complexity of this issue, about which, at the
present time, there are almost as many opinions as there are voices.

At the very least, the editors hope that the four essays in this
volume will assist readers to distinguish between homosexuality and
homosexuals, in much the same way that we are now able, for instance, to distinguish gossip itself from those who gossip. Beyond
that, we believe that an attitude to homosexuality necessarily involves an attitude to heterosexuality—these are not independent issues. They must both emerge whenever we consider human sexuality generally, since they touch on the fundamental configuration of
the human person as he or she attempts the difficult process of integration of the personality. The day has clearly come when the
Church must do more than quote or misquote the Bible—depending
on one's view—to justify a position.

The editing of this particular book has been for us an exhilarat-
ingly informative experience. We have been able to draw on the
wisdom of a great number of people, who have responded in a willing and cooperative manner to what is really a very difficult task. We
were at first surprised and then encouraged to find a common thread
running through the material, and we hope that the Church will
attend to that. For we are firmly convinced that there may be an
emerging consensus here which offers some hope and leadership to
those who must decide how the Church is to grapple with the symbolic interaction of masculinity and femininity in the life and liturgy

of the Church as a whole. Our prayer is that those who read these essays will not react only with their intellect, but will "listen with the third ear" to their own deep responses so that those decisions which must be made will be carried out with an awareness of the emotional and spiritual implications for their personal lives.

Ruth Tiffany Barnhouse
Urban T. Holmes

PART I

A Useful Starting Point

chapter 1

ON THE DIFFERENCE BETWEEN MEN AND WOMEN

Ruth Tiffany Barnhouse

Long ago people took for granted, not only that there was a difference between men and women but that they knew just what the difference was! There is a quaint old Victorian book entitled *Creative and Sexual Science, including Manhood, Womanhood and their Mutual Interrelations, LOVE, its Laws, Power Etc.* by Prof. O. S. Fowler. With innocent confidence, Professor Fowler asserts that manhood is to be defined by what women love in men, and womanhood by what men love in women. (At least he makes it a two-way street!) Women are said to love male strength, size, and a fine physique as well as courage, force, and firmness. They love dignity but hate "trifling," and they dearly love gallantry and generosity. What women love most in men is originality and talent, particularly intellectual initiative, but they also prize sexual vigor and passion.

Professor Fowler then goes on to write twenty almost embarrassingly explicit pages about the female body and men's admiration of it, which he connects with an instinctive sexual appreciation of those figures best suited to maternity. Men are also said to love emotional, exquisite, spiritual women, those who love children and are in general devotedly affectionate. Further, they love piety and religion in women. Men are said to be reflective, women perceptive. Reputation, display, concern about social position, caution, and gratitude are all listed as "female specialties." He sees all of these qualities, physical and mental, as related in both sexes to the primary human task which for him is the producing and rearing of the next generation of healthy, vigorous, intelligent children.

He felt that this distribution of human virtues between the two sexes irrevocably settled the question of their proper roles in society. At the same time, he believed that since both sets of qualities were essential there should be total cooperation between men and women, and that no tasks should be undertaken by one alone. He saw one of woman's most important roles as that of "completing what man commences," taking the sex act as the paradigm of that dictum, with the completion being the delivery of a healthy baby. This principle, he felt, should extend through the whole realm of human endeavor. "As neither can parent or rear children except *conjointly* with the other, so both should participate in all the labors and pleasures of either. Mutuality in *all* things, isolation in none, is the natural law."[1] Commenting on the social ills of his day, he says: "What is wanted is a mutual convention of *both* sexes to ferret out and right up the wrongs of both." While condemning woman's rights conventions as "old maids' parties," he goes on to give a vigorous plea for female suffrage, for women's inclusion in every conceivable sphere of work, and he insists that there should be equal pay for equal work. Generalizing from his view of the intrinsic feminine qualities, he asserts that "in teaching and doctoring women are naturally men's superiors." Applying his principle of mutuality of effort still further to the question of female clergy, he says: "Some religious denominations do, others do not, conform to this law; and those which do not are retrograding."

This is, indeed, a curious mixture of views by modern standards, combining as it does a plea for enlightened cooperation between men and women which is far from being achieved even now, with a rigorous, not to say oppressive, assignment of qualities, virtues, and roles to people purely on the basis of sex. Now in the late twentieth century we are in the middle of trying to extricate ourselves from the unfortunate consequences of such cultural stereotyping, and clearly have a long way to go.

While fathers who fear that a son interested in art, poetry, or music (and not willing to compete successfully on the football field) may be "unmanly" are fortunately far rarer than formerly, it is still tragically rare for a girl to grow up with the feeling that her sex will not constitute a limitation on the career choices available to her. At the same time, she is often made to feel that if she chooses not to have a career at all, she will be "only" a housewife. This begins in the home, is reinforced by the way women are portrayed on television and in advertising, and is sealed by the educational system, from the first grade readers on up through thoughtless advice from guidance counselors in high school. College, and particularly graduate school, is often a nightmare. Paradoxically, things were easier in a former age, which at least believed that women had special qualities and virtues, and which felt that they should be valued just because they were women. In our time, with women no longer on a pedestal or unequivocally perceived as in need of special protection, they are simply seen as competitors in a tight job market, and their devaluation and oppression takes place in cynical and subtle ways. This is reinforced by the excessively materialistic values of a rampantly commercial culture in which, in order to maximize the payoff to the exploiters, it is necessary to have a significant segment of society whose principal task is to be consumers. After the Second World War, middle-class women were the natural choice to fill this role, which very soon began to create in them the first symptoms of the psychological malaise that eventually erupted in the Women's Liberation Movement.[2]

It would perhaps be more accurate to speak of that movement in the plural, since it does not speak with one voice. Some workers confine themselves to the civil rights aspects of the problem, such as equal pay for equal work, reform of the laws concerning ownership of property, the abolishing of discrimination in employment or promotion, and similar issues. At the other end of the spectrum are some very angry, destructive women, the irrationality of whose pronouncements invites the suspicion, if not the certainty, that their apparent concern for a pressing social issue is really a thinly disguised projection of a personal neurosis. No moderately healthy man or woman will be misled by their tactics of dehumanizing men into an impersonal category called "the enemy," their insistence on stimulating women's anger and encouraging them to turn in fury to retributive persecution of their former oppressors. But these women make a lot of noise and have captured a disproportionate amount of publicity. There exists, therefore, a very real danger that they may cause the large majority of sensible citizens, both men and women, to ignore the serious questions being debated by those involved in the mainstream of the movement.

Perhaps the most important of these questions is whether there is any real difference between men and women beyond the biological ones. It is argued by those who think there is not that the apparent differences are all the result of cultural conditioning, of thousands of years of role expectations imposed on women by the patriarchal establishment for the express purpose of maintaining them as second-class citizens whose principal functions in life are to bear children and meet the needs of men. The evidence that can be marshalled from contemporary culture, as well as from historical records, to show the pervasiveness of sexual stereotyping as a powerful factor in determining how children of each sex will be socialized and educated is truly impressive. The process begins in the cradle, pink for girls and blue for boys, and goes on inexorably from there: dolls for girls, toy guns and cars for boys. This differential treatment continues right into adult life, and it is not surprising that some thoughtful people examining these data conclude that all psychological differences between men and women can be traced to such influences and are therefore spurious.

Proponents of this view seem to believe that any admission of innate difference either is, or may be construed as, evidence of inferiority. (Interestingly enough, nobody imagines that the inferiority will be attributed to men!) The reasons for this easy assumption are partly historical, of course. But history has been badly distorted by contemporary writers whose extravagant claims of thousands of years of unrelieved male oppression of women are simply untrue. Nevertheless, in our culture at the present time we are suffering from a hypertrophied development of masculine values and the psychological position of women is considerably worse than it has been in many previous periods. Perhaps this is why so many are tempted to accept the notion that men and women are alike. They have unconsciously accepted the false idea of male supremacy and see no way out of their present social and spiritual dilemmas other than to assert that women are in fact the same as men.

How then can we usefully approach this question? We are confronted with some stubborn facts. Nobody who has even a passing familiarity with the animal kingdom would think of denying that there are clear behavioral differences between the male and the female of the species which are not directly connected with the processes of reproduction. It is hardly likely that human beings constitute the only exception to this rule. Further, every known culture, past or present, has until now assumed a fundamental psychological difference between men and women, and I do not believe that women are either stupid enough or weak enough to have accepted such a difference if it did not have some basis in fact. At the same time, there is an enormous variety of particular cultural assignment of sex roles. Each culture tends to view its own customs as a concrete manifestation of an obvious eternal truth about the sexes. So far, we may consider the hypothesis that there is a difference, but that cultural conditioning has an enormous influence on how that difference is expressed. In the West today we are just beginning to question our own hitherto unexamined basic assumptions about that difference. It is exceptionally difficult to do so, since each of us went through an acculturation process which took for granted the very standards which are now under review. It is, therefore, almost impossible to achieve a reliable degree of objectivity.

The first requirement in approximating objectivity in any scientific endeavor is to learn to separate one's observations from one's conclusions. This is not as easy as one might suppose, since there are very few words in the language which do not have some value judgment connotation. This makes simple, unbiased description very difficult, especially when that which is under scrutiny is some aspect of human behavior. For example, we may observe someone who is engaged in some type of repetitive activity. If we approve of what is being done, we call it "perseverance," while if we do not approve, we are apt to describe exactly the same behavior as "stubborn." Most of the time we will not be aware, in either case, that we have not described the behavior objectively.

In reading reports of research projects done by psychologists, anthropologists, and sociologists to determine the "facts" about male and female behavior, it is particularly important to be keenly aware that the cultural bias of the investigators may, consciously or unconsciously, influence the way they design their experiments and report their findings. It may also influence the way critics respond to their work. For instance, Dr. Daniel Freedman has done a great deal of research on infants to try to discover what differences there may be between boys and girls at an age which precludes sexual stereotyping by the parents having any significant effect on the observed behavior. He found that newborn girls smile more often than boys, and reported this in the following words: ". . . girls are born with a lower threshold to smiling, and ergo, a stronger tendency towards affiliative encounter."[3] But one lady critic of this report said "If it had been baby boys with a higher frequency of smiles the definition might have been that 'smiling is a gesture of confidence, earlier maturity . . .' " (as opposed to "affiliative encounter").[4]

Another example of this kind of difficulty is to be found in the work of Dr. Marianne Frankenhaueser, who heads the experimental psychology unit of the Swedish Medical Research Council. She reports that either under active stress, such as in work or test situations, or under passive stress, such as watching movies or operations, men have a significantly higher increase in the output of adrenaline than women. Experiments done with twelve-year-old boys and girls yield the same results. So far, we are dealing with neutral facts. Her future research, however, is to be based on the idea that these physiological differences are somehow culturally induced before age twelve, and that as women enter competition more, they will suffer more often from stress diseases which are now more common in men. She says this in spite of the fact that in the experiments the women and girls performed just as well as the males, if not better.

It would be equally logical to base future research on the idea that women naturally stand stress better than men, and would therefore be better suited to stressful occupations than men are. Actually, both such research plans have defects, since they both rest on an interpretation of the data which is already believed rather than on an attempt to secure enough facts to draw an as yet unknown firm conclusion. A more neutral way of proceeding might be to conduct tests on younger children in order to determine at what age this effect first appears. Depending on these results, further research could possibly be designed to find out if the difference is innate or if it is environmentally caused. It is not possible to get even fairly objective answers if the right questions have not been asked. Those who are already committed to a particular answer, consciously or unconsciously, frequently fail to ask the right question.

The illustrations given may help to account for the sometimes wildly conflicting results obtained by different investigators in the field of human behavior. When such an emotionally loaded subject as sex or any of its ramifications is involved, it is more difficult, even with the best of intentions, for workers in the field to leave their personal views outside the laboratory. It is far easier for scientists working with nonhuman material to be precise. The study of geology, for instance, is not nearly so fraught with prejudice at the present time, although a few generations ago, when its findings were thought to be in conflict with the doctrine of creation and therefore threatening to people's religious beliefs, it was at least as controversial as sex studies are now.

There is a further reason for the problems under discussion beyond the ones I have already suggested. We cannot examine anything whatever except by the use of our psychological apparatus. But when the subject matter is the psyche itself, or any part of it, the problem is not unlike that of trying to look *at* a magnifying glass *through* a magnifying glass in order to find out what a magnifying glass *really* looks like. To put it another way, the technical problem in doing research on human behavior is that we do not have enough leverage.

But there is still another problem which arises when scientific methods are applied to such issues, particularly to questions which have some obvious moral significance. Let us return for a moment to geology. If it is found that in a certain part of the world nearly all of the rock formations have a particular composition and character, it is perfectly proper to conclude that this formation is natural, or normal, for that region. This conclusion would be arrived at mainly on statistical grounds. In general, the empirical methods of science are designed to deal with those phenomena which either recur frequently in nature or which can be artificially reproduced in the laboratory for repeated study. Up to a point, these methods are fully appropriate in dealing with human beings also, particularly when the aspect under study is primarily physical. But when the issue is one of human behavior or psychology, another variable which it is crucial not to lose sight of is introduced. A comparison to medicine may make the point: physical health can perfectly well be described as absence of disease. But the same thing is not true of mental or psychological health, which are intimately associated with questions of meaning and value. To order one's life not primarily according to *what is,* but according to a higher principle of *what ought to be,* is a peculiarly human trait, one which, for Christians, is an important part of the significance of the assertion that we are created "in the image of God."

Two things are immediately clear. First, it is extraordinarily difficult to be sure of *what ought to be.* We can only keep trying to approximate it, ready at every moment to revise our views in the light of new evidence. Part of the evidence, of course, must be the light that scientists can shed on what it is to be human. But at least as important as that must be the fruit of new theological insights. In our time this task is rendered far more difficult than it ought to be by the nearly complete separation of the two disciplines of science and theology. This separation is not much more than a hundred years old, but is, I believe, responsible for much of our cultural chaos.

Secondly, one can obviously not discover what ought to be by a statistical examination of what is. I have read many studies by investigators who make precisely this error. They will report, for instance, that research reveals that twenty-one percent of all the subjects studied are engaging in some particular sexual behavior which is socially disapproved. They conclude that since so many people are doing it, the time has come to revise the moral code. If doctors discovered that in a certain community twenty-one percent of the people had cholera, they would hardly conclude that cholera may be normal after all. They would realize that they were faced with an epidemic. There would be no doubt in their mind that cholera *ought not to be.*

Still, this example is not intended to give any support to those who would like to return to the sexual stereotypes, either of roles or behavior, which prevailed in former times. This would only re-create the square-peg-in-the-round-hole problems from which both men and women are now struggling to emerge. To be sure, these have been worse for women. Nobody ever told all men that they must, for example, be engineers. But until recently all women were indeed told that the only perfect role for a woman was that of wife and mother, all other roles being departures from, or at best additions to, that basic one. However, men have suffered also, as other writers in this book will describe more fully. Both sexes have been forced into life patterns which did not suit them, as well as being prevented from adopting patterns which would have been congenial.

Clearly we must now attempt to deal with these issues in a manner which is more respectful of individual human freedom of choice than has been customary in the past, because this is the fully Christian direction. This is part of what *ought to be*. (My theological reasons for thinking this way are given in Chapter 20 of this book.) Of what proper use can the sciences be to us in this endeavor? Accepting the earlier hypothesis that on both intuitive and historical grounds it is safe to assume that there are some differences, these are nonetheless not to be described accurately in the excessively concrete and naïve ways which have prevailed until now. It is possible that good research can shed some real light on the differing natural endowments and energies possessed by men and women. It will then be up to the religiously informed conscience of the members of the Christian community to make some decisions (always bearing in mind that such decisions can never be final) about right and wrong ways of channeling those endowments and energies.

The literature of the depth psychologies on the question before us is vast. I will not attempt to discuss it here, since it will be covered in considerable detail by other contributors to this volume.

On the biological side, there is an enormous amount of research currently in progress. Dr. Freedman and his group in Chicago, previously mentioned, seem particularly thorough. Starting with infant smiling, girls go on by six months of age to respond preferentially to human faces, while boys of the same age pay indiscriminate attention to social and nonsocial stimuli. There are also consistent differences in linguistic development and in the performance of visual and spatial tasks. In addition, this group has compared male-female differences in cross-cultural studies among six different ethnic groups, and has also done extensive work on primates. The results show that male-female differences in the human species as a whole are more prominent than the variations which occur between cultures.[5]

Another project worthy of special mention is that being conducted at Stanford University by Dr. Eleanor Maccoby. She and her coworkers have undertaken a series of longitudinal studies in which several groups of children are to be followed from birth to adulthood. The research design attempts either to identify accurately, or to exclude insofar as possible, the effects of cultural conditioning on the results. The first groups of children are now of nursery-school age. Some of the findings are either not statistically significant (but may become so as more children are studied) or are otherwise difficult to interpret. But there seems to be no doubt that boys are more aggressive than girls, especially from the age of eighteen months onward. Even more interesting is the fact that this aggressiveness is between the males. Pairs of female children do not show it, nor do male-female pairs.[6]

Needless to say, this information does not touch the question of how such masculine aggressive energy should be dealt with first by parents and then by society. In this country we have, for instance, accepted the idea that it is natural—according to some authorities even positively healthy—to encourage little boys to play with toy guns. They are also frequently encouraged to fight, particularly if the other child hits first. These child-rearing practices are, I think, at least questionable. We are dealing with a basic kind of energy, which means that it would be useless to try to suppress it, as some extreme pacifists have proposed. But it must be appropriately channeled, so that its expressions will be constructive rather than destructive. It goes without saying that toy choice is only one of many ways in which we currently deal with this factor.

In considering the results of studies such as the ones cited, one must continually bear in mind that such statements as "boys are more aggressive . . ." do not mean that *all* boys have that trait. It simply means that, to a degree that is "statistically significant" the trait is shown more frequently by boys. This holds true for all behavioral differences not directly connected with the reproductive process. For instance, it is well known that men have a different and stronger musculo-skeletal system than women, but this does not mean that there are not some women who are stronger than some men. The curves drawn by statisticians to represent the distribution of particular traits vary enormously, and there is considerable overlap between the sexes. Serious and detailed research on this subject has only recently begun, and reasonably reliable results are still few. There are many traits about which we are curious, but for which no one has yet thought of a good research design. What we may hope for eventually is that, with respect to a number of variables, there may be answers to the following question: How likely is it that on the basis of sex alone an individual will exhibit a particular behavior or possess a particular kind of energy? Sometimes the answer will be:

Very likely indeed. In other instances the purely sexual contribution to the trait in question will be minimal. Many traits will be found to have no correlation whatever with sex—I. Q. is an illustration of this. No doubt many traditional notions will be upset, possibly in ways which even today's most radical thinkers have not anticipated, while others may be unexpectedly upheld.

Since the body and the mind do not function independently of one another but rather are a seamless unity, as the very existence of psychosomatic illness is sufficient to demonstrate, it is inconceivable that the totally different experience of coming to maturity in a male or a female body would not be in identifiable ways determinative for the psychological organization of the individual concerned. This basic disposition must be known and understood much better than it is now before we can improve our present imperfect understanding of the very important role played by cultural and other environmental influences on the total process of human growth. Where human sexuality is concerned, this is of paramount importance, since it is precisely in this area that the biological difference is inescapable. One possible outcome is that in order to bring out the full potential of each individual boy and girl, we may need to drastically overhaul our educational system, which, in its present form, was designed by and for men.

When large numbers of people begin to think seriously about an issue, the likelihood of progress increases. We may yet achieve Professor Fowler's hopeful vision of the ideal relation between the sexes, "mutuality in *all* things, isolation in none."

NOTES

1. Prof. O. S. Fowler, *Creative and Sexual Science, Including Manhood, Womanhood and their Mutual Interrelations, LOVE, its Laws, Power Etc.* (Philadelphia, Chicago & St. Louis: National Publishing Co., 1870). This quaint out-of-print book does not represent the mainstream of thought in the educational establishment of the period. Fowler describes himself as an expert in phrenology and physiology. It is interesting, nonetheless, for its extraordinarily comprehensive treatment of every possible aspect of the relations between the sexes, including unexpectedly specific details about specifically sexual matters.

2. Betty Friedan, *The Feminine Mystique* (New York: W. W. Norton, 1963). See particularly Chapter 9, "The Sexual Sell."

3. Daniel G. Freedman, "Genetic Influences on Human Behavior," *Normal and Abnormal Development of Behavior* (Leiden, Netherlands: Boerhaeve Series Postgraduate Medical Education, Leiden University Press, 1971), pp. 208–233.

4. Donald MacDonald, "The Liberation of Women," *Center Magazine,* vol. V, no. 3, May/June 1972, and discussion of this article in the subsequent issue.

5. D. G. Freedman, *op. cit.*

6. Eleanor Maccoby. Paper presented in May 1975 at the American Psychiatric Association Annual Meeting. A summary is reported in *Psychiatric News,* vol. X, no. 11, June 4, 1975.

PART II

Some Historical Surprises

chapter 2

TOWARD A BIBLICAL THEOLOGY OF WOMANHOOD*

Samuel Terrien

Many books have been written on the great women of the Bible or the position of women in biblical times, but such studies belong chiefly to the fields of biography, psychology, sociology, ethics, jurisprudence, or the phenomenology of religion. Is it possible to develop a biblical view of womanhood that is organically predicated upon biblical faith? Was it in accordance with the thrust of Hebraic theology that every Jewish male over the past centuries has praised in his daily prayers the Lord God of Israel for not having created him a woman? Does the Bible as such lead to the androcentricity of the Church Fathers, the medieval Schoolmen, and the Protestant Reformers? Or is it legitimate and possible to point toward a more positive biblical theology of womanhood?

In Genesis, Yahwism placed the myth of creation of man and woman in the garden (2:4b ff.) at the beginning of its festive liturgy. In all probability, the story was chanted ceremonially in the sanctuaries of Yahweh at the time of the yearly feast before it was incorporated within the literary epic of the Yahwist during the reigns of David and Solomon (tenth century B.C.). Originally, the man (ha-adam) and the woman (ha-ishshah) were not called Adam and Eve.

*Reprinted from *Religion in Life*, copyright © by Abingdon Press. Used with permission.

This textual feature is not often observed but it is highly significant, for it shows that the man and the woman are mythical types. Later on, they became historicized as the first couple (3:20–21). As is well known, a myth is historicized generally under the unconscious wish to dull its bite. In this case, Adam and Eve are no longer everyman or everywoman. They are removed to a distant past and safely put out of the way.

In the early myth, woman is created as help and succor to man's loneliness. Far from denoting the idea of service in a subordinated position, the word "help" (*'ezer*) is generally applied to God, who is *par excellence* the succor of those in need and in despair. Woman is not a mere tool of physiological or psychological delight. She fulfills a function of creative complementariness. Without her, man is created incomplete. It is the woman who brings man to completion. Woman is presented as the completion of man's creation. She is not a secondary being inferior to man because, as some exegetes have thought in the past, she is created after him and out of him. The order of creation goes from the imperfect to the perfect. Woman constitutes the crowning of creation. She is not simply molded of clay, as man was, but she is architecturally "built" (2:22). The meaning of the Hebrew word is usually lost in the translations. The choice of the verb, however, suggests an aesthetic intent and connotes also the idea of reliability and permanence.

The question of the equality or inequality of man and woman does not arise, for sexual differentiation is justified by sexual union. Moreover, sexuality is valued, first of all, for serving the mutuality of communion between man and woman, and not for its function of biological reproduction. Fertility and the procreation of children appear in the development of the story, of course, but that motif is absent from the story of woman's creation itself (cf. 2:18; 3:16; 4:1). It is in the later myth, which includes a fullfledged cosmogony, that the idea of sexuality becomes associated, through textual juxtaposition, with the continuation of the human race (1:27–28).

In the early myth of the garden, the nature and the destiny of woman is placed on a par with the nature and the destiny of man, if not indeed in an exalted position! Woman appears to man as the revelation of his being. The "deep sleep" (*tardemah*) which the Lord God brings upon man is not to be viewed anachronistically as a process of modern anesthesia pertinent to the surgical ablation of the notorious rib. The noun and its verbal root usually connote the idea of divine disclosure in the midst of a deathlike state of unconsciousness. At the same time, the myth indicates that man is aware of a violent disruption at the core of sexual differentiation. The song man sings in the moment of ecstasy expresses in the same breath both the wonder of sexual communion and the wistful and grievous knowledge of the woman's abrupt apartness:

This time, this one! Bone of my bones, flesh of my flesh!
She shall be called Woman [*Ishshah*], for she was *violently extracted* from Man [*Ish*]! (2:23)

The verbal voice, an intensive passive, invites this rendering rather than the traditional and tame word, "taken out of." As in the later Platonic myth of Eros, sexual attraction carries with it the memory of a distressing tearing apart.

Woman is held in such high esteem that the responsibility of man toward her takes precedence over other communal ties, including the most urgent of all social obligations, the duty of a son toward his own parents:

Therefore, the man will abandon his father and mother,
And he will cleave to his woman, and let them become one flesh! (2:24)

Inasmuch as the ancient Hebrews participated in a spectacularly patriarchic culture, it is noteworthy that the Yahwist epic would have preserved the archaic poem on the superiority of the bond uniting man and woman over the filial bond. Very likely, the intention of the myth-maker was to emphasize that woman, far from being mere chattel, a part of man's household, or only a childbearer, occupies in Yahwistic faith a unique position of communality with man.[1]

Even the sequence of the garden story that deals with the temptation, the eating of the fruit, and the expulsion portrays woman in a thoroughly sympathetic and ambiguously admiring manner. It is she who is endowed with the faculty of intellectual perceptiveness and aesthetic appreciation, for it is she alone who sees that "the tree was good for food, and that it was a delight to the eyes, and that the tree was to be desired to make one wise" (3:6). The phrase lingers on her ability to sense the power of gustative and visual arts, and also to respond to the fascination of wisdom. It is not possible to identify the eating of the fruit with the discovery of sexuality, for the knowledge in question is that which God himself possesses. The woman is the prey, not of sexual libido but of theological lust. She is the victim of the desire for infinity.

The story of the garden does not imply blame on the woman rather than on the man. It attempts to depict the tragic situation of human existence. Self-confidence takes the place of faith, with the result that its first consequence is the spoiling of the sexual harmony which hitherto brought man and woman into communion. They now are ashamed of one another.

The myth ignores any psychological faculty of discrimination on the part of man. While the woman exercises critical judgment in her dialogue with the serpent, the man does not even argue with her, although the story explicitly told that the divine prohibition had been communicated to him alone before the creation of the woman (2:16-17). A touch of satire appears in the swiftness with which the man capitulates. After the lengthened description of the woman's discovery, there is only one Hebrew word for describing the man's action, "and he ate," *wayyokal* (3:6b). Woman is a sensitive artist, an intellectually alert individual, a spiritually eager being. She is a real person. Man is a brute.

When challenged for having violated the prohibition, the cad does not hesitate to implicate his mate, and he even displays a feeling of resentment toward the Creator when he says, "The woman, whom Thou gavest to be with me . . ." (3:12). To be sure, the woman likewise evades the issue by pleading, "The serpent beguiled me" (2:13), but she hints thereby at the problem of cosmic evil, and the myth-maker, once again, pays indirect homage to her intuitive qualities.

This is not the place for a discussion of all the elements of the story. Let it be said only that woman's labor pains and subordination to man belong to the tragedy of human existence, together with their common mortality and man's toil in a hostile environment. The rule of man over woman is not accepted as the intended order of creation. It belongs to the realm of historical chaos, like murder, or the Tower of Babel. It is a manifestation of sinfulness, not of creative grace.

The exalted position of woman in the festal catechism of early Yahwism is confirmed in many ways by the theological language of the great prophets, of the psalmists, and of the wise before the birth of Second Temple Judaism.

The covenant between Yahweh and his people could never have been described under the ideology of marriage if the notion of womanhood had been in any way demeaning. The many allusions of the great prophets to Israel as an adulteress and prostitute indirectly pay homage to the dignity of womanhood. The prophet Hosea probably alluded to the myth of the garden when he envisioned the life of the regenerated people in terms of the renewal of confidence between husband and wife. He clearly considered the subordination of woman to man as a symptom of historical corruption, for he said that in the time of her deliverance Israel will call Yahweh no longer "my master" *(baali)* but "my man" *(ishi;* Hos. 2:16). Such language seems to echo the archaic poem of the creation of woman (Gen. 2:23). It could not have been understood, even by the prophet's disciples, unless the Yahwistic ideal of womanhood had received wide acceptance.

Further evidence is provided by the semantics of the feminine in the way in which the Hebrews spoke about God. The terminology of divine mercy among the great prophets and the psalmists makes use of the idea of the maternal womb with metaphorical boldness. The poet of the *Miserere mei* (Ps. 51) throws himself upon God's pardon by crying out, "Have mercy upon me, O God, on account of the multitude of thy motherly compassions" *(rachmim,* plural of majesty of *rechem,* "uterus"). It is probable that the verb itself, *chanan,* from which derives the noun *chen,* "grave," originally meant "to long for" in the sense of the maternal instinct.

The healthy and entirely guiltless lyricism of love between man and woman which pervades the Song of Songs strengthens the validity of the thesis according to which Yahwistic faith until the Babylonian exile entertained the highest regard for womanhood. Whatever may have been the original purpose of these poems, it is generally agreed that their early form is ancient. The romance is devoid of male arrogance, and the erotic intimacies are described with the help of rhetorical devices that leave no room for any knowledge whatever of legal impurity pursuant to sexual secretions or sexual acts. The woman of the Song of Songs is just as free as the man of any awareness of cultic prohibition, ritual restriction, or legal uncleanness. The Song received canonical status because it had been interpreted, perhaps for a long time, as a parable of the covenant between Yahweh and his people. That such an interpretation was possible indicates that, like the great prophets, the poet of the Song looked at womanhood exactly as he looked at manhood. For him both man and woman mirrored the goodness of the Creator.

The wise could not have compared wisdom to an attractive woman if they had not shared with the ancient Yahwists, the great prophets, and the poet of the Song an unrestricted approval of the feminine sex. Wisdom literature is replete with lyrical sequences, not infrequently couched in erotic language, on Wisdom who invites (Prov. 1:20 ff.; 8:1 ff.; 9:1–5), Wisdom who escapes man's search (Job 28:1 ff.), Wisdom who delights man's deepest desires (Prov. 4:8; 8:17; Sir. 4:15; 6:26; 14:20 ff.; 15:2; especially 51:13 ff.; Wisd. of Sol. 6:12 ff.; 8:2 ff.). A rhetorical pattern, so long sustained, witnesses to an ingrained tradition of respect and even fascination for the female of the human species. The wisdom poets detected in the cosmos a certain quality of order, harmony, equilibrium, charm, and even playfulness which suggested to them the feminine principle. Without running the risk of deifying it, they went so far as to picture wisdom as a young girl sporting in the presence of Yahweh at the moment of creation and singing, "I made day after day his delight" (Prov. 8:30). The feminine personification of wisdom allied itself at a later time to the Hellenistic speculations on the hypostasis of *Hagia Sophia*, and both played a part in the development of Mariology.

In the world of the ancient Near East, where the fruitfulness of the soil, the fertility of animals, and a large progeny were signs of divine blessing, woman was understandably considered primarily as a wife and a mother. Nevertheless, several women who left their mark in the religious life of the nation stood out on their own for genius or achievement, and not in relation to husband, family, or descendants.

At the moment of thanksgiving, after the Exodus, the hymnist was a woman, Miriam, the sister of Moses (Exod. 15:21). At a time of extreme crisis, when a Canaanite coalition threatened the central confederation, the national leader was a woman, Deborah, the wife of a certain Lappidoth who apparently stayed home (Judg. 4:4 ff.). At the event which not only led to the reform of Josiah (622 B.C.) but also created the principle of Sacred Scripture, since it shifted the notion of religious authority from the live word of Yahweh to a written code, the cultic official who was called upon to certify the genuineness of the book of the law was a woman, Huldah, wife of a certain Shallum, "keeper of the wardrobe" (2 Kings 22:14). Each of these three women was remembered as a prophetess, which indicates that they were held to have been in the most intimate group of Yahweh's servants.

In wisdom circles and probably elsewhere, married women were not considered only as dutiful housewives and breeders of offspring. The portrayal of the ideal woman (Prov. 31:10 ff.) is indeed that of a wife, whose capabilities inspire the trust of her husband (vs. 11), but she is an individual person in her own right. The fear of Yahweh is the secret of her character. Because she relies on a dimension of transcendence, she is entirely secure in her identity (vs. 30), and she enjoys economic responsibility, political prestige, and social autonomy, all of which even enhance her husband's reputation (vs. 23).

Until the exile in Babylon, Yahwism, Prophetism, and Wisdom point to a theological view of womanhood which was in no way demeaning. Like man, woman shared in the purpose of creation and in the corruption of history. With the birth of Judaism in the sixth century B.C., however, a disturbing transformation occurred.

In his effort to explain the disaster of 587 B.C., the prophet Ezekiel, who was also the son of a Jerusalem priest, employed the language of sexuality no longer as a metaphorical tool but in the sense of ritual purity and impurity. Sin awareness, on the national and individual levels, tended to be related in lesser degree than before to existential failure and social injustice and to be associated with ritual uncleanness, which meant, in effect, physical contact with corpses, foreigners, and women.[2]

While the Palestinian form of Judaism continued to honor national heroines like Esther and Judith, and entertained the highest respect for motherhood, it appears that the androcentricity of worship and cultic regulations increased markedly. After the exile, women were segregated in temple and synagogue alike, whereas before the exile they had been admitted indiscriminately with men within the courts of the sanctuary. With the completion of the Pentateuch, the laws of cultic purity concerning women or the relation between sexes (Lev. 12:1 ff.) assumed an official significance. This legislation led to complex and refined rituals of restriction, prohibition, and cleansing, which ultimately found their expression in the Mishnaic tractates of *Nashim*, "Women," and *Niddah*, the "Menstruant."

It would be unfair to the plurality of trends within Judaism in Hellenistic and Roman times merely to state that cultic rules grossly favored men over women. The rabbinical literature contains a wide variety of sayings, some of which may represent the tradition of early teachers, in which the equality of woman to man is explicitly affirmed, especially in the light of a dynamic view of creation.[3] Jesus and especially Paul may have been exposed to conflicting schools of thought on this subject.

The attitude of Jesus toward womanhood reveals on the one hand the breadth of his humaneness in general and on the other hand the boldness of his hermeneutical principles. Both the Synoptic and Johannine traditions show that he entered into conversation, not only with women at a level of equality with men but with women who were prostitutes and foreigners. The episode of the Syro-Phoenician woman (Matt. 15:21 ff.) suggests that he probably had to overcome a habit of strict separatism from pagans and from women. There is no evidence, however, that he ever was supercilious or even diffident with women as such. The Johannine narrative of his meeting with the Samaritan woman at Jacob's well (John 4:7–30) indicates that his disciples were astonished, not because he was talking to a Samaritan but because this Samaritan was a woman (vs. 27). The Lukan tradition reports that Jesus allowed a woman of ill repute to touch him and that he contrasted her character of openness and generosity to the righteous punctiliousness of a Pharisee (Luke 7:36–50).

The views of Jesus on divorce reflect his respect for the dignity and the rights of woman. He did not hesitate to challenge the Deuteronomic law on divorce, which was entirely male-oriented (Deut. 24:1–4), in the name of the earlier myth of creation. By quoting Genesis 2:23–24, Jesus made it clear that he understood the reality of mutual responsibility and the obligation of love between a husband and a wife (Matt. 19:3 ff.). It is ironical to observe, however, that his insistence on the indissolubility of marriage, which represented an attempt to support defenseless women, has become the ground for a new form of legalism.

Jesus believed in the liberation of women—and of men. The whole of his message and of his activity points to a realistic appraisal of the ailments of the human character, whether of men or of women. The Johannine tradition concerning the woman taken in adultery exemplifies his refusal to follow the unilateralism of the law (John 7:53–8:11). When he proclaimed divine salvation, the proximity of the end of history and the advent of God's realm, he also faced the problems of the disorders of the human personality. By his example, his words, his acts of healing, and his power of prayer, he restored divided selves into whole persons and replaced alienated individuals within their respective communities. Womanhood, like manhood, was for him an aspect of the theology of creatureliness.

The attitudes of the early church toward womanhood reflect the tension of the eschatological fever in which the first Christians lived from day to day, waiting for the imminent Parousia. Paul therefore recommended celibacy rather than marriage (1 Cor. 7:1–4). At the same time, he saw no legal impurity related to married life, nor did he acknowledge the subordination of woman to man in sexuality. On the contrary, he recommended a mutuality of love which is ideologically akin to that of the Yahwist myth of creation (vs. 4; cf. Gen. 2:24). His notorious references to women in the church (I Cor. 11:2–16) appear to have survived from his legal upbringing, although it must be added that some of the antifemale strictures which are now attributed to him represent in all probability the reactionary recoiling of the Deutero-Pauline circles.[4] Paul the Apostle understood the explosiveness of the Gospel: "There is neither Jew nor Greek, there is neither slave nor free, there is neither male nor female; for you are all one in Christ Jesus" (Gal. 3:28). To maintain with some commentators that the writer of this extraordinary sentence was merely thinking of those who were baptized (vs. 7), hence in the presence of God but not in the realm of human society or in the church order, is to look myopically at the context. Paul was concerned in Galatians with the whole of the missionary enterprise in the pagan world. Inasmuch as a man or a woman had "put on Christ," there was no longer any distinction of class, status, race, rite, nationality, or sex. Galatians remains the Magna Carta of the faith, even if Paul himself did not formulate or failed to see the momentous consequences of his discovery in the realm of social ethics (the problems of slavery and of womanhood), although he drew its revolutionary conclusions explicitly in the realm of ritual and racial exclusivism: "If you are Christ's, then you are Abraham's offspring, heirs according to promise" (vs. 29).

A biblical theology of womanhood will not begin and end with the examination of Paul's complex reactions to the problem of law and freedom in the early church. Rather, it will seek to discern the thrust of Hebraic faith in the perspective of the twelve centuries during which Scripture came into being. The significance of the Bible for contemporary Christians does not merely demand the interpretation of isolated texts. It must also fulfill the wider and more difficult task of discovering, beyond the plurality of religious trends, the distinctive tone of loyalty which led from Mosaic Yahwism to the good news of Jesus.

Modern investigation has shown that Judaism should not be confused with Mosaic Yahwism and prophetic Hebraism. Mosaic Yahwism emerged from the liberation from Egypt in the thirteenth century B.C. It began with a gospel and a moral law rather than a ritual law. Judaism arose in the sixth century B.C. during the horrors of the Babylonian exile, when Ezekiel and the Jerusalem priests attempted to preserve from cultural disintegration the surviving Judahites who thus became the first Jews (same Hebrew word). Partly on account of an overreaction to the sexual rites of its pagan environment, nascent Judaism stressed a strict obedience not only to a moral standard of behavior but also to a ritual restrictiveness which led, among other developments, to the cultic degradation of womanhood.

Hebraism and Christianity alike came into historical existence through the power of a gospel of liberation. Jesus found the roots of his teaching in prophetic Hebraism rather than in priestly Judaism. The Bible is "canonical," that is to say, it constitutes at once a normative control and a power to innovate, because it shows in its own pages the constant need and the constant risk of historical change from generation to generation. *Ecclesia semper reformanda!*

The Bible moves across the centuries toward a theology of womanhood organically related to a theology of manhood. Man and woman, created equal, fall under the same dimension of tragic finitude in historical existence, and both are in need of a radical renewal and regeneration.

The poet of Psalm 51, like the poet of Job, refers to the universal solidarity of the human condition and not to the curse of womanhood when he confesses that man is brought forth in iniquity (vs. 5; cf. Job 14:1). The same psalmist applies the myth of cosmic creation to the microcosm of the self in need of rebirth when he asks, "Create in me a pure mind and will" (vs. 10). This notion is at the root of the Pauline view of man or woman in Christ as "a new creation" (Gal. 6:15).

It is from the perspective of their destiny that man and woman discover, not only their equality and their complimentariness but the paradox of their freedom. The Bible does not contain a ready answer to the question of the role of women in the church or in society. The fact that the early church was torn apart by the problem of submissiveness to Jewish ritual should lead the church of today to re-assess the theological validity of an exclusively male ministry of the Word and the Sacraments. While Scripture says nothing about the ordination of women, it is equally silent on a male priesthood. The Old and the New Testaments know only of pagan and Jewish priests. While some New Testament writers use the analogy of the Jewish high priesthood in their efforts to interpret the person and the ministry of Jesus Christ, they do not offer a Christian theology of priesthood, either male or female. A biblical theology of womanhood demands with utmost urgency the formulation of a new theology of the sacerdotal and pastoral ministry of the church. From Abraham to Jesus Christ, biblical faith lays the basis of a theology of womanhood which goes counter to the traditional attitudes and practices of Christendom and challenges the church of today to rethink critically and creatively the respective functions of man and woman.[5]

NOTES

1. See the excellent article by Walter Brueggemann, "Of the Same Flesh and Bone (Gn 2, 23a)," *The Catholic Biblical Quarterly*, XXXII (1970), 532 ff.

2. See my article "The Omphalos Myth and Hebrew Religion," *Vetus Testamentum,* XX (1970), 316 ff., esp. p. 336.

3. A few of the relevant texts have been conveniently gathered in M. Boucher, "Some Unexplored Parallels to I Cor. II, 11–12 and Gal. 3, 28: The NT on the Role of Women," *Catholic Biblical Quarterly,* XXI (1969), 50ff.

4. I Cor. 14:34–35 is placed at the end of the periscope in *Codex Bezae*

and related manuscripts; cf. Col. 3:18 ff.; Eph. 5:22 ff.; I Tim. 2:3 ff.; I Pet. 3:1 ff.

5. This article was completed when I read the excellent treatment of a similar topic by my former student, Dr. Phyllis Trible, "Depatriarchalizing in Biblical Interpretation," *Journal of the American Academy of Religion*, XLI (1973), 30–48.

chapter 3

SEX AND ANTI-SEX
IN THE EARLY CHURCH
FATHERS

Donald F. Winslow

It might be wise to point out at the outset of this brief essay that the
term *patristics* (the study of the life and thought of the early church
Fathers) and the term *patriarchy* (a hierarchy in which the father
occupies the predominant position) are both derived from the same
word, *pater,* or father. Since the great bulk of writings preserved
from the early church (say A.D. 150–600) were written by the Fathers,
and not by their mothers or sisters or daughters, we are somewhat at
a disadvantage in our attempt to spy out an objective picture of what
Christians in this formative period of the church's life thought about
sex. More than this, most of the Fathers whose works survive (such
as Athanasius or Augustine) were also bishops. True, some works
available to us were penned by priests, some by unordained monks,
but, with the major exception of the writings of Tertullian, precious
few by lay persons. A hierarchy, then, which places the male father
at the top of the social pinnacle and the (usually unwed) episcopal
"Father" (bishop) at the top of the ecclesiastical structure, is not
likely to have produced a literature which, in respect to attitudes
toward sexuality, is either balanced or genuinely representative.

In spite of this, the enduring influence of the Fathers of the church
cannot be either dismissed or ignored. We must treat with utter seriousness the evidence with which they provide us. They lived in a
world and society radically different from our own. Many of our
views, therefore, will differ from theirs. But we must not be beguiled
into thinking that we are smarter than they, less prejudiced than

they, or more faithful to the Gospel than they. Ages differ and view-points will differ. We must, in an environment in which our own ecclesiastical and/or social hierarchies are still evolving, seek the truth even as our predecessors sought it, but never may we claim to possess it. With this opening *caveat* now behind us, we can plunge directly into the material at hand.

In Christ Jesus, wrote the apostle Paul, "there is no such thing as Jew and Greek, as slave and freeman, as male and female" (Gal. 3:28). Today, advocates for the ordination of women make frequent reference to this familiar text as their apostolic warrant for challenging the church's traditional exclusion of women from its legitimate ministry, as a call to do away with sexism, patriarchy, and all the societal attitudes or administrative structures which discriminate against women or oppress them. In its own context, however, this Pauline assertion probably cannot bear the weight that is now so often assigned it. There are, in fact, other possible interpretations, no one of them ultimately binding. During the classical period of the church Fathers, for instance, this text was appealed to as often as it is today but for totally different reasons. Rather than being used to support the *equality* between men and women, the Fathers saw in this text an overt attack against what they felt to be the obvious ambiguities (and dangers) of bisexuality. In the angelic state for which every Christian yearned, there would be no marriage or giving in marriage since there would be no males and females as such. The pure estate of the heavenly abode would be sexless. Paul's statement that in Christ Jesus there is no such thing as male and female was interpreted eschatologically; that is, as descriptive, not of this age but of the age to come. Gladly the Fathers made use of this text in order to persuade the faithful as far as possible to emulate in this life the asexuality of the life beyond. Never did the Fathers construe this text to indicate the ideal of sexual equality. The vast amount of patristic literature on virginity and on sexual continence as the higher or more Christian way bears ample testimony to this interpretation, an interpretation which, if placed alongside many of Paul's other assertions as to the inferiority of women or the superiority of the "spirit" to the "flesh," is not without legitimacy. That there is no such thing as male and female means, then, that the person who has accepted Jesus as Lord and Savior, who has "put on Christ," must at the same time, if not actually deny his or her sex, at least transcend it. And to not a few of the Fathers, to transcend one's sex was part and parcel of transcending one's fleshly (or lower) nature. A popular interpretation of the story of the Fall in Genesis was that it was a fall *into* sexuality (with its concomitant lust and passion) out of an original

innocence. It was even possible for an occasional Father to suggest
that the guilt imputed by virtue of Adam's fall to the whole human
race was physically transmitted from one generation to another
through the means of sexual intercourse. There was in general, in the
patristic era, what D. S. Bailey has accurately called an "embarrassment, suspicion, antipathy, and abhorrence" in respect to physical
sexuality. But the Fathers did not invent this attitude, nor did they
create it as an original response to the teachings of the Gospel;
rather, it permeated the Hellenic culture in which they lived and
there was no way for them not to be profoundly influenced by it.

That there is in Christ Jesus no such thing as male and female
finds further expression in the Fathers' understanding of creation.
"So God created man in his own image; in the image of God created
he him; male and female created he them" (Gen. 1:27). Rosemary
Ruether has observed that the Fathers would have been much happier had they been able to expunge the final phrase from this text. It
was a stumbling block to them. If what God had created was "good,"
and if bisexuality was if not in fact at least potentially "bad," how
could this passage be interpreted? Many suggestions were offered by
the Fathers, no one of them destined to win the field but all of them
testifying to the widespread perception of asexuality as more representative of the "perfect" state (either as originally created before
the Fall or as the ultimate state of the sanctified) than bisexuality.
Perhaps there were in fact, *two* creations, the first of which was
spiritual and the second of which was material. Since sexuality belonged by definition to the material order and could not participate
in things spiritual, it quite obviously belonged to the second, and
therefore inferior, creation.

But to divide creation up into two component parts and assign
relative values to each was still to compromise the so-called "goodness" of creation, if not also of the Creator. So perhaps another solution could be offered. Could it not be suggested, for instance, that
sexuality was not in any way a part of the created order but was in
fact a direct result of the Fall? Sexuality belongs neither to the
heaven for which we yearn nor to the pristine prelapsarian paradise
from which we fell. The first two phrases of our Genesis text, then,
belong to the created order *before* the Fall, the third phrase to the
distorted creation which came into being *after* the Fall. There were
many other suggestions as well, all of them offered in the interests of
coming to terms with the ambiguities of sexuality. Sexuality was
seen by some to be a test for man's will, a test provided by God as
an opportunity for measuring one's discipline and obedience. Virtue
is pointless if there is no struggle; only in overcoming temptation can

virtue have any merit. Victory over an enemy is meaningless unless the enemy poses a real threat, so only as the Fathers could win mastery over the very real adversary of sexuality could they rightly claim a moral victory. Not a few Fathers went so far as to suggest that perhaps the "image" of God resided in the male, while the distortion of that image, or the falling away from it was personified by the female. And in some extreme (gnostic) circles, all material things, such as body and flesh were inherently evil and totally opposed to the spiritual principles of the creator God. For them, salvation was a process of constant denial of one's physical or sexual nature so as to return the more quickly to one's true, original, incorporeal state. Or, some suggested, salvation was a process of so indulging the flesh in all sorts of physical and sexual abuse that it would soon disease and perish, and then the spirit would be free of the tomb *(sēma)* of the body *(sōma)*.

As diverse as these possible interpretations of creation are they exhibit one element in common. The "image" of which the Genesis text speaks could not, for most of the Fathers, reside in the *whole* person, whether male or female. It seemed more appropriate for them to assign the image to man's unfallen spiritual or noetic nature, totally divorced from things physical or sexual. Sexuality, therefore, cannot be a part of the true creation, or at least not a part of that creation which God called "good." The paradise from which the human race emerged and the heaven to which the saved progress are joined, in the Fathers' eyes, by one controlling definition: asexuality. Gregory of Nyssa (d. 395) is not alone in his insistence that Genesis 1:27 and Galatians 3:28 are companion texts. The "male and female created he them," he theorized, represents a radical departure from the image or archetype (Christ), since, quite precisely, in Christ "there is no such thing as male and female."

Some serious questions arise at this point. It has often been argued that the patristic attitudes toward sex were an illegitimate capitulation to the early church's Hellenic environment, of which a prevalent spirit/body dualism was one chief characteristic. It has been argued further that this capitulation represented a radical break with the more open naturalism of the Church's Jewish antecedents. As a descriptive statement, it would be difficult to counter such an argument. But if a value judgment is implied, the matter is not so simple. Jewish attitudes toward sexuality as represented, say, in the Old Testament, for all their differences, are not *ipso facto* better than later Greek or Roman attitudes. The Christian church has always existed and developed in a creative tension between its traditional past and its existential present. It has always been radically in-

fluenced by its environment, but at the same time has radically influenced its environment. Simply to say the old is better, and the
new, because it is a departure from the old, is worse, is to avoid the
more real complexities of growth and development within the Christian community. It is perhaps more fruitful to assess the patristic
views we have outlined thus far on the basis (1) of their own merits
or demerits and (2) in comparison, not with an idealized past or an
idealized present but with our own honest understanding of how we
perceive the Gospel to address the questions at hand. We are not
comfortable in rejecting a practice or attitude or doctrine merely
because it represents a break with the past or a coming to terms with
its own cultural and social milieu.

This is nowhere more clearly the situation than when we attempt
to discover in our patristic past what the Fathers thought of marriage. We may disagree with what many of the Fathers wrote about
marriage, but we need not judge them too harshly. And further, our
own, perhaps radically different, views of marriage should at least be
articulated with as much seriousness as were those of the Fathers.
The first thing that must be said is that the Fathers' attitude toward
marriage was profoundly influenced by their attitude toward sexuality. And the second thing that must be said is that there can be
found in the patristic era no one prevailing view of marriage; just as
there was, as we have seen, no one prevailing understanding of sexuality. Yet from the variety of views articulated it is possible to elicit
something of an emerging pattern, a pattern that has been extremely
influential for later generations of Christians, including our own. For
some extreme groups (the Montanists, for instance), Christianity and
the married state were absolutely incompatible. If one became a
Christian as yet unmarried, one could never marry; if one became a
Christian after having married, the marriage had to be dissolved.
Less extreme, but still on the fringe, were those who did not disal-
low the marriage partnership but insisted that it be undertaken
solely in the interests of companionship. Any sexual relations would
destroy the true nature of marriage and were thus forbidden. Marriage, yes, but sex, no. In these so-called spiritual marriages a man
and wife could live together but as brother and sister. There exist
charming stories of earnest young men profitably spending their wed-
ding night persuading their new brides to join them in a mutual life
of sexual abstinence. It is interesting to note that among those who
forbade marriage of any kind, as well as among those who recommended spiritual marriage, were some who saw this as a subtle way
of forcing God's hand so as to usher in the end of the world. If there
were no sexual relations, there would be no children, and eventually

the population of the world would die out. Then God would have to act!

These extreme views, however, were definitely in the minority. Closer to the center of the patristic position were more liberal views. The Fathers often wrestled with the problem of evil, as have generations of Christians since. One solution many of them adopted was to suggest that, while evil was not *caused* by God, it was at least *permitted*. So with their view of marriage. Marriage could not be said to represent the pinnacle of goodness, but neither was it inherently evil. Scripture disallowed the majority of the Fathers from legislating exclusively against marriage. Thus, while they seldom felt called to recommend marriage, they did allow it. Marriage was a "good," but definitely an inferior "good." There was in fact a hierarchy of "goods," and marriage stood on the lowest rung. This hierarchy is clearly expressed by frequent reference on the part of the Fathers to the Parable of the Sower (Mark 4:3–20). The first part of the parable is fairly straightforward. The seed that fell on the footpath was devoured by the birds (by Satan). The seed that fell on the rocky ground sprouted for a while and then, for lack of soil, withered away (fell into temptation). The seed that fell among the thistles was choked to death (by the evil and selfish desires of the world). But then the final part about the seed that fell on the good ground: it bore fruit, some one hundredfold, some sixtyfold, and some thirtyfold. The Fathers seized upon this arbitrary distinction between the productive capacities of the various seeds and allegorized the text radically. The seed that bore fruit one hundredfold was obviously the best, and it represented *martyrdom* as the highest calling for Christians. The seed that produced sixtyfold was also good (but not as good) and it referred to *virginity* as a noble Christian ideal. The seed that produced thirtyfold, because it represented an inferior good (albeit still good), represented *marriage*.

Such an interpretation may strike us as fanciful or as exegetically unwarranted, but it does reflect with some accuracy the general patristic attitude. Martyrdom, especially during the period of persecution, was certainly the highest crown the Christian could win. It was a total surrender of the whole of the body and thus the instrumentality whereby a person's spirit was liberated. It represented an absolute disdain of the flesh and, as a result, an absolute repudiation of sex. There is, for instance, the story of a woman martyr who, just prior to being ravaged by the wild beasts, was miraculously "smoothed out" (that is, de-sexed) by the Holy Spirit so that her heavenly asexual state was achieved even before her actual martyrdom.

If martyrdom was the highest calling (in purest imitation of the passion and death of Christ), virginity was certainly next in line (and also, it might be added, perceived to be imitative of Christ). A friend of mine once remarked that he had always been struck by how many saints in the Christian calendar were referred to as "virgin and martyr." "Is that not a redundant phrase?" he asked. He may not have realized that there was more than just humor in his observation since it was the third-century Methodius (d. 311) who asserted that virginity was in fact a kind of martyrdom. Virgins were martyrs, not just for one painful moment, but for the whole of their lives! Further, that the monastic movement of the fourth and subsequent centuries can be described, by virtue of its disdain for the flesh, as the institutionalized successor to the phenomenon of martyrdom makes this point even more apposite. Short of death, then, virginity was the noblest of Christian ideals, a soil that produced sixty-fold.

The good soil that yielded fruit thirtyfold was marriage. In terms of numbers, it was certainly the most popular option for Christian life but at the same time the least to be praised. Marriage was allowed but not encouraged. Jerome (d. 420), who wrote more letters than anyone today would care to read on the virtues of virginity, claimed that perhaps the saving grace of marriage (or at least of sexual intercourse) was that it produced virgins! "I praise wedlock," he wrote, and "I praise marriage, but it is because they give me virgins. I gather the rose from the thorns, the gold from the earth, the pearl from the shell." That marriage, along with the sexual relations which are natural to marriage, were for Jerome "earthy" and "thorny" perhaps detracts from the genuineness of his so-called praise of the married state. Jerome and his fellow Latins, Tertullian (d. 220) and Augustine (d. 430), are perhaps severest in the denunciation of marriage (allowed) *vis-à-vis* their praise of virginity (recommended). It is also true that they were men who in their youths lived lives that were, by their own confession, hardly distinguished for their sexual continence. Yet even among the more liberal bishops of the patristic era there can be discerned a pervasive attitude which, under the guise of legitimating marriage and sexual relations as a valid option for Christians, succeeds more in underlining the dangers inherent in the married state. First of all, there are those distracting domestic concerns. How can one spend one's time in fasting and prayer if there are small mouths to feed, servants to be trained, and the like?

But more than domesticity, sexuality was an obvious deterrent to true Christian piety. That the marriage relation had as its primary purpose the begetting and bearing of children was accepted by the majority of the Fathers. But when the mechanics of *pro*creation gave way to the experience of *re*creation, that was where the problems began. If only the sex act could be undertaken in a disinterested and passive manner, if only intercourse were a neutrally functional activity, then it would be less dangerous. The Fathers could recommend the marriage bed if it (1) served the purpose of procreation alone and (2) was a function without physical or emotional overtones, not unlike urination. That a person might actually *enjoy* sex was, for Augustine particularly, unthinkable. One detects here a certain fear on the part of the Fathers, a fear, not so much of the sex act itself, but of what might be called "uncontrollability." One's higher (mental or spiritual) nature should ideally always be in control of one's lower (physical) nature. But it is perhaps nowhere more apparent than in the act of coitus that the higher nature loses its control of the lower and is unable to direct it rationally and objectively. And not to be in control is to have one's personhood diminished. It is for this reason that the Fathers would have been more content if intercourse was without the pleasurable sensations which accompany ejaculation and orgasm. No human activity testified more to the inability of the will to hold the passions in check than did coitus. Thus the Fathers' concern was less with intercourse itself than with its accompanying sensations. Procreation, yes, but recreation, no.

So even within the institution of marriage itself there seems to be a hierarchy of different levels. Highest is that marriage undertaken with a mutual dedication, on the part of both partners, to a life of sexual abstinence. Next best is that marriage where sexual intercourse is seen as a conjugal duty for procreative purposes alone, an activity to be tolerated but certainly not enjoyed. Least good is that marriage where sex is a shared pleasure for its own sake.

Martyrdom, as the highest goal to which the Christian can aspire, cares nothing for the whole of physical existence. Virginity (and celibacy), as the second highest good, consciously puts aside that (lowest) part of physical existence which has to do with sex. And marriage, the lowest of the three "goods," allows for sex but only for purposes of procreation and when devoid of pleasurable sensation. So much for the Parable of the Sower!

But two observations must be made at this point. First of all, the ambivalence expressed by the Fathers in their attitude toward sex, even within conjugal limits, suggests an anthropology which is basically dualistic. A person is divided into two warring constituent parts, and it is the task of the higher part so to subjugate the lower part and keep it in control that it will no longer pose a problem. The logical implication of this dualism is that the lower part might best be done away with completely. The Fathers were unable, given this

anthropological presupposition, to see mankind made up of constituent parts which worked either harmoniously one with another or
functioned as a whole. An example of this dualism can be found in
Basil of Caesarea (d. 379). There are three states of life, he said. The
mind (or spirit), in which resides the image of God, is assigned the
role of pilot, leader, guide, physician, master. The *flesh* is the source
of most of our problems because it is so unruly. While not evil in and
of itself, the flesh is a threat because it can so easily persuade the
mind to acquiesce to its urgings. Between the two, therefore, is the
soul, which is the neutral mediator between the mind and the flesh,
the means by which the temptations coming from the lower nature
are rebuffed, and also the means by which the divinely inspired
intentions of the higher nature can be communicated effectively to
the lower. There are countless variations in patristic literature to this
anthropological theme, but all of them underline the element of conflict (Gregory of Nazianzus called the flesh a "friendly enemy").
Harmony can be achieved only by severe subjugation. The tendency,
therefore, is to define mankind, essentially, solely in terms of the
higher nature. Accordingly, sexuality itself, as well as sexual activity,
are ultimately excluded from what it means to be human. What we
look for in vain in the writings of the Fathers is a healthy respect for,
or even appreciation of, the whole person as created. We miss that
attitude which allows "goodness" to be assigned to all the levels of
human existence and which therefore admits that "badness" can
operate equally on all levels (not just the flesh). It is impossible to
avoid the conclusion that much of the patristic antipathy toward sex
arises out of this "doctrine" of creation, a doctrine which few of us
today would countenance.

A second observation is this: If the Fathers were afraid of that lack
of control which was so clearly manifest in the sexual act, they were
also at the same time patently, even if unconsciously, unable to come
to terms with their own (male) sexuality *vis-à-vis* women. The writings of Jerome and Augustine, for instance, are replete with references to the attractiveness of the opposite sex. Their admonitions to
women, therefore, that they dress modestly, cover their heads, eschew cosmetics were reflections, less of their convictions as to how
Christian women should behave than of their fear of what womanly
behavior might arouse in them. They responded, therefore, by seeking to eliminate in women the one thing which was a potential
source of passion in their own (male) sexuality. Gregory of Nazianzus
(d. 389) writes of a dream in which he was visited by two "lovely"
women who sought to persuade him to adopt the celibate and temper-
ate life of a monastic. But he adds (a little too quickly), so that his

reader may not misinterpret him, that their loveliness was not of the kind that would arouse the passions! What one discovers here is an element of irony: the Fathers admonish their female counterparts to cover up or even deny their sexuality but only because they (the Fathers) are so aware of their own (never fully repressed) sexuality. Sexual attractiveness was not just a threat to the uncontrollability of male response, it was also a threat to episcopal power!

It is perhaps in this light that the growth of clerical celibacy (more pronounced in the Latin West than in the Greek East) can best be interpreted. The development of celibacy as a canonical norm, and subsequently as a canonical imperative, took place alongside a parallel development of increasing canonical legislation against sexual abuse. If the Fathers were afraid of the "loss of control" that was symbolized in the phenomenon of sexuality, it is difficult to avoid the conclusion that an underlying motivation behind much of their legislation against sexual malpractice was enacted so as to protect those areas of life over which they sought to retain control. The punishments assigned specific sexual misdemeanors are a case in point. They are directed more to the "rank" of the offender than to the nature of the offence. The continual fornication of a harlot was viewed less seriously than the single fornication of a confessed virgin. The adultery of an ordinary believer was punished less severely than the "falling from grace" of an ordained priest. It may in fact be asserted that, more than any element, it was the early church's attitude toward sexuality which was the major cause behind the development of the so-called "double standard," the hierarchy of moral expectations which demanded greater perfection of the ordained than of the laity.

E. R. Dodds has called the patristic period an "Age of Anxiety." He sees in these formative centuries of the Christian church the attempt to arrive at an understanding, as over against the non-Christian world, of one's own Christian identity. In this attempt, sexuality was a potent source of ambiguity and ambivalence. More than this, it was a continual source of personal and corporate conflict. Given the environment in which the Fathers lived, it was easier for them to do away with the source of conflict than to deal with it openly and creatively. Accordingly, they adopted an "I-wish-it-weren't-there" approach to sexuality. There is no question that this attitude has had a subtle but enduring influence on the Christian church throughout the centuries. We might be at that "fullness of time" today, however, when we can, without unduly criticizing the patristic enterprise, take a fresh look at sexuality in its Christian context and arrive at some conclusions which will result in the responsible liberation of the

whole person, male and female, and no longer be afraid to acknowledge and affirm the miracle of humanity in its wholeness. It will, for
us, be neither a "patristic" nor a "patriarchal" undertaking and therefore more balanced and representative than much of the material
which has here, in all too brief a span, been presented.

SUGGESTED READING

Augustine, *The Confessions*
Gregory of Nyssa, *On Virginity*
Jerome, *Epistle* 22

D. S. Bailey, *Sexual Relation in Christian Thought* (New York: Harper,
    1959)
E. R. Dodds, *Pagan and Christian in an Age of Anxiety* (New York: Cam-
    bridge University Press, 1965).
Samuel Laeuchli, *Power and Sexuality* (Philadelphia: Temple University
    Press, 1972)
Rosemary Ruether (ed.), *Religion and Sexism* (New York: Simon and Schus-
    ter, 1974)

chapter 4

MALE AND FEMALE IN CHRISTIAN TRADITION:

Was There a Reformation in the Sixteenth Century?

Eleanor L. McLaughlin

The arguments against change in the status and role of women in the Christian community and, in particular, the opposition to the opening of priesthood to women, are grounded ultimately in our perceptions of God and how God is appropriately symbolized in the language of word and body. Christians today assume the maleness of metaphors and names for God to have been an unvarying constant in Scripture and tradition. Furthermore, this male "God-language"—Father, Son, Begetter, King, Word, Initiator, Lawgiver, the Wholly Other—is felt to tell us something real, having to do with the very being of God. Consequently, the priest, who stands as an icon of God, representing not only God's people but the royal priesthood of Jesus Christ, would seem to be necessarily male. According to this view, only a male Christian could be the appropriate sacramental symbol of the divine when God-language is restricted to male metaphor. The supporters of this position do not argue that God is male, only that God symbols are male, symbols that may not be altered without endangering the communication of the divine. The core of the argument for a male priesthood resides in the issue of God symbols. Scripture is reinterpreted; tradition does change; women can and do bear teaching authority; the patriarchal family structure headed by the father/provider is already disappearing; all of these bulwarks of the male priesthood ultimately fall before the single argument of the Fatherhood of God and Sonship of Christ. Language and body are the parameters of our meaningful existence.

The student of Christian history has some new chapters to add to this story. The tradition is not as unequivocal in its God-language as our recent theologians and liturgists would suggest. Just as students of the Scriptures have been uncovering, in the Wisdom literature, for example, long unrecognized feminine references to the numinous, so also our common Christian history reveals a tradition of female God symbol and metaphor which reminds us that the exclusively male and overwhelmingly transcendent imagery of recent theology and spirituality is an exaggerated and one-sided departure from Catholic Christianity. The watershed was in the complexity of emotional and intellectual change which overwhelmed the West following the Protestant Reformation of the sixteenth century. To provide a glimpse of "the world we have lost" is the purpose of this paper. We look to recover a past which may be usable and freeing for us as we attempt to follow the guidance of the Spirit into the future.

First we must look at the negative aspect of our inheritance, a part of Christian tradition which needs to be made conscious if we are to be free. The pre-Reformation church, the medieval church, conjures up images of a brutal warrior society in which the patriarchal subordination of the girl-child to father and the child-bride to husband was barely relieved by romantic stories of queenly majesty, the mysteriously powerful fairy godmother or the witch of the folktales. Our investigation of the names of God in the spirituality of the medieval church has to be prefaced by a word about the formal theological structuring of male/female relationships in that world. Prayer grows out of life, but it is also not unconnected with the intellectual work out of the Schoolmen.

The woman in medieval society was virtually the property of the male. She was "given away" by her father at the canonical age of consent (thirteen) into the keeping of her husband. The church tempered the economic realities of feudal marriage, an institution for the adding of field to field, by insisting that neither boy nor girl could be married without his or her consent, nor could a woman (as in pagan Germanic law) be repudiated at the whim of a dissatisfied husband. However, the subordination of the woman to the male sex, and her inherent mental and moral inferiority by which that subordination was justified, were given a rationale by biblical exegesis and in the theology of the church. The woman, as daughter of Eve, was a secondary creation in time and substance, derived from Adam, the archetype of humanity. The Genesis story of the Fall was interpreted in a way to deepen this inferiority, with the tendency of medieval exegesis to associate the woman in particular with lust, a punishment for the primal sin. The daughters of Eve were long considered unclean and dangerous as creatures who mysteriously bleed without dying, and therefore unfit to enter the Holy of Holies or serve at God's altar. To this primitive fear, reflected in Old Testament Levitical laws excluding women from cultic function, was added the Christian inheritance of the sin of Eve. According to some popular myths, it was Eve, inflamed with lust by the devil, who taught Adam the art of sexual intercourse, by which original sin was thought to be transmitted. The woman, throughout medieval story and theological tractate, was ever the temptress, dangerous to male virtue, destructive of celibate male spirituality, and when married was typically depicted as the lascivious, cuckolding, untrustworthy wife of Bath.

Despite the canon law which protected marriage and the sacramentalizing of the marriage bond, the Middle Ages saw little idealization of family or motherhood. The woman was reduced to an aid in procreation and physical nurture. As soon as the child was weaned, the prime responsibility for the moral and mental nurture of offspring as children of God was the father's. According to Thomas Aquinas, only the man has the necessary authority and force to teach either the young child or the community. The woman was thus reduced in family and society to her biological being: positively seen, an aid in procreation; negatively regarded, the arouser of sinful sexual feelings.

I have taken the time to sketch out this negative view of the woman from the Christian theological past in a paper ostensibly devoted to a recovery of positive feminine imagery because we are still living with the burden of fear and projection and exclusion symbolized by Eve, the witch, and the shrew. That doctrine of human nature which allocates sensuality, receptiveness, and response to women; and initiative, intellectuality, and headship to men, was derived from a Christian adaptation of Greek philosophy which associated woman with fleshliness and emotion, men with rationality and spirit. This dualism has been as disastrously dehumanizing for men as for women in our culture—forbidding sensitivity and emotion to the "real man" and disallowing leadership or aggressiveness for the "feminine woman." That destructive anthropology must be raised up and made conscious if we are to experience the empowering wholeness promised by Christ to those who in Baptism become a new creation, one and whole and free of the alienation of race, sex, class, nation; free also of the alienation of flesh from spirit.

For those who object that I conjure up medieval ghosts irrelevant to twentieth-century Anglican Christians, one can only point out the fear voiced recently by two English priests, that the ordination of women would symbolically call into question the headship properly

exercised by the husband in every Christian family. They rightly
recognize that patriarchy is threatened by women in priesthood. The
theological justification of this patriarchy is explicitly set forth by the
many churchmen who understand the subordination of the female to
be a reflection of the created order and of the relationship between
Christ and the Church. As Karl Barth expressed it, ". . . she recognizes that in order she is woman and therefore B, and therefore
behind and subordinate to man. . . . Properly speaking, the business
of woman, her task and function is to actualize the fellowship in
which man can only precede her, stimulating, leading and inspir-
ing." One must recognize that this "difference" between the sexes,
this subordination of "self-giving, receptiveness, and response," this
complementarity, has historically, in fact, been inseparable from inferiority. Separate has meant functionally unequal. More to the point
for Christians, separate and different have meant that a woman is not
free to say "yes" to God's will in her life, for the church has defined
the way in which God may validly speak to women! Unlike the
medieval church, which experienced the eruption of radically new
forms of religious vocation—as, for example, in the Franciscan break
with Benedictine monasticism—the church today seems to have lost
that exciting openness to the scandalous innovations of the Spirit.

Until we as a church own and confess this negative burden—the
body-denying dualism and misogyny of traditional Christian anthropology, and our faithless anxiety in the face of innovation—we cannot take the next step into the fullness of personhood for both sexes,
which is Christ's promise. Having confessed this burden which a
theologizing of patriarchy and ancient Greek physiology (that the
woman is a "misbegotten male") has placed on men and women—
denying the one feeling and forbidding the other spiritual and intellectual maturity—we as a church must look beyond the negative in
our tradition. We need to discover what the Spirit has taught us of
God in other times, and how the divine has been experienced and
expressed in the created human image. As a Christian woman and an
Episcopalian, I am sick of reciting the bad news. What does the
tradition have to tell us of the good news?

If we turn, in the literature of the pre-Reformation church, from
theology written by clerics (male and celibate), to the witnesses of
spiritual experience, the church at prayer, we enter a wholly different world. The records of Christians meeting God, unlike formal
school theology, come from the hands of lay and cleric, women and
men, married and virgin. Especially in the later Middle Ages, the
thirteenth through fifteenth centuries, a large body of this literature
of religious experience was produced by women—nuns, anchoresses,
and the semi-regular Beguines who lived and worked in the world

but under the discipline of poverty, chastity, and obedience. The spirituality of the medieval church was shaped by women and men together far more than is the case today.

One crucial reason for this common life lay in the existence of an institution and vocation to the religious life of the nun and monk, to which men and women were called equally. The life of Christian perfection was open to all baptized Christians, all who were called to total commitment to Christ. It was not the bureaucratic, worldly, and male clergy, but the religious, brothers and sisters together who dominated and shaped the life of prayer and good works of the pre-Reformation church. The fruit of their experience—prayers, visions, autobiographies, saints' lives, works of instruction for seekers after God—this literature speaks forcefully to our contemporary confusions on sexuality and the life of the Spirit in two different areas. We discover in these writings a God who is strongly androgynous, a use of language and symbol which points to a God who is feminine as well as masculine in attribute and action. We discover also in pre-Reformation spirituality a more androgynous image of humankind. In particular, medieval men spoke of themselves easily in feminine modes. There seemed to be much less nervousness than is felt today about responding to God and the created world in the manner of the opposite sex. Before God, every Christian soul was the bride of Christ and the mother of the Child of Bethlehem; before God every Christian soul was a son and heir of Christ, a soldier called to fight against the world, the flesh, and the devil. The medieval church in its life with God experienced Christ as mother, and men and women could experience themselves as women and men.

Let us look first at the divine androgyny. One of the earliest witnesses in the Middle Ages to the tradition which knew the Second Person of the Trinity in a feminine mode was St. Anselm of Canterbury. This eleventh-century English bishop, theologian, and monk, refers to Jesus as "our Mother" in his prayers, in three different modes of divine action. Through his passion and death, Jesus gives birth to the souls of faithful Christians.

> And if you had not died, you would not have brought forth.
> For longing to bear sons into life, you tasted death,
> And by dying, you begot them.

Anselm's motif of Jesus our Mother is found repeatedly throughout the literature of mystical piety.

A second theme found in St. Anselm depicts Christ as our caring mother who comforts, gentles, revives, consoles.

Christ my mother, you gather your chickens under your wings; this dead chicken of yours puts himself under those wings. For by your gentleness the badly frightened are comforted, by your sweet smell the despairing are revived, your warmth gives life to the dead, your touch justifies sinners. Mother know again your dead son, both by the sign of your cross and the voice of his confession. Warm your chicken, give life to your dead man, justify your sinner. Let your terrified one be consoled by you; and in your whole and unceasing grace let him be refashioned by you. For from you flows consolation for sinners; to you be blessing for ages and ages. Amen.

Anselm takes the biblical image of Christ the Mother Hen (Matt. 23:37) to draw a parallel between the care and nurture of earthly mothers and the work of Christ in the soul, as our Mother of Mercy. This Mother of Mercy is not as in Marian piety, the Lord's mother Mary, but is the Lord Christ. The experience of unquestioning, accepting love is here found in God rather than in the auxiliary, subordinate figure of the Virgin.

A third aspect of God's feminine action called forth by St. Anselm in his prayer is that of feeding. In Anselm's experience, the divine nurse is symbolized by St. Paul, who feeds us as our "sweet nurse, sweet mother," with faith and instruction. For St. Bernard the miraculous experience of being fed with the milk of Mary's breast symbolized and complemented the blood from the side of Christ which washes and nourishes every Christian. A fourteenth-century British monk from the Isle of Farne locates the nurturing act of God in the crucified Christ who suckles Christians with blood from his riven side. "Do not wean me from the breasts of thy consolation as long as I live in this world."

A thirteenth-century prioress, Marguerite d'Oingt brings the common experience of women into her life with God as she identifies Christ's agony with that of a woman in labor.

> Ah, who has seen a woman give birth thus!
> And when the hour of birth came, they placed
> You on the bed of the Cross. And it is not astonishing
> your veins ruptured, as you gave birth in one single day,
> to the whole world!

The birth of the soul through Christ's death is here enlarged into the Pauline insight of the redemption of all creation, and both are seen as processes of a divine maternity.

These witnesses to the God who gives us birth, who accepts and loves us without question, who nurtures and feeds and trains us up into maturity are neither unorthodox, nor are they all women. We can now recognize that Dame Julian of Norwich, the fourteenth-century English anchoress who has lately been so often cited for her experience of Christ as our Mother, was not a lonely or peculiar voice. She stands in a long tradition of Christians, men and women, who experience God in a feminine way. However, Julian moves beyond the metaphor of religious experience to a reflective spirituality which gives theological substance to the meeting with Christ our Mother. Jesus, like a human mother, gives us our creaturehood.

"We owe our being to him, and this is the essence of motherhood." In pain he bears us into eternal life.

Thus he carries us within himself in love. And he is in labour until the time has fully come for him to suffer the sharpest pangs and most appalling pain possible—and in the end he dies . . . and we ourselves have been born to eternal bliss.

And finally, God in Christ feeds us with, and by means of, his Body, the Church.

The human mother will suckle her child with her own milk, but our beloved Mother, Jesus, feeds us with himself, and, with the most tender courtesy, does it by means of the Blessed Sacrament, the precious food of all true life. . . . The human mother may put her child tenderly to her breast, but our tender Mother Jesus simply leads us into his blessed breast through his open side, and there gives us a glimpse of the Godhead and heavenly joy—the inner certainty of eternal bliss.

The experiences of human motherhood and of divine motherhood in the free, self-giving sacrifice of Christ reinforce each other. The work of human mothers is given sacramental meaning and the action of God in the lives of men and women is felt in the maternal modalities familiar to all human beings. The mother in all of us is affirmed. Repeatedly, in the popular vernacular literature of prayer, Christ's sacrifice is experienced in a maternal way. The mother pelican, who was thought to feed her young with flesh and blood from her own breast, is still a figure of the sacrifice of the Cross. Catherine of Siena witnesses to the sophistication of fourteenth-century folk medicine as she describes the action of Christ on the Cross as that of the mother who swallows bitter medicine too harsh for her suckling child, then gives the child the breast, knowing the milk to contain a weakened and sufficient potion of the saving dosage.

Christ is not only our Mother. Medieval Christians experienced God in a wonderful variety of emotional relationships. They passed easily in prayer from Jesus the Lover of the Bride-Soul, to Mother of the Creature-Child, to Brother and Sister who stands with us in our creaturehood, to the Child who is born within in the castle of the soul, and to Father, Lord, and King. Nor is there a hierarchy in these images. Rather we encounter a rich mixture of sexual and natural metaphors of intimacy, from Friend of the Soul, to ". . . an immense ocean of sweetness . . . [where I] lose myself in the flood of thy living love as a drop of sea water." Yet even these impersonal God-pictures from the natural order often carry feminine overtones, the all-embracing water and fire and earth balance the Word from the Cloud or Burning Bush that is more typical of the Hebrew experience of the Father God of Abraham, Isaac, and Jacob.

The God of medieval piety was a Mother/Father, Sister/Brother, Lover/Child, a God of demanding *and* accepting Love, a God who is born within each of us and who bears us into life as a travailing mother. A British theologian, Eirene Willis, has recently commented on this tradition of spirituality as necessary for an adequate doctrine and experience of God.

> . . . we need to develop belief in a matrix of unconditional love within which demanding love operates—a matrix, something ultimate, not a subordinate kind of love that mitigates, wards off . . . as was that of the Virgin Mary. *Both* loves must be ultimate, both must be God's.

She goes on to ask whether a priesthood which is female and male might not more adequately incarnate, sacramentalize, and convey God's love to us. "Parental love, if it is to convey God's love to us, must be a sacrament in two kinds" (she cites H. A. Williams in an article from *Soundings*) and then adds: "If there were spiritual fathers and spiritual mothers we would have 'the two kinds . . .' and the two loves being exercised within the one priesthood would strongly and consistently imply their operation in the one Ultimate Reality."

Before we ask what happened to wipe away this more whole, more adequate image of God in the Church's prayer, a word must be said about the androgynous "people-language" which flourished along with the tradition of Christ our Mother-Father, Sister-Brother, Servant-King, Child-Lover. H. A. Williams, in the essay cited above, assumed that the "Herm-Aphrodite" (his term) God-language disappeared because: "It had nothing in human experience on which to fasten. The grotesque cannot evoke love." As an historian, I question this judgment; it reflects an anachronistic absolutizing of contemporary concepts of the natural and the grotesque. We assume the rigid and polarized definitions of masculine and feminine current in our society to be biological, ontological givens, and these assumptions carry over into our conceptions of God.

Yet we see that feminine God-imagery has had a long history in Christian piety, and associated with that tradition was the fact that medieval men and women seemed to experience *themselves* in a more androgynous, even a more feminine way. St. Francis bade the obedient soul to be a spouse, joined to Christ by the Holy Spirit, to be a brother to do his will, to be a mother to carry Christ in his body and give birth to him by enlightening others through example. This letter was addressed to friars, men, pastors, and preachers who were to be mothers in their ministry. St. Bernard also bade priests and prelates to be mothers, to whom the wounded resort as to the bosom of a mother. Whether in male or female body, the Christian's soul *(anima)* was always feminine in grammar as well as personification. Therefore, even the medieval man was continually knowing himself as a bride of Christ, the vocation of all Christians.

The androgynous self-image of the Christian woman is more familiar to us. From the time of Jerome's designation of a holy woman as one who had become, as it were, a man *(vir)*, to the moment of our own commitment ". . . manfully to fight under his banner . . ." Christian women have known the reality of male models of personhood. The woman in a patriarchal society, then and now, has always had more opportunity than the man to develop her contrasexual potentiality.

What is striking and perhaps of great significance for us today, is that medieval men and women, especially men, were apparently comfortable about perceiving themselves in either sexual mode. The medieval "conceit" of finding the soul, a "she," at the center of what it means to be a human being, meant that every Christian had the possibility of experiencing reality as the receiver as well as the giver, the bride as well as the groom, the mother as well as the father. Must there not be some connection between this more whole sense of human nature and the more adequate symbolization of the God of love who accepts as well as demands, who is mother and father, which was witnessed to by Christians of the pre-modern world? As illustration, John Donne writes of a newly ordained Anglican priest:

> These are thy titles and preeminences,
> In whom must meet Gods graces, mens offences,
> And so the heavens which beget all things here,
> And the earth our mother, which these things doth beare,
> Both these in thee, are in thy Calling knit,
> And make thee now a blest Hermaphrodite.

What happened to this divine and human wholeness—for it is certainly hardly any longer with us. These are new questions. Reformation scholars have just begun to address themselves to the role of women in the religious movements. We are asking something far more difficult. We are inquiring after the fate of "the feminine" in the post-Reformation church. At this stage, one can only make some tentative suggestions, not offer certain answers.

If we consider first the negative misogynist inheritance from classical and Christian antiquity, the impact of Luther and Calvin seems at first glance to have changed little. For Luther, the woman is defined as in Thomas Aquinas, principally as a means of procreation and a remedy for sin; that is, the wife in marriage tames the lust which otherwise would lead a man to fornication. Luther makes an important theological concession to the original integrity of Creation in finding the loss of woman's equality with man in the results of Eve's sin. However, he continues to follow the medieval tradition which associates the woman's mental, moral, and physical inferiority with her defining purpose in life, the procreation of the race.

Men have broad and large chests and small narrow hips, and more understanding than women, who have but small and narrow breasts and broad hips to the end that they should remain at home, sit still, keep house, and bear and bring up children.

Despite Luther's positive view of the family, he never escapes the deep pessimism toward the sexual act, and therefore toward women, which the Church had read out of Paul and Augustine.

We can hardly speak of her without a feeling of shame, and we surely cannot make use of her without shame.

Calvin also follows the medieval tradition in holding that by God's eternal law, the female sex is subject to the male.

Let man exercise authority with moderation, let woman be satisfied with the state of subjection and not take it amiss that she is made inferior to the more distinguished sex.

It is this view, that woman was created "to be a distinguished ornament of the man," which lies hidden within the theologies of contemporary exponents of sexual complementarity. The Reformation has passed on to us a logic by which sexual difference is grounded in inferiority. The Church today acts as if she holds

Luther's view, ". . . the woman appears to be a somewhat different being from the man, having different members *and a much weaker nature.*"

Yet much more needs to be said of the Reformers' impact on the relationship between the sexes. The inheritance is indeed ambiguous. Many have remarked on the Protestant rejection of the medieval ethical double standard, monasticism and celibacy for those who pursue Christian perfection, married life for the ordinary mortal. Calvin and Luther, in particular, coupled an insistence on the universal calling of *all* Christians to a total commitment to God with a celebration of Christian family life. The home becomes "the little school of charity," replacing the monastery as the center of Christian nurture and ". . . father and mother are apostles, bishops, priests to their children, for it is they who make them acquainted with the Gospel." The Christian woman thus is given a spiritual vocation in motherhood, though Luther's praise of the fruitful mother has for us some of the ambiguities of the celebration of martyrdom. "Let them bear themselves out. This is the purpose for which they exist." The woman, ". . . built out of Adam's rib" is the builder of the household, the home, which in Reformation theology has now a religious dignity. The "work" of childbearing and child rearing and providing a safe haven for the husband take on spiritual meaning.

We spoke of ambiguity. The two-edged character of these innovations must be recognized, for, in fact, the Reformers had reduced the possible vocations for Christian women by half. The freely chosen consecrated virginity of the nun is gone, only marriage and motherhood remain as full Christian vocations. No longer could a woman of Protestant faith opt for a life devoted to God alone. No longer could she live either as an autonomous anchoress or in a sisterhood, a bride of Christ only, subject to a self-imposed rule of obedience to God and ecclesial superiors, yet free of father, husband, and family. In practice, the only religious vocation beyond that of childbearing for women within the major Protestant confessions came to be that of the minister's wife. (Among the so-called radical sects of the sixteenth and seventeenth centuries—for example, the Quakers and Shakers—women functioned in ministry and leadership alongside men. The reasons for this community between the sexes form an as yet unwritten chapter in our common history.) Not until the missionary movements of the nineteenth century, the revival of religious orders, the abolitionist and social reform movements, do we find Protestant women moving out of the home into positions of religious leadership and responsibility.

A glance at our own revised church calendar, revealing the total absence of women since the sixteenth century among those we commemorate as saints, symbolizes the way in which the destruction of the religious life in Protestantism and the Anglican Church deprived those Christian communities of the spiritual creativity which women had exercised in the pre-Reformation church. This is not to say that there was no contribution to church life by faithful Christian wives and mothers. But one must insist that we miss the innovative, formative, and reforming roles taken in the community by women like Hilda of Whitby, Brigid of Sweden, Joan of Arc, Catherine of Siena, Teresa of Avila, Angela Merici (founder of the Ursulines), and Madame Guyon, the controversial seventeenth-century French mystic. Roman Catholic women after the sixteenth century continued to shape and contribute to the community, for their church retained the theory and structures which enabled them to respond to a diversity of callings within the pursuit of holiness. But for Protestants, the Reformation destroyed the one structure within the institutional church where men and women functioned as equals before God, the monastic life, leaving the church to be led and formed by the all-male clerical order.

A second aspect of our ambiguous inheritance in the area of human sexuality from the sixteenth-century religious revolution lies deeply embedded in the Protestant shifts in the doctrine of God and God's relationship to the world. Roughly speaking, Protestant doctrines of justification tended to move sharply away from the immanental divine presence of late medieval mysticism toward the Father God whose extrinsic historical acts justify the human being from without, independent of our cooperation. This is the Wholly Other God whose inscrutable judgments were symbolized by a renewed emphasis on the doctrine of predestination and a preference for the Word over sacrament as the chosen means of God's saving presence among us. Historically, the language and imagery of Protestant God-talk tended to come from the very male and patriarchal inheritance of the Old Testament rather than out of the medieval literature of religious experience mediated by women as well as men. Psychologically, this renewed focus on transcendence, the otherness, the arbitrary judgments of God was most naturally symbolized by patriarchal fatherhood. God the initiator, the lawgiver was especially the gift of Calvin and later Lutheran orthodoxy to Protestant Christianity and Anglicanism. We have drunk deeply at this trough, most recently under the guidance of Karl Barth. This theology of transcendence with its one-sided male emphasis may have been a necessary corrective in the sixteenth century. It has in the last years come to be destructive of and unfaithful to the God experience of those twentieth-century

Christians, men and women, who feel and know the One within, the God of boundless mercy and love, the ground of our being who seeks us out of the fullness of creation and the stillness of our soul. The Protestant focus on the God of transcendence has helped undermine and deny our experience of the feminine in the Ultimate and in ourselves.

Lastly, the Protestant Reformers, or their followers, again reacting against serious abuses, embarked on a theology and a praxis of iconoclasm which ultimately weakened their own sacramental theology and obscured the truth that lies in an experiencing of the divine indwelling in ourselves and all creation. There was a rationalistic and spiritualizing tendency abroad in the sixteenth century, an attack on the physical—relics, crucifixes, the Real Presence, the purchase of pardons, honor to the Virgin—which carried antifeeling, antifeminine tendencies. The mood was one of distinction, analysis, criticism, rather than integration and rediscovery of wholeness.

No sharper example of this can be found than Ulrich Zwingli's diatribes against music in the liturgy. In his early life as a Benedictine choir boy, music had moved Zwingli himself, but in later years, as a leader of the Reformation in Zurich, he came to believe that the potential of music for the stirring of strong emotion was seriously destructive of true religion, which Christ tells us is of the spirit. Music touches the emotions and is of the flesh. Therefore, it was disallowed and Zwingli ordered every organ in Zurich smashed. He went so far as to forbid the singing of the popular, rousing Lutheran chorales lest the pure worship of God be marred by fleshly feeling. Even Anglicans, with our sacramentally ordered life, our linguistically elegant Prayer Book, and our heritage of Byrd and Gibbons and Vaughn Williams, have not remained untouched by this Puritan and ultimately docetic heresy.

If we are honest with ourselves, we will have to discover that opposition to women in priesthood bears some deep relationship to this fear of the body, of emotion, of that which stirs within when we contemplate a man and a woman together at God's altar. We may laugh at Zwingli's anxieties about organs and choirs, but his denial of the Real Presence and his heretical christology, like our common fear of the conjunction of the woman and the holy, are functions of an unwillingness to take seriously the Incarnation, that God became flesh in our humanity. It is not, I believe, too farfetched to suggest that since the eighteenth century, Anglicanism has imbibed all too much of this humanistic rationalism with its male, antibody, antifeeling bias. In so doing we have abandoned our own heritage, of St. Anselm, Dame Julian, John Donne, Richard Crashaw, men and

women whose sense of divine indwelling preserved for them an
experience of the feminine in God and in Creation without losing
that vision of the God who is beyond all creatures, being, or language.

The Protestant Reformation was a necessary cataclysm in the life
of the Christian church, which had lost in many areas a just balance
between worldliness and holiness, between the all-sufficiency of
God's actions and our response, between the transcendent Father
God of judgment and the immanent, homely mercies of the saints.
But correctives frequently overshoot the mark, and in the issue of the
right relationship of masculine and feminine, which now so tears at
our peace in the church and the world, we suffer from a serious
obscuring of the Catholic tradition. Until recent centuries, the
church at prayer had found it possible, despite a patriarchal social
setting, to name God Mother and Sister as well as Brother, King, and
Lover. The naming of God is an awesome and powerful human act—
in some way it names every human possibility. We need to recover
today, not an artificially resurrected copy of fourteenth-century God-
language, although liturgical reform in this area is absolutely necessary. No, we need to recover the reality which that naming reflected,
an experience of God within, God our Mother, God who uncondition-
ally accepts our and her broken world, God who takes into herself
and affirms by her wholeness the full potential of man and woman to
be God-bearers. We need to be led, in this spiritual adventure, this
twentieth-century fulfillment of the Reformation which failed to take
place in the sixteenth century, by explorers of that inner space where
God is born in the self and in the cosmos. These Reformers will be
found among the laywomen and laymen, male and female priests,
deacons and bishops who are in touch with and can symbolize the
reconciling, mediating, integrating *anima* of God and humanity,
without which there can be no life.

chapter 5

A HOMEOPATHY OF SEX

R. M. COOPER

Sex and death are powerful. There is no news in that, and I have nothing new to say about either sex or death. Our time, in its discovery of the fact that sex and death *are* powerful, is not substantially different from any other age. It is a necessary condition of human beings, of persons, that the power of sex and the power of death be discovered. That sex and death are closely associated is something that has been known for millenia, and the hackneyed literary phrases do not even bear repetition now. However, the human opportunity of finding life and living remains. The closeness of the relation between sex and death can be readily seen in our culture, our films, and our literature. And both films and literature are language in a broader sense. The close connection between sex and death can be seen in the pathetic common wisdom that sex is healing, i.e., that it is therapeutic. Such therapy is, however, as I shall attempt to show, the healing of my people's wound lightly. Sexual contact, sexual intercourse of whatever sort, *is not necessary for a particular person,* though every person remains incurably, aboriginally, sexual. There are no perfect orgasms for imperfect people, and no achievement of technique will heal a technician.

Such assertions require some substantiation. In arguing that sexual contact is not finally therapeutic, it would be necessary to say something about how our time differs from others in its view of sex. That would be essentially a descriptive task and, for the most part, I limit myself to such a task. A description of how we value or disvalue ourselves with respect to others would be a normative task. In the language of some anthropologists, the former is a task of ethnography, the latter a task for ethnology. Or: *What,* in fact, are we dealing with? And *how* do we understand that "what" in terms of other human expressions of sexuality?

I will speak of these things in terms of "contemporary films and literature"—an enormous undertaking. It is clear that not everything that is in print is "literature," for there are traditions and methods for making such determinations that have been fashioned over centuries. But what about our films? What criteria have we there? We have criteria, to be sure, but they are far less secure. No one, I think, would want to say that everything that is on film is art. To say so is to introduce another difficult term, namely, art. In an essay as brief as this one it is necessary to avoid the attempt to say what is literature, and what is art in film. It can be said, however, that everything that is in print or on film makes some statement, conveys some meaning about humanity directly or indirectly.

John Henry Newman observed that literature "is the Life and Remains of the *natural* man, innocent or guilty." He continued:

> If then by literature is meant the manifestation of human nature in human language, you will seek for it in vain except in the world. Put up with it, as it is, or do not pretend to cultivate it; take things as they are, not as you could wish them.[1]

I propose that the same thing could be said about films, and that the same warning can be issued concerning our treatment of them. This is difficult to do. We are never able to question what we take for granted, for that is what is meant by being taken for granted; namely, that which is assumed, that which is virtually inarticulate. A writer shares to some degree what is taken for granted in his own age, and interpretation is, therefore, always difficult, if not perilous. Description, for the same reasons, is also difficult.

I will speak of two recent films and of two recent novels; and in doing so I must assume my reader's acquaintance with them. The films are *Shampoo* and *Alice Doesn't Live Here Anymore*. The novels are Iris Murdoch's *The Sacred and Profane Love Machine*,[2] and Erica Jong's *Fear of Flying*.[3] In making my selection, I claim only that these are recent works, and that they have to do in some explicit ways with human sexuality. There is a common motif in them all: that human sexual contact is fulfilling and therapeutic; that everybody wants "to get it off (or on)"; that everybody is entitled (has a right) to it. Sex is a commodity. It is something to be acquired. And since everybody already has it, he can be a giver as well as a taker or getter. In short, sex is divorced from the deepest roots of our being.

Two examples from the current cinema will show that that is, in fact, the way we think about our sexuality; namely, in that we use the word "sex" for "sexual intercourse," or for the more basic one-syllable terms which probably cannot be printed in this modest volume.

Three items—an advertisement, a review, and a poem—point the way to our understanding of these two films. It is not the sexuality that we are, but the "thing" we "use" or do not "use," as the case may be. The same sense of sex is employed by Richard Hughes, in a review of a Tom Wolfe book. He writes:

So in *The Printed Word* Wolfe tries to come across as the little boy looking at the Emperor's new clothes. In fact, his account of the art world reads more like an eleven-year-old's written report on a pornographic movie. The lad is spry and attentive at first. He can see things moving up and down and in and out, buttocks heaving, breasts jiggling. *He has heard about sex but never had any.* Consequently he has no inkling of what the real transaction between these absorbed couples might be, or why the glazed audience is staring so raptly at the screen. His state is incomprehension, broken by fits of naughty giggles.[4]

"He has heard about sex but never had any." Not so! Ever since conception he has "had" sex, and he does well to either giggle or to lapse into inattention, for what he sees (in Hughes's example) is essentially boring—as boring, finally, as the clown who will not give up the laughs he got for attempting (interminably) to staunch the flow of blood from an amputated leg with a Bandaid. He is bored because boredom ensues inevitably in a world that either knows no limits at all or endlessly focuses attention upon very narrow limits.

The following brief poem by D. H. Lawrence, which I quote in its entirety, generalizes the issue of the divorce of our culture from life (and I quote it without subscribing implicitly to all of Lawrence's doctrine about sex, blood, life, etc.):

When I went to the film, and saw all the black-and-white feelings that
nobody felt,
and heard the audience sighing and sobbing with all the emotions they none
of them felt,
and saw them cuddling with rising passions they none of them for a moment
felt,
and caught them moaning from close-up kisses, black-and-white kisses that
could not be felt,
It was like being in heaven, which I am sure has a white atmosphere
upon which shadows of people, pure personalities
are cast in black and white, and move
in flat ecstasy, supremely unfelt,
and heavenly.[5]

Lawrence's heaven in this poem is bodiless; for him, such a "heaven" is a hell. It is the place of death. For Lawrence, films are fundamentally pornographic for they concentrate only upon surfaces.

They can tell very little about the depths of persons, but they *can* depict us in a partial, and therefore not insignificant manner.

George, a hairdresser, is the principal male character of *Shampoo*. He is a caricature of a human being, and he partly knows it but is too stupid to change. He knows that he has—and well beyond the common measure—what every woman wants: male sex. He enjoys "doing it," and he is helping out the women. And, besides, they like it. He meets their needs. He is a species of healer. Part of the alleged comedy of the film resides in his putting off one paramour by telling her that another has a serious malady and that he must leave their bed in order to go minister to her. Hairdressers are healers, and they are generally cheaper to hire than psychiatrists or analysts—especially when they can moonlight as the latter. God knows, we need all the comedy we can get about sex in our times, obsessed as we are with it. *Shampoo* is *de trop*, and we are finally bored.

A deadlier species of healer is Alice's disingenuous cowboy in the film *Alice Doesn't Live Here Anymore*. For him, sex is the instrumentality of power, as one would employ a scalpel or a hammer, and it is close to death-dealing because it is fundamentally sadistic. The sex he has is for him the means of exercising control over women. Sadism is always, at least almost always, an assault upon the freedom of another, which assault finds its limits in not being able to coerce the victim into *liking* what is perpetrated upon him or her.[6] (Though I do not have space to treat it here, the most interesting aspect of *Alice Doesn't Live Here Anymore*, from the point of view of human sexuality, is that of the various relations women without husbands have with their children. There are three such characterizations in the film; the most developed is that of Alice and her adolescent son.)

The punk lover of Alice, who brutalizes his own wife, knows what every single woman wants—No, needs!—male sex. And by God, he is going to give it to her, force her! It is not surprising that if death and sex are powerful, cruelty, which is close to both of them, is going to be present in some measure.

A January 1975 issue of *Paris Match* notes in an article[7] that the big money in films is now moving from pornography (for example, *Emanuelle*, which is advertised in this country as a film that "leaves you with a singular lack of guilt"—probably, I would observe, because it can only touch you on the surface of your life) to horror films. Cruelty—the helplessness of a victim placed under pain by another—is a frequent, if not a constant, companion of "horror." (See Joseph Conrad's *The Heart of Darkness*.) Pain always involves some caricature of human being. When we are in pain we experience it as the demand for the attention of our organism to a given portion of the organism: namely, where the hurt is. The part overwhelms the whole. Pain is the impairment of actual or hoped-for wholeness.

What is felt by us as sexual urgency, or need, is a species of pain in the sense in which I have been speaking of pain; that is, as that which demands a disproportionate measure of attention, thereby rendering us caricatures of human beings, caricatures of whole persons. Not infrequently it is more pleasant to cherish and coddle the pain, because to be released from it will require of us a more dreadful and difficult thing: the exercise of the freedom that persons *are* upon a wider range of themselves and their world.

The relationship of sex to pain leads up to Erica Jong's novel, *Fear of Flying*. There are no persons and no characters—only caricatures. Jong is better as a poet, for as such she *is* the place where the painful and hurtful piecemeal nature of our human experience is felt, recorded, and voiced. The book is an episodic record, discontinuous, like all of the names that "people" her novel. It is hard for me to care what happens to Isadora Wing, the principal female in *Fear of Flying*; as difficult as it is for the reader of *The Story of O* to care for the concatenation of orifices that passes there for someone.

In contrast, in the work of D. H. Lawrence there are *characters*, persons struggling to become whole. *Women in Love* is profoundly erotic, and the reader can believe that he is in the presence of persons, persons he can care about: love or hate. The same could be said about the majority of the characters in, for example, George Eliot's *Middlemarch*. Sexuality struggles in Lawrence's characters to come to birth untrammeled. The labor produced its own fruits and has its own integrity, but when one looks to Erica Jong, abortions litter the landscape of Europe and America. The vapidity of the characters can find nothing substantializing for them in her claim that *Fear of Flying* is "a female picaresque."[8] Readers can still care about Don Quixote and Sancho Panza and the host that peoples Cervantes' great work, but with Erica Jong it is impossible to care about the bodies which seem only so many addenda to so many pudenda, bodies attached to genitals, bodies uninhabited by persons. There are no characters in *Fear of Flying*. Jong's novel is a caricature of human being. It is essentially pornographic in that it focuses upon genital caricature. Lawrence, I am persuaded, would have loathed it.

Jong herself claims that her *Fear of Flying* is a novel about "unfulfillment," that it "is not really a very sexy book."[9] I would agree. But *why* is it a novel of unfulfillment? Too much is freighted on sex. Human sexuality will not bear all that we try to make it carry. *Everything that is human is sexual,* and there can be no successful substitution of any part for the whole. Sex will never replace the whole of human being. I have said that her characters are, in fact, nonexistent, that they are bodies following their genitals to such chic places as New York City, Heidelberg, Paris, Vienna, London. Isadora Wing is married to a psychiatrist, and the novel is in part set in an international meeting of psychiatrists. She finds no therapy in her various liaisons, with either her psychiatrist husband or her psychiatrist lover. The therapy of venereal liaison is a failure; she remains "unfulfilled." She remains so, because that is the way we are made. The part cannot heal the whole.

Iris Murdoch's novel, *The Sacred and Profane Love Machine,* has as its principal male character, Blaise Gavender, a psychotherapist. He who cannot heal himself is a healer of others. He has led a double life for nine years: with his wife and their son, and with his mistress and their son (again, mothers and sons without fathers in a conventional sense). Blaise's life with his wife is presumably sexually conventional, while with his mistress we are led to believe that it is "kinky," involving "bondage." Just as there is no healing sex in *Fear of Flying,* there is no union of sexual gratification and love in *The Sacred and Profane Love Machine.*

In Murdoch's novel there are reports of sexual gratification—the reader being spared the details—but what is missing is the uniting of love and sexual gratification. The characters are left in their hells, where the author found them. Presumably, healing would result from the uniting of sexual intercourse and love, and thus a measure of authentic but piecemeal life could ensue. Monty Small, a character of Miss Murdoch's, makes numerous references to hell, and is spoken of by Blaise as Mephistopheles. Having just been referred to by Blaise under that designation, Monty remarks, "Well, intelligence does help in hell. It helped Milton's characters. Once you can start thinking about the situation instead of being crushed by it, you'll immediately suffer less."[10] What haunts this passage, and many others, is the old Christian view that hell is wanting your own way, and getting it. In three of these four movies and novels I have mentioned, we have physicians who cannot heal themselves. The homeopathy of sex cannot heal our condition. That much, at least, I see in Newman's *"natural* man" as he is found in these works. In short, human sexual contact can be many things—good and bad, healing and hurtful—but never a medicine of immortality, never finally therapeutic. To repeat: Our sexuality cannot bear all that we have freighted upon it.

Sex and death are powerful, and coming to deal with them, I have said, is a necessary condition for personhood. I wish to conclude this brief essay with reference to the remarks of those wiser than I which address the point that sex as a possession does not heal as we think, but conveys a deathly meaning. In a recent interview with Michel Contat, Jean-Paul Sartre said:

I am not talking about the language of sex properly speaking. As for language itself, it comes from the deepest place, it comes from sex, when a love relationship is involved. With a woman, the whole of what one is is present.[11]

The critic, George Steiner, has recently observed that:

To speak and to make love is to enact a distinctive twofold universality: both forms of communication are universals of human physiology as well as of social evolution. It is likely that human sexuality and speech developed in close-knit reciprocity.[12]

For Steiner, an assault upon language is always a spear thrust at the heart of human being; it is essentially death-dealing. The same holds for an assault on our sexuality, which is what we see in *Shampoo, Alice Doesn't Live Here Anymore,* and *Fear of Flying.* He states that "the kinds of things said about death offer a grammatical and ontological parallel. Language and death may be conceived of as the two areas of meaning or cognitive constants in which grammar and ontology are mutually determined."[13]

As for language, so for sexuality; destroy the necessary relationship between lovemaking and sexuality and the only alternative is death. While Steiner's is high doctrine, it is but another way of instancing the powerfulness of sex and death, and their intimate connection with language. In the language of the films and novels that I have considered so superficially here, we see the persistent symptoms of a disease of which we are dying. We are sufficiently fascinated with the pornography of our own deaths that we continue the remedy that is killing us.

NOTES

1. John Henry Newman, *The Idea of a University Defined and Illustrated* (London: Basil Montagu Pickering, 1873), pp. 227–228, 232.

2. Iris Murdoch, *The Sacred and Profane Love Machine* (New York: The Viking Press, 1974).

3. Erica Jong, *Fear of Flying* (New York: New American Library, Signet Books, 1973).

4. *Time Magazine,* June 23, 1975, p. 40. My emphasis.

5. "When I Went to the Film—" in *The Complete Poems of D. H. Law-*

rence, edited by Vivian de Sola Pinto and Warren Roberts (New York: The Viking Press, 1964), vol. I, pp. 443–444.

6. I am relying here on the important book by Philip P. Hallie, *The Paradox of Cruelty* (Middletown, Conn.: Wesleyan University Press, 1969).

7. *Nouveau Paris Match,* January 4, 1975, p. 42.

8. Erica Jong, *Here Comes & Other Poems* [originally published as *Fruits & Vegetables* and *Half-Lives*] (New York: New American Library, Signet Books, 1975), p. 275.

9. *Ibid.*

10. Murdoch, *The Sacred and Profane Love Machine,* p. 130.

11. Jean-Paul Sartre and Michel Contat, "Sartre at Seventy: An Interview," trans. by Paul Auster and Lydia Davis, *The New York Review of Books,* vol. XXII, no. 13 (August 7, 1975), p. 16.

12. George Steiner, *After Babel: Aspects of Language and Translation* (New York: Oxford University Press, 1975), p. 38.

13. Steiner, *After Babel,* p. 124. See also Steiner's *Language and Silence: Essays on Language, Literature, and the Inhuman* (New York: Atheneum, 1970), especially the essays, "Night Words," and "A Note on Günter Grass."

PART III

Some Contemporary Issues

chapter 6

CHANGING PATTERNS OF MARRIAGE

John Snow

The danger in discussing changing patterns of marriage is that one may suggest by the topic itself that there is some sort of orderly, conscious, ideological shift from one marriage pattern to another. This is probably not the case even where couples, or even whole communities, believe that they are involved in precisely this. No institution is more conservative than marriage, because it lies at the heart of social organization. Marriage is concerned with ordering the relationships between the sexes, the procreation and raising of children, and the orderly transfer of both culture and property from one generation to the next. In the past, precisely because of its crucial importance, marriage has proved to be extraordinarily adaptive to its environment, but in all cultures the adaptation is achieved slowly, and once an equilibrium is found it tends to be maintained fiercely.

What we are experiencing in Western society, and with a vengeance in many regions of the United States, is the disruption of the core institution of marriage, and what seem to be changing patterns of marriage are in reality frantic, impulsive, desperate attempts of this core institution to maintain its equilibrium—or even more frantic, impulsive, and desperate attempts to find a new equilibrium. What we are experiencing at present is chaos at the center of society. To state the issue less radically is to avoid it; and to avoid it is cruel, for marital agony is currently experienced and understood most often as a private, personal inadequacy.

In order that some new and nonalienating equilibrium might be discovered, we must understand what is happening to us. Only then shall we be able to begin to deal with the chaos and to move rationally toward a newly viable institution.

Among human beings, all sense of meaningfulness and purposefulness is found in continuing relationships. As Peter Marris points out in his book *Loss and Change* (Pantheon Books, 1974), when we suggest to recently bereaved persons that they should cheer up and go out and have some fun, they look at us uncomprehendingly. They actually do not know what we mean. What could they possibly do without the person they have lost that would be fun? Their agony is that they can't really see any reason for doing anything. Radical discontinuity in human relationships, whatever its cause, results in an at least momentary loss of purposefulness, and the restoration of purpose and meaning will depend on establishing some new relationship with the lost past, on seeing oneself in a new way in relationship to it. In American life, innovative technology causes many such discontinuities, and they are largely unplanned and undealt with. The disruption of the core institution of marriage is primarily a result of these discontinuities, and the history of this disruption is not hard to trace.

During World War II, American business and industry discovered that transportation in the United States had reached a level of sophistication that made it possible to move a large labor force wherever it was needed by offering sufficient wages. They discovered, too, that management was equally amenable to moving about. indeed, the whole country seemed to find a new exhilaration in its wheels and wings and movement. Soldiers and sailors stationed in a once lovely California vowed to return, and did when the war was over. The G.I. Bill sent millions of young men to college who otherwise might not have gone, and these young men and the women they married felt no desire to return to the small towns and cities of their birth when they could go into junior management jobs and partake of the joys of suburbia wherever suburbia was.

Business and industry also discovered that a transient management was a more efficient management. The newly arrived manager had no investment in things as they were, no embarrassing friendships with peers or subordinates. He could shake and move his department in ways impossible for the manager buried in an enclave of relationships. By the early 1950s it was accepted that to go up in a large company was to be willing to move and move often. Most people wanted to go up, and most people moved.

And children were born. Lots of them. School systems strained, first to meet the demands and then to anticipate the demands of the population explosion. More and more teachers and administrators were hired, and these, too, began to get in the habit of moving, or, if they were the wives of industrial management, moved whether they wanted to or not. Children were faced with a bewildering array of discontinuous relationships which they were expected to regard as normal. Television became the most dependable relationship they had, even though it lied to them constantly and they knew it.

By the third move, many of the mothers and children of transient suburbia began to show signs of combat fatigue. Mothers complained of irritability, constant fatigue, an inability to feel much of anything. Doctors prescribed amphetamines. Mothers complained of sleeplessness. Doctors prescribed tranquilizers. Drug companies cooperated by supplying blends of the two. Children became listless or hyperactive or developed learning problems. Some mothers innocently shared their drug expertise with their children. Television urged pills of whatever kind on everyone. Emotional disorders became too numerous for psychiatry, and counseling of one kind or another became a growth industry. Martinis became dryer and dryer and larger and larger.

The men began to burn out, to drink too much, smoke too much, work too much; and finally, by the middle 1960s as their children reached adolescence, to die too much. They had a good deal of money by now. The economy was booming. Many had lost interest in their work and felt they deserved some diversion. The death of peers and the gnawing of their own ulcers had made them aware of their own mortality. Many chose sex as their diversion, but since most had been brought up to be responsible people, the sex led to divorce and remarriage—a new life. Their ex-wives, too often out of despair, became sexually predatory, hoping against hope to be married again because marriage was all they felt prepared for—although they suspected they weren't very good at that either. The "togetherness" family, the most successful advertising hoax of history, that brave little band of consumers out to vanquish the world, was no longer together. In its place was a plastic jungle, a competitive hell.

So much for the picture, the sociological image. It is not, of course, any more accurate than the manufactured mythology of the togetherness family. It leaves out the heroic, the quietly heroic, resistance of millions of middle-class Americans who were, during this time, trying to make sense out of their lives and the society within which they lived their lives. It leaves out the unnumbered families who tried to build a sane community around worship and sacrifice and service and mutual care. Worst of all, it trivializes the innate seriousness of individual human beings. Yet the dark sociological picture is part of the way even the most serious suburbanites see their own life experience, especially if an angry child, home from college or commune, has spelled it out to them in graphic, ruthless terms.

The picture also leaves out the life experience of most Americans
—the urbanite of whatever class or color, the people who continue to
live in small towns or cities, the farmers and rural people in general,
and the entire laboring class. But this picture is a part of their fantasies and dreams as it filters through the media, and it influences their
marriages as well. If we are talking about changing patterns of marriage, the classical image of the suburban togetherness family falling
apart is the source of whatever new patterns of marriage are developing; for only the children of these marriages, the parental survivors
of these marriages, or the Korean War generation influenced by them
are affluent enough to experiment with new forms. To some degree,
the new forms are all reactions to this image or variations on it.

The first technological development to affect marriage, then, was
in the area of transportation, and resulted in a mindless transiency
which made the American middle class an essentially rootless, dis-
enfranchised, and powerless sector of society. The best educated and
politically most sophisticated people in the country were removed
from its political life and placed in pleasant enough camps where
they managed the middle levels of its economic life. In their affluent, consumptive impotence these people lost any felt sense of
meaning or purpose, and in too many cases their marriages (and
families) began to disintegrate. But while this was happening, two
other technological innovations occurred which were to affect radically the lives of their children and, to a lesser but still important
degree, their own lives.

The first was the computer, all the social results of which we have
not yet begun to understand. Nevertheless, one result of it was a
raised ecological consciousness which was to have devastating consequences for the self-image of the American middle class. It was out
of computer projections that we came to understand that we lived in
a finite cosmos, and that what we had come to regard as the good life
was in reality an impulsive squandering of limited planetary resources which, in turn, resulted in a rapid poisoning of the earth's air
and water. To describe the situation in less brutal terms would be to
do injustice to how it was apprehended emotionally by the younger
generation, the most intelligent and sensitive of whom saw their
future and the future of humanity ripped off by our mindless greed.

The second technological innovation was the mixture of effective
birth control and safe abortion. Those who had children were made
to feel irrationally guilty, and those who continued or began to have
children were made out in the media to be irresponsible. Parenthood, the most sanctioned and legitimated estate in Western society,
was under question. What, in its inevitability, had been regarded as

a blessing and source of hope and commitment to the future, very suddenly became an option, and as an option, a possible threat to the future. An unquestioned core value of society was, if not removed, radically modified, and women began to wonder what on earth they were here for. The extent to which men were made to feel the same way has not yet surfaced so violently. But both men and women became considerably less convinced that they were here to be married until death should them part.

New patterns of marriage, then, can be seen as attempts of couples to deal with the psychic and institutional wreckage brought about in the society by interpersonal discontinuity and a heightened sense of cosmic doom. These new patterns can be divided into two categories. The first might be called passive-adaptive, and the other, countercultural.

Passive-adaptive patterns of marriage are based on the assumption that human beings can adjust to discontinuity and cosmic meaninglessness by arranging a set of secondary interpersonal adjustments centered around the single value of hedonism. People choosing the passive-adaptive modes of marriage feel that the discontinuity is essentially liberating, and that the need for any sense of cosmic meaning or purpose is not basic to human life but an anachronistic, learned construct which binds people to static social institutions by causing them to identify with these institutions and to be blindly loyal to them. To rely on any form of institutional identity or continuing relationship is to be trapped. To remain sane and free, it is held, one must forge an identity together enough to avoid any commitment to any institution or other person which might begin to interfere with one's personal fulfillment or growth. All this is best summed up in the much quoted extrapolation from Fritz Perls, often referred to as a "manifesto" but certainly not to be taken as Perls' last word on the nature of interpersonal reality:

I do my thing and you do your thing. I am not in this world to live up to your expectations, and you are not in this world to live up to mine. You are you, and I am I. And if, by chance, we find each other, it's beautiful. If not, it can't be helped.

It must be remembered that those who quote this manifesto with most passion are of that generation who, from the time of their birth, were in too many cases never permitted to have a relationship of more than a few year's duration with anyone but their parents, and who often had no continuous relationship with either parent. It must also be remembered that in the bewildering discontinuities of their growing up they were continually meeting with conflicting expectations of who they should be and how they should behave. Although these people view this manifesto as something new and liberating, it is hardly more than a confirmation of their own experience; but this confirmation of who they are is understandably reassuring. The children of discontinuity and loss simply do not know if they are capable of a lasting relationship, and this manifesto at least gives them the courage to make a tentative beginning.

Marriages entered into under this rubric, then, are tentative. The institution of marriage is no more to be trusted than any other, and the people who believe this, even though they may have gone through the forms of marriage required by law, do not regard themselves as "married people." Marriage does not become a part of their identity. They do not feel much obligation to live up to the classical expectations of this institution. They may have quietly made a contract with each other, renewable, say, in five years, and to be renegotiated at that time. Or they may have agreed upon an open marriage, hoping that it would "work" and be a continuing relationship, but assuming that the classical role-expectations of traditional marriage would be destructive rather than supportive to a continuing relationship. The breadwinning male and the child-rearing, homemaking female and the whole concept of lifelong sexual fidelity are not role-expectations to be trusted, particularly since sex and procreation no longer have any inevitable connection, and having any children at all in an option. The marriage relationship, then, is more like a friendship spiced with sex and with interchangeable roles and functions. If there is a child or two, all aspects of the parenting will be shared. Possible extramarital sexual experimentation is agreed upon from the start, with the proviso that it will not be done secretly and will not be persisted in if it begins to prove threatening to the primary relationship.

It is important to note that the trend toward agreed upon extramarital sexual experimentation began in traditional marriages during the middle 1950s with the advent of the pill. This was before role-expectations had broken down, and just the term "wife-swapping" expresses the male dominance involved in the process. Within a traditional marriage this kind of experimentation proved to be destructive to women, increasing their sense of submissiveness and exploitation. It was a reflection of the generally competitive atmosphere of the suburbs which was already doing them in, and the matter of "who was the best lay" was determined by the men. Women began to feel like another consumer item, and their gathering resentment, whether the experimentation led to divorce or not, was to give a particular vehemence to their participation in the liberation of women a few years later.

Indeed, the open marriage is, among other things, an attempt to find a secondary adjustment to the hazards of competitive, extramarital sexuality by giving the woman as much choice as the man in the matter of extramarital sexual partners. Whether it simply removes the competition among men and puts it between spouses is still an open question. The issue of jealousy is not yet resolved, but in the open marriage it does not have to be resolved. If the jealousy of either spouse becomes obsessive and cannot be resolved by using encounter-group techniques or by repairing to a marriage counselor, there are always the options of fidelity or divorce. If the divorce begins to become sticky, there are divorce counselors to ease the passage and help with an amicable settlement. Indeed, it is held that both partners may "grow" in awareness and self-knowledge in the process of divorce.

The passivity in passive-adaptive patterns of marriage is most certainly not within the relationship itself. Partners work endlessly at improving their sexual techniques and interpersonal skills. They may attend encounter or sensitivity weekends. They read books about new patterns of marriage, evaluate and negotiate and schedule the roles and functions of living together in a household, and try to encourage each other's personal growth. In many respects they take marriage more seriously than it has ever been taken before, or, to be more accurate, they take their relationship as spouses more seriously than such relationships have been taken before. Their passivity manifests itself in their acceptance, basically a despairing acceptance, of the status quo of a society which they themselves regard as corrupt and dangerous; and for all their secondary adjustments to it, it is just as dangerous to them as it was to their parents. Often hating their work, they nevertheless want to succeed in it in order to indulge themselves in a good life that consists mainly of elegant play requiring untold consumption of expensive gear.

It is true, perhaps more true than ever with the present economic downturn, that to succeed, to make more money, one must be mobile. But with more and more wives regarding their own careers as of primary importance in their self-realization, it is often not possible for a husband and a wife to find new and better positions in the same city or even the same state. Career conflict has become a major issue for couples who have chosen to live and work in the mainstream of American economic life, and the centrality of hedonistic values in the passive-adaptive marriage makes the "commuter marriage" a very perilous arrangement indeed. The inevitable loneliness of such arrangements has a way of turning convenient sexual liaisons into companionate relationships which eventually take precedence over marriages that have become weekend and vacation affairs. Eventual divorce is normative for the commuter marriage among passive-adaptive spouses.

The types of countercultural marriages are so diverse and numerous that they defy even listing, to say nothing of description. What they have in common is a basis in revolt against the economic-institutional life of the free-enterprise system as it currently operates in the United States, and an ideological core which throws them into conflict with it or into alienation from it. The politics of people in countercultural marriage ranges from underground revolutionary to John Birch reactionary, with a religious commitment to the apolitical in-between. Countercultural marriages are entered into with the belief that marriage cannot have any human value for either spouse if it exists apart from meaning and purpose. For most people in these marriages it is understood that meaning and purpose depend upon a trustworthy community as well as upon an ideology, that an ideology without consensual validation is powerless.

Perhaps an example is in order. A group of ten young professional couples with a political activist orientation in a large university city are closely allied in their efforts to effect social change. These lawyers, professors, doctors, and clinical psychologists had, during their early years in the "movement," become very aware of the oppression of women ("The only place for a woman in the movement is on her back"). They decided to meet regularly with a psychiatrist (also a political activist) to work out among themselves the nature of an "egalitarian" marriage. Their original assumption, deriving from their political orientation, was that in a traditional marriage both husband and wife were regarded as each other's property. Their logical conclusion from this premise was that the group should share themselves sexually with each other. This practice proved hugely disruptive to their relationships and most gave it up. (Those who didn't were eventually divorced.) They arrived at the conclusion that marital fidelity was the authentic activist style and agreed, as a group, to live this out. It is easy to trivialize this by saying that five years' expenditure of energy and intelligence had succeeded in re-inventing the wheel, but to do so is to miss the point. The point is that for these people marital sexual fidelity was given strong emotional consensual validation. There was no aching doubt in their minds—as there often is in the minds of an isolated, maritally faithful Christian couple—that they were hanging on to some crazy, anachronistic custom.

Other significant conclusions were reached in this closely observed group. They found that the equal sharing of all tasks was impossible within a family, and that the tasks one spouse did better and liked better should be taken care of more (though not exclusively) by that spouse. This was particularly true in the matter of raising children. It was not that the more "parental" spouse should raise the children, but that that spouse should spend more time with the children than the other. Only mutually loathed tasks were to be shared equally.

All this is gone into in some detail because it is typical of the intentionality of most countercultural marriages. As one communard remarked, "Whether a commune lives or not depends on whether the people who got it together did so intentionally or wishfully."

The distinction between willing and wishing is an important one in any marriage, as it is in any community, but what creates this distinction is more important. Where loss and discontinuity lie at the heart of motivation, as Peter Marris explains, people will at all times be trying by what they do in the present to establish continuity with the past. In passive-adaptive marriage patterns one still sees a kind of nostalgia for the suburban life of the 1950s, the childhood decade of the people who choose these patterns. But nostalgia is wishful, not willful, and will accomplish little toward making sense out of either the past or the present.

From a Christian point of view, the issue of intentionality, will, commitment, must be considered of primary importance in evaluating changing patterns of marriage. It is present, of course, in both the passive-adaptive and the countercultural patterns. But in the former the commitment is to self-realization or personal growth, often understood entirely in hedonistic terms; and in the latter, it is usually to an ideology, whether philosophical or political or, in the widest sense, religious. There is also a theological dimension to both these marriage patterns, to be discovered in their mistrust or institutional loyalty. Christians have traditionally been warned against worshiping—that is, giving ultimate loyalty to—principalities and powers; but at least within Anglicanism a strong sacramental tendency has kept this institutional distrust from amounting to a creed in itself. Indeed, if there is an Anglican heresy, it may be found in a too high doctrine of institutions. It was Richard Hooker who described the church as the state at prayer. Nevertheless, St. Paul was of two minds about institutions. Although his dictum that it was better to marry than to burn cannot be described as a high doctrine of marriage as an institution, it was to this institution that he turned as a metaphor for the relationship between Christ and his Church, which is certainly to give it primary importance.

Marriage, then, for the Christian, is a secular institution with potential theological significance. There is no such thing as a Christian marriage, but a marriage can be committed to the sovereignty of Christ and blessed as Christian. The spirit of the marriage, not the form, is Christ's. There is then no very profound theological reason for Christians to adhere to one form of marriage as Christian, and there may be very good theological reasons for Christians to abandon a form of marriage which is in direct conflict with what a Christian believes. A marriage which has submitted itself to the sovereignty of the economic ideology of a particular nation, as was the case with so many American middle-class marriages in the 1950s and 1960s, cannot also be considered Christian even though it may have been blessed by the church and endured with sexual fidelity. Christians saying of divorced people: "What has happened to the concept of sacrifice and self-denial?" might ask themselves as well: "Why should a wife sacrifice herself for a corporation which is unaware of her existence as anything but a potential consumer, and why should a husband sacrifice himself and his family to maximize profits, his own and the corporation's?" There are answers to these questions: "To put the kids through college." "To succeed." "To have access to the good life." Perhaps the most honest and profoundly felt answer would be "to survive in a wildly untrustworthy and competitive society." This last is how many, many people perceived their predicament, and how a few articulated it. But none of these answers has proved adequate. None, certainly, is Christian. The nuclear family, the famous "togetherness" family, as a competitive, mobile unit in an economic system which serves itself far more than it serves the society that supports it, should be abandoned. But the church must give much more thought to what should take its place, and perhaps less attention to the futile task of trying to hold it together.

Perhaps the church should begin by taking another look at the custom, usually tolerated, of the young living together out of wedlock. There seems to be about the same amount of commitment to a relationship among such couples as there is among couples who marry; but there is far less motivation to take the best-paying job available, however hateful it might be—which was the gateway to the primrose path for so many young couples who rushed to get married two decades ago. The children of discontinuity and loss have little confidence in their ability to sustain a lasting relationship, too often having had little opportunity during their lives even to know one, to say nothing of having experienced one. Their tentativeness is understandable and perhaps commendable, and makes it possible for them to avoid becoming an extension, a reluctant agent, of a solipsistic economic system—however much their privilege is supported by this same system. The postponement gives them time to discover what they are called to do, and there are many more things that need doing than were apparent a quarter of a century ago. Some of these things require a specialized education, others require an apprenticeship, and still others require a newly recovered genius for entrepreneurship. But freed from the economic urgencies of early marriage, young adults are given time to make some sense out of their life work. For the Christian, this means the serious providing of goods and services, humanly necessary goods and services, or a serious, serving vocation to medicine, law, education, politics, government, or ordained ministry. This freedom is, of course, not an unmixed blessing and can be used for aimless "swinging" or for simply going to pieces. Again, it is a question of intentionality and values, as much as of given psychic strength.

When the direction of both partners' life work is set, the couple who have maintained a relationship through the tentative stage of vocational discovery will often marry, and will often bring to this marriage habits of mutuality and sharing that include, not just each other but a number of friends—paired, married, or single—who share their value system. Where such people are Christians, as in some urban charismatic communities, eucharistic worship is the ordering dynamic of their shared lives. These marriages are open in the sense of being hospitable, generous, and socially concerned. They do not regard themselves as little islands of intimacy in competition with the world for survival, but as part of a community concerned with the redemption and renewal of that world for whom Christ became incarnate, suffered, died, and rose again. These marriages, like the community within which they exist and from which they draw continuous support, are open and trusting toward the people of this world, but bring a kind of creative mistrust, a critical restlessness, to its institutional, political and economic life.

Particularly in the matter of child care and education, young people seriously concerned with discovering more humane, or even more Christian, forms of marriage are taking quite a different tack from that of their parents. In the 1950s, serious parents were concerned that their children should have the best in education, and they were willing to endure higher taxes if they were in the suburbs, or higher private school tuitions if they were in the city. As for preschool care, concerned mothers believed it was irresponsible to let anyone but themselves take care of children under four. Concerned young parents today are more inclined to entrust their children from an early age to group care, but a rationalized group care they have taken part in planning, and in which they continue to involve themselves as volunteer assistants or in some other capacity.

In the matter of schooling, a distrust of the public schools as they developed in the last twenty years is very widespread among this generation of young parents, from fundamentalist Christians in Appalachia to agnostic Ph.D.s in the suburbs. What is new about this discontent and distrust is that it is not with "bad" teachers or administrators, it is with the actual content of the curriculum, particularly with the value assumptions of the curriculum, both as they are revealed in the content of books and in the methods of teaching. To disagree with something so deeply at the center of an institution means involvement, and a surprising number of young parents across the country have shown themselves willing to give endless hours of work to alternative education, whether within the public school system or outside of it. People with a commitment to stay in the same place are able to effect institutional change in ways that were impossible for their nomadic parents.

What is described above is neither a passive-adaptive nor a thoroughly countercultural marriage. Neither is it as rational or utopian as the brevity of description makes it sound. There is much painful trial and error involved, and there is not a great deal of communication between the communities within which this pattern of marriage is taking place. Thus, marriages in one community may be struggling with issues which have already been coped with creatively by marriages in another. Nevertheless, this pattern of marriage, wherever it exists, is based either consciously or unconsciously on a dynamic of repentance and a new life rooted in mutuality, cooperation, and shared concern.

The similarity between these marriages in community and marriage as it was understood in the early church, as we know this church through the New Testament, is too strong to be dismissed. Yet even where the communities within which these marriages exist are consciously and explicitly Christian, they seem to show a surprising reluctance to identify with the institutional church as it is represented by the parish. To the extent that it is helping young people in their quest for more humane and viable patterns of marriage, the parish seems more concerned with helping passive-adaptive couples discover secondary adjustments to a sick society than in facing the extent to which any economic overdependence on this society, or any trust in its current hedonistic goals and values, will eventuate, for Christians especially, in a value conflict out of which no one can make sense.

If the Anglican communion has shown any special genius, if it has made any essential contribution to the whole church, it has been in its determined incarnational insistence on historical continuity, involvement in the life of the world, and the ability of Christianity continuously to help human beings caught in the chaos of the present to find a new and comprehensible relationship to what has gone on in the past. Human beings are not genetically programed to know why they are born and how they are to spend their lives. In the human beginning was the Word, and words are all that humans have to communicate from generation to generation what it is to *be* human. Radical historical discontinuity resulting in a failure of communication between generations also results in a universal purposelessness, an aimless wandering toward death.

The Anglican communion, from Hooker to F. D. Maurice to William Temple to Reuel Howe, has resolutely refused to let theological or political or economic-technological discontinuity cast humanity blind into the wilderness. And neither has it demanded of its adherents an orthodox lockstep toward heaven oblivious to the chaos and suffering of the world. It is not that society should not change, but that the change should in some way, perhaps quite a new way, make sense in terms of what wisdom humans have garnered from the past. And the church has insisted that the core of this wisdom, an extraordinarily enlightening and spirited core, has been given to the world by God through it in Jesus Christ.

The responsibility of the church in such a critical matter as marriage, the primary social agent of human continuity, cannot be denied. But until it bases its own community, as that community is reflected in the parish, on something more profound than trying to make people caught in a demonic value conflict feel better about themselves—rather than continually and lovingly pointing out that value conflict and the need to choose one way or the other—it is hard to see how the church will be of much help to those who need it most and would perhaps respond most receptively and vividly to its message.

chapter 7

LIBERATING THE FEMININE

Robert M. Stein

Times are changing. Marriage, particularly for women, seems to have become more of an oppressive prison than a sanctuary. And no longer is the education of little girls solely for the purpose of teaching them the arts of pleasing and winning a man, homemaking, and motherhood. Still, mating, nesting, and family-making are deeply rooted instinctual needs which cannot simply be tossed aside. The archetypal roles which both women and men have lived out in our culture are not only due to education and conditioning; these are ancient roles and have instinctual parallels among many other species.

The Woman's Liberation Movement is primarily concerned with freeing women from these roles, and with attaining equal rights and status for women. What are some of these roles? In what way are they oppressive? How have they developed? Are they oppressive only to women, or are men equally oppressed by them? Are men responsible for forcing women into these roles? Have women perhaps had a need to assume these roles and for men to assume their corresponding roles?

From the archetypal research of depth psychology, we have learned that all long-established social forms and institutions are instinctually rooted, even though they may have become oppressive to the evolution of the human spirit. If these archetypal feminine and masculine roles have emerged in order to satisfy certain basic needs, then we might do well to explore the nature of these needs and how they may be affected by change. Whenever changes threaten basic needs, human nature will resist them. So, we might better effect the necessary changes if we know more about the resistance. In addition, just as our scientific and cultural progress has had detrimental effects on the balance of nature, so too must we be careful about the consequences of changing these archetypal patterns in the male-female relationship. We must attempt to find the most creative way of effecting these necessary changes so that they do not backfire as have our technological advances.

The great Swiss psychologist, C. G. Jung, is responsible for introducing the ancient concept of the archetype into modern psychology. I use the term archetype to express the presence of a divine force within the human soul which manifests itself in all the typically human patterns of thought, feeling, imagery, and behavior. This implies that the directing energy and intelligence within the soul comes from a divine source, and that human instincts are one of its manifestations. So, when we say women are stuck in archetypal feminine roles, we must recognize that these roles are not simply human creations, but that they also express an aspect of the divine. Every culture, every religion has attempted to express the archetypal masculine and feminine in their gods and heroes. The ancient Greeks were particularly gifted in their ability to describe divine activity—every state and every capacity, every mood, thought, act, and experience was mirrored in a deity. In our attempt to explore some of the archetypal roles in which modern women are caught, we shall take advantage of this Greek perceptiveness.

The most obvious role that women have had to accept is that of mother. Every religion has had mother goddesses. What are the divine qualities contained in the image of mother? Mother is soft, warm, loving, gentle, sensitive, receptive, nourishing, and supportive. She is all-accepting and always there to respond to the needs of the child. She has no life of her own apart from her child. She lives only to give birth to children and to nurture them until they are ready to be on their own. Surely women are the natural carriers of this maternal function, especially since men are unable to give birth to children. But the maternal involves much more than giving birth to actual children. Giving birth, for example, is as much a psychic or spiritual phenomenon as it is a literal act—such as giving birth to an idea, a vision, or any creative work. The maternal is a powerful force which expresses itself through a wide range of human attitudes, emotions, and behavior. The qualities just listed are certainly not exclusive to women. A man too must develop these qualities or he is not quite human. Unfortunately, in our culture women have been burdened with the responsibility of being the sole carriers of these essential maternal qualities.

Woman has also had to carry the almost equally heavy burden of love goddess. As a consequence she has had to put an enormous amount of energy into attending to her physical appearance and developing her capacity to stimulate erotic desires in men. Now this too has instinctual parallels among many other animal species—is it not the scent of the female in heat that arouses the sexual desire in the male?

While the maternal capacity and the need to evoke erotic desires in the male through her physical charm and beauty are certainly instinctual dominants in women, to be forced to identify with these roles prevents a woman from developing her individuality. Furthermore, a creative evolving male-female relationship is impossible as long as women remain in these archetypal roles and men in their corresponding "macho" (physical or intellectual) roles.

The fact that women have largely identified with these roles and men have generally remained on a similar primitive level, relating to women only as maternal or erotic archetypes, has contributed much to the sterility of modern marriages. The traditional patriarchal marriage was a viable institution as long as it was contained in a larger community and the couple found their meaning in raising children and perpetuating the life of the community. But since the breakdown of community, since marriages have become isolated city-states cut off from all the meaningful, renewing rituals of communal life, couples have become more and more dependent on each other for intimacy, companionship, and spiritual renewal. Furthermore, after the children are grown and leave to form their own isolated units, marriage for the older couple no longer has any meaningful function as an essential nucleus for family life. For a woman identified with the roles of mother and love goddess, this can be catastrophic. Her function as mother begins to lose its central importance, and her aging body makes it difficult for her to maintain her confidence in the powers of her erotic charm. What then is to hold the marriage together once motherhood is no longer so important and her youthful body is gone? Even young girls worry about this inevitable course of events. Once a woman is stripped of the power of these archetypal roles she has only herself to offer in a relationship, and if she has left herself undeveloped as she has played out her roles over the years, she feels empty and worthless. This is why the Woman's Liberation Movement has become such an important force.

The tendency in the movement to place the blame for the oppression on men is, I believe, a great mistake. Clearly, basic instinctual needs have been fulfilled for both men and women as they have lived out their respective roles. And in the past these roles have not necessarily been any more oppressive than are the instinctual patterns governing animal relationships. Historically, men and women have been not only biologically dependent on each other but they have been dependent on each other for psychological completion— men have carried the so-called masculine qualities and women the feminine qualities. I believe the breakdown in traditional marriage, family, and community relationships is part of an evolutionary process leading toward higher levels of psychological integration and wholeness.

The inherent differences between male and female tend to become obliterated when women view their oppression mainly in terms of the male's need to dominate, to keep women in an inferior and servile position. What madness to denigrate the instinctual attraction which every woman feels for a strong and courageous (physical or mental) male! And how can we simply dismiss the male's attraction to a warm, receptive, loving and/or sexually seductive female as merely a product of cultural conditioning? But I do not intend to argue this point further in this paper. Rather, let us attempt to explore the nature of the oppressive force which has not allowed women the freedom for psychological development.

If not men, then who or what is responsible for the inferior economic and social status of women? And who is responsible for the prevailing attitudes that women are intellectually inferior to men, that they are irrational, guided more by emotions than reason, therefore unstable, weak, childish, and morally inferior to men? Let me go quickly to the point. Depth psychology has established that both masculine and feminine qualities are contained within the soul of everyone. In our Western culture there has been an overdevelopment of the masculine perspective, which has resulted in a glorification of reason, objectivity, detachment, noninvolvement, and a denigration of all the subjective feelings and life-involving emotions. Now this powerful masculine force or spirit is primarily responsible for the oppression of women. But this distorted masculine perspective is deeply embedded within the psyche of both men and women. All the social, economic, and political changes will be worthless if this spirit that has been so oppressive to the feminine continues to dominate. Having made this necessary shift to the psychological arena, our main concern now becomes the oppression of the *feminine,* not of women.

Let us briefly explore the nature of this spirit, this masculine deity which has finally provoked the wrath of so many women. One god in particular comes to mind: the ancient Greek god Apollo, who is still very much alive and kicking—at least for the modern physician who, on his graduation day, must recite the Hippocratic oath which begins, "I swear by Apollo . . ." Apollo is a god who views the universe from afar, from a position of complete detachment and impersonality. His main concern is with clarity, order, and moderation. From his remote Olympian heights he is a dispassionate observer as we poor mortals struggle with our individual fates. Spiritual loftiness is an essential part of his essence, and he is oblivious to the eternal worth of the human individual and the single soul. His concern is rather with what transcends the personal, with the unchangeable, with the eternal forms. Now this Apollonian deity, which I believe dominates our Western consciousness, has, as we have seen, no concern for the needs of the individual human soul. The soul's needs for involvement, entanglement, proximity, melting, merging, exuberance, excess, ecstasy are obliterated by the brilliant beam of this hypertrophied Apollonian perspective.

Apollo personifies a particular tendency toward detachment and impersonality in the masculine spirit. In his world the clarity and the breadth of the mind hold sway. The feminine spirit on the other hand, tends to move with the Dionysian thrust of life as it involves and entangles us with all living things. Dionysus, by the way, was a bisexual god, who was worshiped mainly by women in ancient Greece. His world is the life and mystery of blood, and of the powers of the earth. He personifies proximity and union, in contrast to Apollo's distance and detachment. While Apollo's distance and clarity emphasizes cognition, Dionysus plunges us into immediate contact with others, and with the quick of life.

Apollo and Dionysus need each other. Without Dionysus, Apollo leads to the neglect and abuse of basic human needs, to the destructive manipulation of nature, and to a severe alienation from the earthy, maternal life-source of our own natures. Dionysus without Apollo leads ultimately to the obliteration of reason and culture. The Greeks knew that these two gods belonged together, and they were both equally honored in Delphi. Theological speculation even identified the one with the other.[1]

One of the most important consequences of our modern Apollonian distortion of life is that our world has become de-souled. Only the rational mind has been left with a bit of soul. The body, feelings, emotions, instincts, earth, nature, matter, living creatures, have become mere mechanisms totally devoid of any directing intelligence.[2] This final lofty Olympian elevation of the mind is the product of the Enlightenment and of Cartesian philosophy: *"Cogito, ergo sum."* (I think, therefore I am). For Descartes, the body, with its animal-sensual nature, is viewed as a substance distinct from the mind and subject only to mechanical laws—the body is passive while the mind is active and capable of free will. The rational mind is superior to the emotional-bodily roots of human nature because it can control and overcome the animal passions. The mind, says Descartes, is moved by soul while the body is moved only by animal spirits. Only the mind has soul. And the prime mover is God, whose directing intelligence is continually manifesting itself in the rational mind. God has implanted motion in the human body and all other matter, but then he has abandoned all matter. "Mechanical laws govern the material world—man obeys the same laws since he is nothing but a more complex form of organization of the same processes that dominate other aspects of nature."[3] Now, these metaphysical assumptions have had an enormous influence on the development of Western science, and they still underlie most of modern Western thought. Any woman who buys this Apollonian distortion automatically devalues and mistrusts her so-called "irrational" feelings and intuitions, as well as the mysterious intelligence of the emotional-bodily roots of her nature. Of course, the Cartesian split between mind and body, and soul and body, is equally damaging to men. This brings me to the difficulty I have of talking only about woman's liberation.

One can hardly talk about the Apollonian oppression of women without recognizing that men have been at least equally oppressed by this ruling spirit of our times. The feminine in both men and women is suffering. The liberation of the feminine, rather than women, is really what is needed. While the economic, educational, and social advantages which men have had over women are obvious and need to be corrected, I don't believe this is the main issue. As long as our culture and its institutions are ruled by a depersonalizing, dehumanizing spirit, the feminine will continue to be abused and devalued no matter how many gains women make toward social equality.

One of the main tasks of my profession, psychotherapy, is to help liberate, redeem, and heal the oppressed and rejected feminine within the individual soul. It is no accident that modern psychotherapy originated out of Sigmund Freud's attempt to cure hysterical women. Certainly in those days women were still attempting to live up to some Victorian image of the proper lady, which was a terrible violation to the feminine soul. The feminine cannot be confined to one-dimensional images. Let us further explore some of the attributes of the feminine so that we might better understand the nature of the psychological task.

We have already discussed some of the qualities of the mother archetype, but we have only touched upon the nature of the love goddess. Behind the current image of the "playgirl" ideal, which is so clearly a perverse masculine distortion of the feminine, there must exist an important essence of the goddess. Of course, these plastic, sexless, playboy models of the "golden" goddess are a far cry from the enchanting beauty, the smiling charm that radiates from Aphrodite and enraptures the senses. The cool detachment, the unmovable, untouchable distance which the playgirl maintains, has no connection at all to the Greek goddess. Quite the contrary. The great appeal of Aphrodite is her eagerness to surrender, to voluntarily bend toward the love-stricken with an undisguised yearning which is itself irresistible.

Aphrodite symbolizes a divine gift that does not belong only to women, but belongs to all of life. Walter Otto offers us a larger, richer image of the world which she inspires with her spirit:

From her comes not so much the ecstasy of desire as the charm which kindles and propels it. She is the enchantment that radiates from things and beings and enraptures the senses with its smile. Not only men and beasts but plants, inanimate images and appearances, even thoughts and words, derive their winning, moving, overwhelming sweetness from her.[4]

Thus, the world loses its sweet, yielding, enrapturing beauty when this divine feminine quality, which the Greeks called Aphrodite, is so denigrated that it becomes the bitter, sterile, hollow plastic husk of the "playgirl."

When I think about the feminine, my initial images are of softness, gentleness, sensitivity, receptivity, warmth, moisture, responsiveness, containment, nurturing. Nothing sharp, probing, pushing, abrasive, phallic in any of these images. Rather, water, receptive fertile earth, the womb. Now, this certainly does not exhaust my images of the feminine, but these all-accepting, all-embracing and nourishing maternal womblike aspects are basic. The exciting, bewitching, erotic charm of Aphrodite is certainly not unfamiliar to me. I have also experienced a very direct, quick, clear, pragmatic type of logic which focuses sharply on attending to an immediate situation involving my own or someone else's welfare. I believe this usage of the intellect, in contrast to the impersonality and total disregard for the individual of the Apollonian intellect, is feminine. Let us once again turn to the Greeks for support and elaboration of this view.

Pallas Athene, the goddess who never had a mother but was born from the head of Zeus, is such a clear-sighted goddess as I have described. Although she is equal to Apollo in her clarity and capacity to reason, unlike him, she is a goddess of nearness. "She inspires man to boldness, a will to victory, courage, but always with directing reason and illuminating clarity."[5] She is always near and involved with the person: sharing, advising, helping, encouraging, and rejoicing in success. In comparing her to Apollo, Otto gives us an insightful view of her world:

In Apollo we recognize the wholly masculine man. The aristocratic aloofness, the superiority of cognition, the sense of proportion, these and other related traits in a man, even music in the broadest sense of the word, are, in the last analysis alien to a woman. Apollo is all these things. But perfection in the living present, untrammelled and victorious action, not in the service of some remote and infinite idea but for the mastery over the moment—that is the triumph which has always delighted woman in a man, to which she inspires him, and whose high satisfaction he can learn from her. The divine precision of the well-pleased dead, the readiness to be forceful and merciless, the unflagging will to victory—this, paradoxical as it may sound, is woman's gift to man, *who by nature is indifferent to the momentary and strives for the infinite.*[6]

Athena is oblivious to what we call tenderheartedness. "Neither wisdom nor vision, neither devotion nor pleasure is her will. *Consummation, the immediate present, action here and now—that is Athena.*"[7]

Another important aspect of the feminine is related to a free, wild, independent, youthful, unspoiled-nature spirit which has no interest in merging with a man. For the Greeks this world was reflected in the virgin goddess, Artemis. Many young women nowadays tend to identify with her. The need to return to the pristine beauty and wonder of nature also belongs to her world:

Here everything is mobile and withdrawn and pure. The lucidity of the goddess hovers over meadows and lakes; her bright spirit is wafted in the solitude of forest, in the lonely lights of mountains; she causes the mysterious magic of solitude in nature and its breathless tremor, its playful tenderness and the sternness into which it can suddenly transform itself. To her belong the beasts of field and forest, which she protects maternally in their need, and harries to death as game with reckless pleasure. But man too belongs to her realm. Her manifestation is the tart sweetness of the young body and the young soul, the loveliness that shrinks at the fervor of the lover and turns cruel if he approach too near. Inspirited by her is lightness of foot, which can only run or dance: hers is the morning freshness with its shimmer and clarity, in which, as in a dewdrop, the colorful fire of the heavenly rays glint and gleam.[8]

While we have only touched upon a few of the basic qualities of the feminine—the maternal, the erotic, the elusive spirit of the wood, and bold pragmatic reason—what they all share in common is: close-

ness to the earth and involvement with living things; the need to
nurture, to promote growth; the need for closeness, for union with
another or with nature. For the most part, the feminine seems to
move most comfortably and freely when it is close to the earth and
nature. In contrast, the masculine tends to seek distance from the
earth, to find freedom in pure spirit, in the realm of abstract ideas
and universal principles. Once again, let me stress that I am speaking about masculine and feminine as qualities which belong to both
men and women. Anyone who identifies with only one of these opposites cannot really develop psychologically.

As symbols, masculine and feminine are the root metaphors, *par
excellence,* for the fundamental affinity and polarity of all opposites.
In my recent book,[9] I present the thesis that the most important
function of the incest taboo is to promote the formation and internalization of images in the human psyche of the sacred union between the divine couple. This internalization of the archetypal
image of the harmonious union between the masculine/feminine opposites is essential for internal balance and wholeness, and for the
experience of intimacy with others.

In this same book, I also speak of the *incest wound,* a term I use
to describe the wounding developmental splits between the mascu-
line/feminine opposites, love/sex, mind/body, spirit/matter, inner/
outer. One of the consequences of the incest wound is the prevalent
internal split in our Western culture between the maternal-spiritual
and the erotic-sensual aspects of the feminine—between the Virgin
Mary and Aphrodite. As a consequence of such wounds, a man then
tends to associate purity, softness, comfort, and tender loving senti-
ments with wife-mother; and erotic aggression, sensual abandonment, excitement and passion with the promiscuous hussy or the
"other woman." Now this same split occurs in a woman as a consequence of the incest wound, so that women too suffer from this
fragmented perspective in our culture. Hand in hand with the split
feminine goes a similar split within the masculine; that is, between
the understanding, protective, paternal and the aggressive, phallic,
sensual, dynamic aspects. The healing of these splits has much to do
with the redemption of the feminine. In contrast to the masculine,
the feminine cannot tolerate being stuck in a fragmented, compart-
mentalized state.

Let us return now to the psychological task of the redemption of
the feminine. An appreciation of the basic feminine attitude of acceptance of and harmony with nature is absolutely essential. The
feminine always respects and honors nature's mysteries. Unlike the
masculine, the feminine seldom attempts to go against nature or to

penetrate and dissect the mysteries in order to gain control over nature so that it can manipulate it to its own advantage. In this sense the feminine is submissive to nature, and unable to alter or change the course of natural events. But it is just this apparent submissiveness and helplessness, this complete acceptance of *what is*, that has not been respected by the masculine spirit in our culture. Above all, we must confront that inner masculine voice which continually makes us feel ashamed and inadequate about those aspects of ourselves which appear weak, helpless, dependent, impotent when viewed from some perverse masculine perspective of strength, intelligence, potency. While the feminine may not have the power or inclination to go against nature, to alter the course of nature, its relationship to nature gives it a strength which the masculine lacks. The spirit which enables a woman to flow with the rhythm of her monthly moon cycle, to patiently and joyfully endure the nine months it takes to give birth to a child, is something a man must develop or all his best-laid plans and creative efforts will be constantly aborted. Without the feminine respect for nature's ways, the ingenuity of the masculine spirit soon becomes destructive to life.

Openness, receptivity, responsiveness to life's forces are characteristic of all aspects of the feminine. While the capacity to initiate action is contained in the feminine (certainly in Athena, as we have seen), the generative life force is essentially phallic. Understanding the reciprocal relationship between the masculine and feminine aspects of the soul is important to the psychological process of feminine liberation. If we neglect and denigrate the soft, open, receptive feminine aspects of ourselves, our lives become progressively more rigid, empty, sterile, inert, and filled with meaningless action. By the same token, if we fear opening up to the sudden, spontaneous, irrational influx of our phallic energies, nothing moves, nothing changes, and our lives become stagnant. A positive relationship to the phallic root of the masculine spirit is absolutely essential for creative development, for the liberation of the feminine and for the liberation of women.[10] As long as a woman is afraid, angry and rejecting of the masculine within herself, as long as she continues to fight the battle mainly "out there" instead of inside her own soul, she will never really become free of her oppressive dependency on men, because she has essentially cut herself off from the phallic source of her own power and potency. Furthermore, she will continually provoke men to incarnate and act out the very thing she fears, which, of course only intensifies her conviction that men are nothing but "male chauvinist pigs."

Above all, the feminine places the highest value on relationship.

Consistent with the masculine fascination with the infinite is its tendency to view relationship in terms of purpose and accomplishment. In contrast, relationship is an end in itself for the feminine spirit, and it feels violated when a relationship is being used primarily for any other purpose, even a worthy one.

We have touched upon some of the psychological factors involved in woman's liberation, on the nature of the feminine and on the need to differentiate more clearly between the *feminine* and *woman*. As long as a woman does not distinguish and differentiate herself from the feminine, she will continue to experience men as the enemy. And she will completely miss the psychic dimensions of her oppression, which are far more important and in more urgent need of attention.

NOTES

1. Walter F. Otto, *The Homeric Gods: The Spiritual Significance of Greek Religion* (London: Thames & Hudson, 1954) p. 203.

2. This notion that "the behavior of man depends on reason, whereas all animals are governed by instinct" (St. Thomas Aquinas), which has such deep roots in Western tradition, is absolutely foreign to the Eastern mind and in oriental religions.

3. Frank Thilly, *A History of Philosophy* (New York: Henry Holt, 1927) pp. 272 f.

4. *Op. cit.*, Otto, p. 161.

5. *Ibid.*, p. 53.

6. *Ibid.*, p. 55. In this and other quotations from Otto, let me suggest that feminine and masculine be substituted when he uses woman and man.

7. *Ibid.*, p. 56.

8. *Ibid.*, p. 161.

9. Robert Stein, *Incest and Human Love: The Betrayal of the Soul in Psychotherapy* (Baltimore: Penguin Books, pap., 1974).

10. *Op. cit.*, Stein. For a detailed discussion of this issue, see the section on Phallos.

chapter 8

MY BODY/MY WORLD*

Penelope Washbourn

I begin with my body . . . my body is me. I can think of my body as a porous membrane, not separated from the world, as an organic body pulsing . . . opening and closing . . . taking in and giving out. It is like a flower as it turns to the sun, responds to light, growing, absorbing, expelling. . . . I am breathing gently and with such ease . . . until something happens to tense me, and my breath becomes shallow and labored. My skin is open, each of my cells in hair and skin is intimately connected to air, moisture, sun, dirt, hot, and cold.

The lines that define me as separate are the same lines that connect me. In gestalt exercises I become aware of the *connections* . . . the breath and its rhythms, the movement of its in and its out, the body as it moves and sits and stands in relation to its own weight and to the floor. I feel sweat for the first time. I let my hands explore, and I allow touch to be the prime sensation. I close my eyes . . . eyes that have thought that *they* are the superior sense. I touch, I taste, I smell. I close my eyes. I am silent. I learn that seeing and hearing can interpret the other senses, but they cannot substitute for them.

I don't often think of my body as an organic reality intimately connected with everything around it. I think of it more as a separate body with boundaries. My problem is to find the connections again, to find the other without losing myself. That's the fear, the fear of risking too much of myself, fear of trusting. That fear keeps my neck muscles tense, keeps me from sexual fulfillment. It will keep me finally from being able to die in peace.

As I am aware of my body, I am aware of it as a sexual body, and it is to that aspect of my bodily awareness that I wish to address myself. One question I ask myself often is: Does it make any difference, being a body with a penis or a body with a vagina? Does the body and its structure affect the way I perceive my world and the way I relate to my world? Yes, I think it does. If I am fat or small or thin or tall or grossly overweight or lack one hand, I will physically move and relate to my world in a physically distinctive manner. My attitude to my fatness or tallness may vary greatly from person to person and from culture to culture, but the body itself will be what *it is* and will affect my perception and action in my world. It will also compensate for any missing or dysfunctional parts.

My body is my possibility and my limitation. To the extent that "I" control "its" actions, I forget that "it" controls "me." We are what we eat and sleep and drink and smoke and exercise and touch. Body awareness . . . that means my being aware of the total organic structure and my being able to feel *bodily* what it needs. I know the hunger signs, the sleep signs, but do I know the exercise signs, the touch signs? How strange it is that I am an "I," a "person" who has the responsibility of feeding my body, washing it, putting it to bed! I "decide" what the body needs. I don't know anymore how to listen to its needs or respond to its rhythms.

As a child I was so *aware* of my body in contact with the new-mown grass, the dampness of it, the glorious smell of it . . . swimming is marvelous . . . the feel of water on my skin exhilarates me. Sun warming my skin, wind in my hair . . . my vivid awareness at the age of eight of the sweet smell of lilacs in bloom, or lying on my back in the grass looking up at the blue sky and seeing white blossoms . . . all the things that I remember as a child are of *intense* bodily feelings, of being alive to my body responding to its environment, of *delighting* in my body as it felt and smelled and tasted and touched. These memories are etched into my consciousness with such brilliance. They are part of my lost selfhood that I fear I can never recover.

I have a baby daughter. She is one-and-a-quarter. Her world is all body. She has a soft blanket she loves, she plays in mud, she splashes in the bath, she walks and explores and finds so much thrill in discovering everything by touch and taste. Her relation to me, to her world, is through her body. Everything is a physical experience for her. As she learns to trust her physical world, she will trust herself and develop her own selfhood.

This first year has reminded me of my own forgotten body. From our organic oneness through pregnancy, to birth, to breast feeding, to holding and bathing, her body, now on its own, emerged from *our* bodies, but particularly from mine. She was nourished from my body and now finds delight in our bodies, their warmth, their size, their security. My daughter accepts touch without question: in fact she demands it when she needs it, in physical terms and with yells. I wish I could come with such ease and say I need to be held.

My body and my world are one. They are one for Stephanie. Her body depends on mine to be fed, washed, and put to bed when she is tired. I suppose babies get trained out of their natural ability to fall asleep by our clock-time schedules. (I often think we would all snooze in the afternoon if we listened to our bodies. Instead I must resort to coffee to prop myself up.)

Body/World and the Understanding of Reality My body is my world. What does that mean for my experience of sexuality? I think that people have different perceptions of reality; different gods, theological systems, myths, social structures, forms of self-understanding based on simple things like climate, landscape, type of food eaten, size of body, shape of body, contact with means of food production, ease of sustenance. All of these things appear to affect the way we talk, the words we have, our thought patterns, our customs, social structures, and perceptions of selfhood. (I saw an obese girl at the beach the other day: obesity can be a self-imposed condition, or culturally imposed, but it then becomes a physical factor radically affecting the manner in which reality and self are experienced.) The size of my body as a child also affects my relation to the world.

The question I have been asking myself is this: Does the structure of the body and the forms of its contacts with other bodies also affect my views of reality? I believe that it *does*. Insofar as I am a female body with a female sexual structure, I believe this affects my understanding of myself and my world. I believe that as a woman I must relate to the world not only in terms of my *unique* body structure but also in terms of the sexual structure of my body. This gives me a sense of identity with other women. I can know from inside the skin how the femaleness of body is experienced. I can never know what it would be like to have a penis. (Once, when I was sixteen, I accidentally hit a boy in the balls. The look of pain on his face was so excruciating, and I was totally bewildered and confused because I had no physical awareness of the kind of pain I had caused.)

I have come to the realization that whatever type of cultural values, social roles, or interpretations I place on my body, the body itself does affect my behavior, my action in relation to my world, my fears and my possibilities for the graceful experience of reality. I wish to own my female body and its female sexual structure. On the level of sexual structure I can speak only for women, for men will perceive reality in and through having a male body.

MY BODY: MY POSSIBILITY

As a woman I *organically* relate to the world with the body of a female. I menstruate. I can choose whether or not and when to have children, but nothing will prevent the menstruation process or menopause, and I must deal with the potential fertility of my body. However I deal with it, whatever myths or attitudes I place on those experiences, menstruation must be dealt with—the fears about it as a child, the relief of it if I thought I was pregnant, the discomfort of it. The more I tense up, the more I feel the need for brown paper wrappers on Kotex boxes, the more shame I have, the more I will create tensions for the body and menstrual cramps. The fact of it is a reality. The attitude to it—and thus the experience of it—is somewhat a matter of choice.

I am sometimes afraid that the contemporary emphasis on equality with men is based not on an acceptance of the structure of female sexuality but on a curious denial of it. (I'll show you I'm not a sex object. I'll show you I'm as good a mind as you, and my body isn't weaker than yours.) If I can control my sexual weakness, that is, my liability to become pregnant, then I can almost become disassociated from my female body. I feel the danger today is that I begin to see only the problematic aspect of having female sex organs, and not the possibilities. The possibility that is offered to me is to be able to enjoy the bodily experiences that go along with being a female body. I can enjoy my female sexuality in its orgasmic potential. I can also enjoy the functions of my female sexuality. I think enjoyment means being able to relax into, to accept and not to resist. Menstruation becomes more painful the more tension and shame are associated with it. Labor becomes more difficult and more painful the more resistance I give to it.

I learned with my husband how to prepare for "natural childbirth." The fact that I had to learn how to be natural again, how to trust my own body, is a testimony to the fact that the natural lore of women has been forgotten. Learning how to cooperate with my uterus during labor and not to resist it meant learning how to relax and how to adjust my breathing to the needs of my body. I learned to imitate the panting breath of a pregnant dog. As I experienced it, labor was learning to trust my body again, to respond to the contractions of the uterus, not as pain but as intense energy directed toward an end, and to aid that energy through relaxing. It was learning to experience reality in a new way. Letting one's body do it, cooperating with it, trusting it, meant that labor and childbirth was not terrifying pain but an experience of great force.

The effort of my body was intense; I felt an ability to share in that effort in its most productive moments. It *was* the groaning of creation, not as pain, but as the emergence of life. Many women told me of loneliness, intense pain and horror associated with childbirth. In fact, it seemed to me that women made a point of telling me about the pain. No one described the graceful dimensions of that whole process, the bearing of the child, the labor, and the birth. All of these bodily experiences were worth it for their own sake, and not just bearable because of the desire for the end result—the child. Indeed, I did not really know what that end result would be. Even if the baby had died at birth, it would not have changed the experience.

I don't believe that I am alone in writing of childbirth as an ecstatic experience of my own body and one able to be shared with my husband. For me as a woman my body taught me to surrender myself to the processes of life and to trust them. Surrendering did not mean submission or passivity or giving up of myself or lack of activity. It *did* mean allying myself with the natural flow of energy. In that effort I discovered the inner dynamic of the process of life. "I" did not "have" a baby. She is not "my" daughter. My body became the instrument, the means by which the graceful, giftful dimension of life is experienced. To be taken over, to allow oneself the physical experience of the body giving birth. "I" did not "have" the child. The baby was born *through* me and with my assistance.

I found this experience caused me to reflect on the meaning of the word "creation." To create is not something I "do" insofar as it is directed activity performed by me, a process that involves me, takes me up, and from which something new emerges. As I experienced it, the bodily process that is called "giving birth" was genuinely "creative" ... I experienced my body taking "me" with it ... I experienced myself as being caught up and participating in the creative action of life that moved me with it insofar as I was open to it.

I used to think of creation and the image of God as Creator as one who made, fashioned, or shaped. I feel now, however, that the image of creation is best understood as being open to, sharing, participating, working with, surrendering to the movement of life, which will then give us more than we could ever gain by our own agency. This, ultimately, is the graceful dimension of existence, of relationships, of artistic creation, and I feel that through my body, specifically through the natural functioning of my female sexual structures, I have been given a perception of these graceful dimensions.

I find myself apologetic for writing so extensively of the enjoyment and graceful dimensions of one aspect of female sexuality: child-birth. I feel, however, that to speak from female experience insofar as it is distinctive means to take the female body and mind as a whole. I think our society hates the female body. Menstruation is to be hidden, pregnancy is often experienced as the ultimate symbol of female submission to male dominance, and nursing a baby in public is a rare event. To expose one's breast in a strip show may be fine, but for me to nurse my baby on an airplane felt like an act of courage.

True liberation of myself as a woman means, for me, the ability to delight in my body. It means the ability to accept the pleasures associated with my body, to control the procreative functions of my body until the internal and external structures can accept the preg-nancy. In this sense childbirth can be an experience that I can look forward to as a pleasurable body experience.

It is also a cosmic event—a glimpse into the nature of life itself, into my own birth and into my own death. It is a physical and psycho-logical experience in which I am most rooted, grounded in my flesh, in the blood and sweat and cries and breath and push of my own body. This is ecstasy. To surrender ourself, to participate in and to feel the force of creative action. It is the spirit. In the femaleness of my own body I have experienced creation groaning, the spirit mov-ing. I know it and am thankful for it. Fathers who stay away from the birth of "their" child out of a sense of fear should not be afraid. They can participate in the end action of their own generative movement. To experience the birthing of a child together is like a mutual or-gasm: We are both transcended and left panting! Fathers should not tolerate being separated from this event.

I wish to be liberated in my body. I want to be able to experience pregnancy as a glowing state—worth it for its own sake. I want to be able to live in my body and to celebrate its unique possibilities for menstruation, orgasm, pregnancy, childbirth, nursing, and meno-pause. I want to be a sexual body and be able to experience the fullness and potential of the female sexual structures. It is here that I can experience in a uniquely female way the graceful dimensions of my own body. It gives me pleasure; that's why I do it. I enjoy it. A female has a right to know and understand and derive as much pleasure from her body as she can. But more than that, childbirth in particular may be the only time that I may be dramatically presented with a glimpse into the essence of life itself.

Opening myself to my own body, being responsible to it, caring for it, and creating a situation in which its body-based experiences can be trusted is my most sacred obligation to myself. To open myself to myself is the same as opening myself to others. As a child it is through close physical contact and organic relatedness with my parents that I can learn to trust my own body. I must be open, relax into being an organism interconnected with others. It is through being open that I can breathe in and out, that I can digest, defecate, experience orgasm. All these openings, taking in and giving out, can be experienced as gifts and as signs of the interconnectedness of myself with others.

MY BODY: MY FEAR

There is fear, however. Fear of relaxing, fear of opening, fear of trusting myself and others. I feel there is particular fear associated with being female in the experiences of my sexuality. I don't believe it all boils down to a fear to "love" and "trust" and "communicate," and that the focus on sexuality is really a disguise for a more basic issue. I believe that the particular problems of trusting and my special fears as a woman are connected with the unique female sexual structure. I feel that there are innate fears associated with being a body with a vagina, just as there are unique fears and pleasures associated with being a body with a penis. For a child the vision of animals engaged in the act of coitus is not necessarily a reassuring one. The female is passive, and there is a goodly amount of force and exertion on the part of the male. The female never looks as if she is "enjoying" it.

To be a woman means that I must open myself, desire to be penetrated. My deep-seated fear, of course, is that entry will be forced; I won't be ready. The possibility of sexual violation of the female by the male is based not only on the superior strength of one over the other but also on the nature of the sexual organs—one has a penis, the other a vagina. In this enlightened age of karate and female sexual initiative I still cannot get over the fact that it is I who open myself to being entered. The sexual act of coitus involves force—penetrative force, ejaculatory force, straining, pushing, wild, wanted, shared force. Ultimately, however, the penetrative force of the male member is the necessary force of procreation. It is my possibility for enjoyment, but also my fear. My fears as a woman will be associated with violation. I can be raped. For the male his fears may be associated with death, with being consumed, absorbed, smothered in the sexual act. He must trust entering. I must trust being entered; I must trust the force, must welcome and open the deepest center of myself to the "other."

My body: my problem and my possibility, the source of my fears and my deepest joys. I think accepting my body as a woman means knowing that there is continual risking, for there is a dark side along with the graceful dimensions of my sexuality. To be grounded in my physical selfhood may mean knowing the fears of opening myself, knowing the desire and yet the fear of receiving the other into myself. This element of the need to open—to surrender oneself to the natural structures and processes of one's body in coitus, pregnancy, and childbirth—is not unique to females, for on a symbolic level it is an image of what it means to trust in life, to trust in the other. It is in and through my body as a woman that I can share with other women and attempt to share with men the graceful experiences of my own sexuality.

I can share with you how nice it is to breast-feed the baby, what a pleasurable sensation comes from the baby sucking on the breast. I can tell you these things. I can suggest that you too hold the baby close to your skin to allow its warmth and yours to melt together. This baby will bring you a new sense of your body as a man, teach you again your own love of softness and touch and warmth. This baby in your arms will reveal new dimensions of your own lost childhood; it will in its helplessness show you your own tenderness, your own simplicity.

For me as a woman the special experiences that belong to my own female sexual structures are mine. They can reveal to me more about the dark, the demonic, and the fearful than anything else can. They can also show me what the holy means, what ecstasy means, what creation means, what life and death mean, what trust and love mean. In a way, nothing else is as clear to me as the experiences of my own body. Theology, God, doctrinal discussions only make sense if I know the ground from which I am speaking. The meaning of life and death, the question of a transcendent dimension, the experience of grace become most real on the visceral level, and most particularly so in the experience of my female sexuality.

chapter 9

A RETURN TO
"FATHER KNOWS BEST"

Robert S. Ellwood, Jr.

I

A bright and cheerful image haunts the hearts of many in these tempestuous days for church and society. It is a luminous image of what they sense deep down is the way things should be, an image, shall we say, of the Jones family. They live in a pleasant, leafy American suburb or small town. Their spacious house has a green lawn and white picket fence around it.

On Sunday morning the Jones family goes to church, Mr. Jones in his dark suit driving the car, his wife at his side, his two children in the back seat. He and his family worship the heavenly Father devoutly as the rector stands as Christ's priestly representative at the Holy Table, and explicates God's Word from the pulpit. Afterwards, the Jones family repairs to the parish hall where the church ladies serve coffee and tea, with Kool-Aid for the children. Some of the men informally discuss vestry matters while their wives talk children or shopping.

Back home, Mrs. Jones sets Sunday dinner on the table. Mr. Jones presiding, offers thanks to the Father above for the meal. He subsequently keeps the children's manners and conversation respectful with benign firmness, while considering his wife's query about whether he would like her to order a new sofa.

This picture gives a capsule version of what, for many, is the way things should be. Admittedly, in this world of mass starvation, rising divorce rate, child abuse, race conflict, and the alleged breakdown of moral standards, it is not always the way they are. Like many such haunting images, the picture is made up of three parts: it is a composite of some present reality, some pure fancy, and some remembrance from a past as recent as the 1950s but already beginning to be idealized into an object of romantic nostalgia. (One of the most powerful of the mind's myth-making processes is its well-nigh irresistible tendency to join together its idea of the way things should be with its idea of the way things used to be, making the present a "fall" from a better, more virtuous past—even though this generally grossly distorts the way it really was.)

More important, this picture serves for those to whom it appeals as a paradigm of an archetypal model which, as a picture of the way things should be, need not conform to present reality but is the measure to which present things ought to be squared. The picture clearly gives a hierarchical, patriarchal paradigm for church and family: it suffuses that pattern of married life with a pleasing aura of family closeness, devoutness, prosperity, and respectability. It suggests that if one adheres to the right pattern, he and his will be blessed in this world and the next; husband, wife, and children alike will inwardly be happier and more secure in accepting the hierarchical, patriarchal pattern—letting the husband/father be the quasi-priestly head of the house and final decision-maker—than those who try to short-circuit the powerlines of authority God has set for human society.

This is the point of view of a position being heard increasingly today as a self-conscious intellectual position, particularly in conservative oriented sectors of Christendom and among some Neo-Pentecostalists. It could be called "Neo-Patriarchalism." This position stands in opposition to the highly individualized views of happiness and meaning in human life which seem to say that one's personal self-fulfillment is more important than family or other structural commitments, and that "liberation" or flat-out equality is more important than any relationship of authority/subordination. Neo-Patriarchalism sees that sort of self-fulfillment or liberation as a deceptive Lorelei that can never really deliver what it promises, but goes against both the will of God and the true roots of human happiness—which, of course, are finally identical. It speaks with the advantages of being able to present a fairly exact, yet workable, plan. Buttressed as it is by an immense weight of authoritative sanctions—scriptural and traditional—Neo-Patriarchalism gives uncertainty-racked moderns the added strength of thinking they are acting in accordance with God's will, in an absolutely and not just a relatively right way. Finally, Neo-Patriarchalism has the asset of presenting the usages of the more conservative and traditional segments of society, which can at least outwardly appear appealingly happy and self-assured to those who wander from them.

Neo-Patriarchalism affirms a divinely ordained hierarchy of authority in the universe. The God we are taught to call "Father" is sovereign over heaven and earth; kings are the biblical and traditional archetype of sovereignty below (however scarce they may be today); a male priesthood is the outward, sacramental sign of the church's authority and supernatural vocation; the husband and father is head over his wife and children. Only when human life is structured to conform to this hierarchical model, we are told, will it attain to that deepest joy which comes from truly fulfilling God's will in the pattern of one's life—for God has not only sent down a miscellany of individual vocations, but also a precise overall pattern for society. He has set the solitary in families, ordaining them society's basic unit, and made the father head of each. The family headed by a father is the model for all other social relationships, and even for the language God desires us to use toward himself.

The defence of this position, Neo-Patriarchalists would say, is particularly important today because God's pattern is being challenged anew by several deceptive idols which promise greater freedom or benefit by making something other than the family the prior and pivotal social unit. Recently some voices have urged that larger units —state, race, class—should be one's chief identity, and both family and individual life must be subordinated or even destroyed for their sake. Other voices go to the opposite extreme to infer that only the individual has real meaning, and the family with its lines of authority (not to mention larger units) is to be accepted or discarded only as it advances or hinders one's individual objectives or supposed happiness.

Related to this is a deeper contemporary dissatisfaction—also deceptive in the judgment of Neo-Patriarchalists—with the idea of playing "roles." The idea is abroad that the self has a virtual aseity or total self-sufficiency, and that whatever comes out of the self—one's own drives and wishes and goals—is sincere, meaningful, sacred; but whatever is imposed on one's life by prior structures—family and the institutions of society—is by definition the opposite: empty, role-playing, even a form of slavery. But this presumption does not fit the empirical facts, since all human beings are deeply interdependent at every level from the cradle up. Neither does it fit the assumption that is at the basis of any discussion of moral philosophy, that given this interdependency there are decisions about behavior relative to it which can and must be made, and which every being makes in effect one way or another. Neo-Patriarchalism says the decisions ought to

be made with structuring the interdependency along the right lines
—family and father—in view. To do this avoids the idolatries of both
the larger and generally more dehumanizing units, and of a falsely
autonomous noninterdependent self. To be a father, mother, husband, wife, or child in *this* context is not just "playing a role"
(though it may involve some squelching of nonconforming urges),
but is being who you really are and are meant to be by the Source of
all being when, in the course of human events, you come into that
office. The father *is* a father; the wife *is* a wife; the child *is* a child—
not just something else acting like one. So says Neo-Patriarchalism.

It will not be my purpose to criticize or defend Neo-Patriarchalism
on theological grounds. But to put it into perspective, especially in
its view of male-female relations, as a historian of religion I would
like to look at it in the light of what history shows us about the
religious meaning of being male or female.

II

The picture of the way things should be, according to the Neo-
Patriarchal vision with which we started, can be contrasted with its
opposites. These are pictures called into being by words like goddess, priestess, or matriarch.

What we shall actually be investigating now are the consequences
of the fact that human religious and image-perceiving consciousness
has two sides, which may be called masculine and feminine. Each
has a particular style of spirituality, type of religious archetype or
paradigmatic image, and an implied critique of the social order. The
masculine typically presents a monotheistic God or universal absolute who regulates the cosmos; its hallmarks are structure, judgment,
intellect, logic, law, obedience, and affirmation of the social order.
The feminine tradition offers a feminine archetypal image, an immanent mystic Oneness, though also open to polytheistic pluralism
under the One. It is more oriented to nature than society, more
mystical and affirmative of emotions than of logic and intellect, sometimes bending toward apocalyptic change rather than stability.

Needless to say, there are numerous major exceptions to these
generalizations. One is the apocalyptic side of the Judaeo-Christian
God, though that is linked to the masculine attribute of judgment,
and is associated with some profoundly feminine imagery—like birth
pangs and the woman of the Book of Revelation. Another is the
association today of Neo-Pentecostalism, with its affective, spontaneous, immediate, and apocalyptic overtones, with a quite masculine
image of God, and indeed often with Neo-Patriarchalism. But the

movement is infused with the Holy Spirit, and some theologians have noted that the Holy Spirit—like the Wisdom of the Old Testament, which is a prototype of the Spirit of the New—mysteriously conjoins masculine and femine faces of God. If Neo-Pentecostalism is in fact partly a new discovery of what may be called the archetypally feminine side of the Christian God, as I believe it is, Neo-Patriarchalism may be, humanly speaking, an almost necessary compensatory stability in the outward realm of the social order for some who have set sail on its inward seas.

It is very important, also, to stress that we are talking about the sets of attributes that tend to cluster around masculine and feminine divine figures and religious leaders, not necessarily about the religious attitudes of all human men and women respectively. There is some correlation in the latter, but nothing like uniformity, partly because everyone has both masculine and feminine psychological characteristics in varying proportions regardless of biological gender, partly because everyone regardless of sex is influenced by the general bent of his culture. (For that matter, these two caveats apply to deities as well.) But particularly since Neo-Patriarchalism unapologetically offers such a classic example of the claims of the masculine paradigm in the social order, a contrast and comparison of these two may be instructive in this discussion.

According to early post-Darwinian theories of social evolution, matriarchy—society dominated by a mother with several lovers and many offspring in tow—was the next stage after the "primal horde." It was often portrayed as a rather sinister state of affairs, at least for the males. To be at the mercy of a ruling woman was a risky matter, for women lacked stability, going from one extreme to another, now smothering mates and children with love, now reaching out at them with irrational destructive rage.

Anthropologists universally agree today that matriarchy of this sort never existed. To be sure, some archaic societies traced descent matrilineally, but political rule was still in male hands, passing perhaps like the patriarchate of the Assyrian ("Nestorian") Church from uncle to nephew. But the fascinating and terrifying vision of feminine nature in control has rich expression in the goddesses who have dwelt as embodiments of the feminine archetypes in the psyches of humankind.

We might evoke before our mental eyes Aphrodite with her passions both for love and, paradoxically, also for Ares, the god of war, and her promiscuity with many lovers. Or we might conjure up the Hindu Kali, who (representing the phenomenal world) combines all extremes of tenderness and fury. Like Saturn devouring his progeny, she can fondle her child and nurse him at her breast, then suddenly shift mood and wring his neck. Her mood is suggested by the reeking sacrifices of goats—all male—which lie before her altars, and by the warm devotion of her devotees, some of them saintly mystics, who call her Mother. They believe she represents the ultimate source of the universe, better defined as maternal and feminine than anything else. It is said that unless one can face the dark side of life in its unending cycle of conception and consumption, one can never fully comprehend the mysteries of what transcends space and time.

But generally religion seems to reach a sort of stasis between the spiritual forces engendered by male and female sexuality. Both are recognized as highly charged, standing off against each other like positive and negative magnetic poles. Interaction must be carefully controlled so that it is creative instead of becoming, as can easily happen, destructive. (In some Melanesian villages, the holy places of the men and women are at opposite ends of the village, where the youths of each sex respectively are initiated; the homes of married couples are at the point of equilibrium in between.)

Within the broad world of Hinduism, devotion to Kali and other forms of the mother goddess is balanced by the hereditary priestly authority of males of the Brahmin caste, who alone can perform the most ancient and sacred rituals and who preserve the holy lore of the Vedas.

In China, the two most influential classical philosophies, Confucianism and Taoism, whose nominal founder was Lao-tzu, represent the two poles vividly. Confucius presents one side in teaching family, loyalty, good citizenship, community rituals, and adherence to traditional morality as the basis of a good society and a good life. The fundamental virtue for Confucius was "filial piety," the obligation of a son to reverence and obey his father, the head of his house. If this relationship was set right, he said, the rest of one's relationships—to ruler, brother, wife, and friend—would fall into place. Like the Neo-Patriarchalists of today, Confucianism stresses that the salvation of society and the individual lies in fulfilling one's *given* role. "Let the father be father," said Confucius, "and the son be son. Let the ruler be ruler, and the subject be subject,"—the doctrine known as "rectification of names."

Based on precepts like these, traditional Chinese society endured from before the time of Christ until the Communist revolution. But Confucianism alone was not enough, for the Chinese found they could not live only in unrelieved sober virtue and patriarchal rectitude all day every day. In Taoism a romantic, feeling-oriented, individual-oriented side of their character appeared, among other outlets finding expression in gorgeous fairy tales and lovely goddesses. It was said that mandarins were Confucianists at work and Taoists on vacation.

The counterphilosophy to Confucianism and everything similar to it has never been put more forcefully than in the book, *Tao Tê Ching* ("Teaching of Tao"), attributed to Lao-tzu, traditionally an older contemporary of Confucius. Here we are told that the conventions of society corrupt nature and that to live either by rule or competitive ambition is to be rigid and easily broken, like a dead branch. One should instead flow with God or nature (the *Tao*)—subtle, deep, self-effacing, flexible. The best leader, Lao-tzu says, is not the authority-laden patriarch but he whose people are scarcely aware of his existence and say, "We did this ourselves." It was only when people lost touch with how to live attuned to the *Tao* that they began to talk of moral codes. When "morality" came in the spontaneity of nature was lost; a son uncorrupted by moral advice naturally admires and wants to emulate his father, but the son who is told he must be obediently filial probably will hate his father instead.

It is interesting to observe that Confucius, with his emphasis on moralism and the social order as the place where value is found, makes the father-son relationship the key to his system, and filial obedience the key virtue. But Lao-tzu, for whom the relation of mankind and nature is the pivot, often uses the mother-child metaphor. He says one must live with nature as a child nursing at the breast, for the *Tao* is a continually bearing, maternal womb.

Confucianism was generally the official "establishment" philosophy of the Chinese state, taught in the schools and enforced in the homes of respectable families. Taoism was like a perennial counterculture—a different point of view with which to tap off pressure built up behind the hard and straight Confucian dams.

A comparable contrast has developed over the centuries in Roman Catholicism. The official ecclesiastical structure is based on a male hierarchy, as is its teaching and sacramental authority. (The priesthood, of course, is celibate; celibacy and monasticism as male ideals, whether in Christianity, Buddhism, or Hinduism, have some relationship to social patriarchalism and bear a complex psychological kinship to the masculine as well as the feminine side: it says not only that males should be sovereign over females but that males, while they may be devotees of the Great Mother, can be spiritually fulfilled independent of actual females.)

But beside the official Roman Catholic structure is the celebrated cultus of the Blessed Virgin Mary, Mother of God. Particularly in its nineteenth- and twentieth-century forms, so much centered on the great apparitions of the Virgin Mother at places like La Salette, Lourdes, Knock, and Fatima, this devotion has been relatively independent of the official institution, and perhaps psychologically very independent. The percipients of the apparitions were generally untutored young women or children and the sites were mountain glades or isolated villages far from the centers of ecclesiastical or political power. The messages of Our Lady have sometimes skirted the edge of heresy, and have had less to do with the official sacramental or doctrinal systems than with apocalyptic signs, miraculous healings, and extraliturgical devotions.

Yet the cultus has been immensely popular, showing clearly that it answered to some deeply felt yearning. The hierarchical church has had to come to terms with it. Marian fervor has declined somewhat since Vatican II. But for a time it was almost as though there were two religions conjoined in popular Catholicism, mirror images of each other—one patriarchal and one matriarchal; one linked to the centers of power and one leaving its signs miraculously among the humble; one of the city and one of the peasant countryside; one working chiefly through regularized structure and the other redolent of unexpected marvels and unmerited boons; one negotiating this world and the other shot through with portents of radical apocalyptic event.

Elsewhere the spirituality of the feminine side of human consciousness has distinguished itself from the masculine in still other ways. In the northern part of the Sudan, and in neighboring Muslim lands, a cult of *zar*, or possessing spirits, is common among women. Women here have little outward security or power; the rules of society and the course of individual lives are determined by men, from the lawgivers of the Islamic community down to individual fathers and husbands. The whole tone of traditional Islam, with its absolute God, its legal emphasis, and its assumption that only men take responsibility for the course of events, is heavily masculine. But here women have a response of their own; they can go into dissociated trance, believing themselves possessed by mighty spirits who can bless and curse. The spirits often make demands of the entranced woman's husband —for new clothes or jewelry or whatever—which he dare not refuse lest the invisible guest curse him with sickness. This cult can be compared with other mediumistic faiths the world around, like Vodun in Haiti or Umbanda in Brazil, which while not exclusively feminine have high levels of feminine participation and leadership in contrast to the exclusively male-led "official" religion of the society.

Compare the role of women in American religion. Three important religious or spiritual movements have been founded by women on these shores: Spiritualism, by the Fox sisters; Theosophy, and the various occultisms derived from it, by the Russian-born Madame Helena Blavatsky; Christian Science by Mary Baker Eddy. All three movements have had substantial feminine leadership and participation since their founding as well, not a few of the leading women having had unhappy marriage experiences. Probably there are twice as many women as men spiritualist mediums and ministers. Needless to say, all three have been considered highly heretical if not demonic by the male-dominated mainline churches, and it is a striking fact that they have much in common with the "underground" feminine cults around the world, like the African *zar* faith.

III

The feminine religious mystique tends to emphasize the unity and immanence of the divine. Rather than a transcendent, highly personal Lawgiver, God is more like an infinite Sea or Womb within which all things rise and fall, and with which to merge is perfect peace. Under the infinite God, though, there often dwells a great household of lesser entities visible and invisible, spirits or saints, with whom one can commune or who can speak through one in dissociated states. This style of religion is highly oriented toward the cognitive significance of states of consciousness, mystical or ecstatic or mediumistic—out of them can come power to teach, prophesy, or heal, and immediate gifts like healing are important.

Ethical teaching and moral codes, while given recognition, are relatively less emphasized than in the masculine-dominated religions which have responsibility for the ordering of society as a whole. The tone in feminine faiths is generally one of a more intuitive, feeling-oriented, accepting attitude toward behavior, like that of a wise mother who knows how to comfort her children even when they have been bad. Mercy holds a precarious lead over justice, as in the case of Our Lady of La Salette, who spoke of being able to restrain the just wrath of her Son against sinful mankind only a short while longer. Such apocalyptic emphasis, found also in some wings of Theosophy and Spiritualism, is characteristic; to feminine religion, the world is less a stable structure than one that is growing, changing, and capable of shifting unexpectedly into the birth pangs of a new age heralded by new revelations.

Within Christianity, widely influential feminine leadership has been mostly in Pentecostal and "healing" movements. Their emphases on immediacy of power and experience, flexibility of structure, and continuing revelation obviously have more in common with the pattern than other forms. One thinks of Aimee Semple McPherson, Katherine Kuhlmann, and now some of the leaders of the Roman Catholic charismatic movement.

To what extent this pattern is rooted in woman's basic psychology, or to what extent that psychology has been itself shaped by woman's position in society, are complex questions that we cannot attempt to answer here. It may even be that the pattern, which always tends to be nonrational, feeling-expressive, and apocalyptic, is simply characteristic of the religious expression of submerged groups, both male and female, having little access to power structures. Indeed, it is impossible to answer any of these questions empirically, since there is really no example of a feminine-dominated "establishment" religion to serve as control. Be that as it may, it is this submerged but universal feminine pattern which must be contrasted with the vision of Neo-Patriarchalism.

To the Neo-Patriarchalist, the feminine religious pattern is disturbing because it suggests a universe too fluid, too susceptible to the winds of feeling, and too polymorphous to be secure. He prefers a firmly hierarchical universe in which, in the moral and spiritual as well as the natural realms, definite and clear rules obtain, and there is a dependable chain of command. Someone needs to be in charge whose natural bent is for firmness and justice. It is all right, after father has scolded and punished his child for good cause, for mother to dry his tears and slip him a piece of candy. But the latter action has significance only because the former was prior; we are not ready yet for a world of nothing but tear-wiping and candy. (Much traditional Roman Catholicism suggests a similar contrast between God, or even Jesus, and the Blessed Virgin Mary.) At least on the surface, the Neo-Patriarchalist's desire is for a hierarchical society more than for masculine dominance; it is just that male leadership seems to be the only hierarchical option available that could possibly work as well as being the one ordained by God. He emphasizes, of course, that the feminine role is intrinsically just as important; it is only that it is different.

IV

Today we are in a situation of changing values and life styles, and even more, of uncertainty about them. For one thing, the feminine side is coming back to the Western consciousness, and not only as veiled in Marianism. The values of many quite secular people, as well as of many churchmen, who do not explicitly worship goddesses bespeak what has traditionally belonged to the feminine archetype:

emphasizing therapeutic "caring" more than legalistic morality; thinking it good to express feelings rather than suppress them; openness to the spiritualistic and psychic, Taoistic, "ecological" rapport with nature; feeling great apocalyptic changes are afoot. But all this is also baffling. The basic problem for many is one of "placing" themselves. With so many value alternatives and life-style options available—so many that one could virtually try out a new one every week—one hardly knows who he or she *really* is or where one's right place in the world is. The kaleidoscope turns and seems never to rest. One feels first the excitement and then the sickening vertigo of this spinning; he wants somehow to make it stop somewhere.

The way to stop it is to affirm, with the "Jesus movement," that there is One Way. There is one image which is *the way things should be*.

Here it is that Neo-Patriarchalism makes its appeal. Certainly it has helped many who have come to affirm it as a more Christian pattern to find out who they really are. It has worked to dim the dazzle of the kaleidoscope, and has brought balm to the anxieties of some who formerly accepted the popular notions that one's only ethical imperatives are to be "caring" and "self-fulfilled." These dicta can produce the same sort of guilt and anxiety St. Paul experienced under the law, or Luther under "works righteousness." One can never know whether he is "caring" or "self-fulfilled" enough. Moreover, the two values often seem to conflict in real life.

But the patriarchal way things should be produces a structure to which one can, with relief, subordinate one's bafflingly open-ended drives and know who he or she needs to be and what attitudes and actions come first. More than one husband, unsure of himself and like so many moderns wanting above all not to dominate anybody, unhappy and feeling more like a cipher than anything else but afraid to assert himself, has found self-confidence in accepting the rightness of the much-scorned patriarchal pattern, and to his surprise found his family really liked and respected him more for it. More than one wife, not quite knowing why she is irritable and frustrated with a husband who tries only to be "caring" and wants her to do whatever she thinks she wants, and who is torn between what she thinks she wants inside and outside the home, has found a way out of an impossible dilemma by accepting the priority of wifery and homemaking on the authority of the Word of God. Children, contemptuous and wild because their parents were so fearful of being authoritarian as to abdicate all authority and seemed virtually to ask for contempt, have found greater joy in accepting the reaffirmed authority of parents whose strength they could honor.

One final observation. The whole issue has been presented here in archetypal terms. We have not talked about individual men and women—who may well be as different from others of their sex as from the opposite sex. Some men may rejoice in modern pluralism and others be terrified by it. Some women are no more attracted to unitive mysticism than the most rationalistic male. But archetypal language is appropriate, for the whole point of Neo-Patriarchalism is its univocal reliance on archetypes.

For this reason it cannot, for example, concede that a man and woman could reach a pragmatic but genuine relationship of shared decision-making with each other, or acknowledge that each has some archetypally masculine and some feminine personality traits or needs. Unlike Jungian analysts, they would hold that the archetypal possibilities within one cannot make domestic covenants and form mandalas or round-table committees with each other. Each person can, they apparently hold, only enthrone one familial archetype (or obviously coregent ones like wife and mother) at a time, and the mandala is the family. These archetypes are kings rather than cabinet ministers, and have divine right, though they can and should make feudal external treaties.

So in effect, Neo-Patriarchalists speak not of this man or that woman, but of The Man, The Priest, The Father, The Woman, The Mother. These categories, more than the refractory diverse individuals in concrete existence, can be arranged into close-knit hierarchical patterns. Many individuals in turn feel better exchanging individuality for an archetypal slot. They are content to be The Father, The Priest, or The Mother. If they accept Neo-Patriarchalism's hierarchy running from God through The Father, and symbolized in The Priest, it is not necessarily because they are unaware of the immense suffering (as well as immense good) which women and children down through the ages have received from fallible human patriarchs. But to these people the meaningless abyss of a world without archetypes and hierarchies giving one place and pattern is more terrifying.

One feels the issue of ordination of women has produced such bitter passion precisely because it has become an issue symbolizing the confrontation between the church's traditional role of presenting archetypal paradigms and the modern affirmation of individuality. If history teaches anything, it is that symbols arouse in people the deepest emotional responses of all, far more than mere practical or empirical goals. Starving people may kill for food, but for the sake of symbols well-fed people will torture or lay down their own lives. No symbols run deeper than those grounded in the male-female relationship.

In fact, men and women themselves easily become symbols, becoming The Man and The Woman to each other and even to themselves. This is nowhere more the case than in religion, for religion is rightly the first and final home of archetype and symbol. Knowing archetype and symbol to be bright windows elucidating God and his ways (themes too vast for ordinary language), religionists sometimes forget that even what seems an angel of light can conceal an enslaving demon. The ordination issue, like Neo-Patriarchalism, forces us to ask precisely to what extent assimilating men and women to archetypes is viable and in accordance with the intention of the God who made them male and female.

Do we think primarily of a person of female sex as an archetype, as The Woman, who as such has a certain place even as does The Man in the splendid hierarchy of heaven and earth? Or do we think of her as another individual in an extremely pluralistic society, who like so many others may have an untraditional vocation, and who may (but again, may not, for no one is conventionally "feminine" just because she is female) bring to a male-dominated institution something of the feminine spiritual tradition, which may do it some good?

The conundrum is not easy, for we know that nothing human is more glorious than a person liberated by affirmation of an archetype to accept herself and her vocation, and nothing more dehumanized than a person who has reduced himself and his views of others to nothing but archetypes. The former may be a person reborn in Christ; the latter may reach the level of a Nazi racist. If we give up the archetype, quite apart from theological considerations, we may surrender the capacity to proclaim to people lost in modern multiplicity a divine pattern for family and society that gives them a sense of "place" and meaning. If we save the archetype by giving up individuality, we run the risk of making persons into The Man, The Woman, The Good Guy, The Bad Guy, The Jew. We could also conclude that indeed The Father and The Priest are archetypally masculine, and The Mother and The Mystic archetypally feminine, but that biological gender is one thing, and archetypal identity or identities is another and more complex matter. The latter may follow the biological or may not. More likely they are struggling to compose a potential symphony with major and minor themes, trills and continuos and codas, which does not have to be played all in one key—though one can make as good a symphony in C Major as anything else if that's what the music seems to be saying.

People can get lost in archetypes, and they can also get lost in their separate individualities. They can find themselves in both. We will be much blessed if the Neo-Patriarchal appeal and the ordination issue force us to sort out satisfactorily these two sides of human identity.

chapter 10

A WOMAN'S VOCATION
TO THE PRIESTHOOD:
"How Can This Be?"

Elsa P. Walberg

"You have a vocation to the priesthood." My rector didn't say that to me back in 1958 when he tried to persuade me to attend seminary. His own seminary had just opened its doors to women, and somehow he and I both knew that theological education ought to be the next step for me. But I fought it then—it just didn't make sense to interrupt a well-established career in teaching simply to pursue a consuming interest in the Bible and theology. I saw no future in it.

"You have a vocation to the priesthood." The members of my parish didn't say that either when, a year later, they saw me off to seminary. I had by then persuaded myself that in order to handle increasingly challenging assignments as a lay leader in my parish I needed to become theologically more responsible. As an educator I'd been "turned on" by my involvement in the church's new teaching series, which disclosed to me and to many a God who was active in our lives. As an adult who'd already made conscious decisions about vocation and life style I now found my faith quickened and stretched by the high seriousness of a new experience—the Parish Life Conference. Within the parish I discovered a community of faith which embodied for me the love of God. Suddenly three years of seminary seemed little enough to undertake in order to be responsive and responsible to the new life I was experiencing as a valued member of a parish family. Yes, I *could* go to seminary. I had found my reason for doing so.

"You have a vocation to the priesthood." That was hardly the way my fellow seminarians greeted my presence in their midst. Few thought I had any business being there at all. I spent much time and psychic energy simply justifying my presence. I discovered that postulants and candidates for Holy Orders were a very special breed; an informed laity was an abstraction to which they paid lip service. That any of its members should participate in the same process of theological education which shaped their vocations was somehow quite threatening. Time and again my motivation was questioned. In fact, I began to question it myself. What was I doing there? Didn't I know my place? What would become of me?

The joy and excitement of being loved and affirmed as a member of a community of faith—my recent parish experience—gave place to an atmosphere in which I experienced myself as the "other." The fact that there were so few women on campus in those days—I myself had one female classmate—intensified our sense of isolation. A seminary that prided itself in offering the same curriculum to women as to men could not know how wholly different would be the experience a woman might have in that male-oriented, male-directed, male-dominated, and male-affirming institution. In those days I was not entirely conscious myself of the many ways in which I died to the person I was and hoped to be in the midst of so many who found it so difficult to accept and affirm me.

"You have a vocation to the priesthood." In 1960 women seminarians never said that to each other. It was clearly unthinkable! Whenever such fantasies entered our consciousness we quickly repressed them; they were threatening even to ourselves. (It was far more appropriate to suggest to each other that we had come to seminary to find husbands!) We had been taught too well even before we entered seminary that womanhood and priesthood were mutually exclusive, while our brothers learned the equally damaging "truth" that priesthood would, by definition, confirm and verify their manhood.

Most of the women in seminary in the early sixties were really not sure why they were there. Like our male counterparts we were deeply committed to our Lord and his church, we were excited by the growth of the Episcopal Church during the fifties, and we took seriously its urgent need and concern at that moment in history for more laborers in the vineyard—more people who were willing to commit their lives to full-time service within the church. What this calling might mean for Episcopal women pioneering in the church's seminaries was as yet unknown. How might they serve? Like myself some of them hoped to return to the local parish, but in what capacity? What did it mean to have studied theology, liturgics, and preaching along with Bible, church history, and Christian education? Dimly we began to perceive where we might be headed, but most of us were unable to acknowledge these intimations even to ourselves. Women weren't *called* to priesthood—it was as simple as that.

There were no role models to whom we could look or could point. We practiced denial of what was happening to us. We could neither admit it to ourselves nor to each other. We knew no sisterhood, and we found acceptance from our brothers only as we put ourselves down and played the dilettante or the coquette. In the early sixties it became increasingly acceptable, even for male seminarians, to prepare for ministry in nonparochial settings. As we neared the completion of our seminary years, we began to focus on vocations in education, social work, publishing, and specialized chaplaincies. I was the only woman graduate in the seminary's first three years to enter fulltime parish work, although at least two of our number achieved reentry as clergymen's wives.

"You have a vocation to the priesthood." That was what the members of the faculty said to my classmates as they commended most of them to their respective bishops and standing committees for ordination. The seminary's general exams were behind us at last, and while I was busy packing up my books and learning to drive a car, most of the male seniors were still studying hard, anxiously facing diocesan ordination exams. I had already watched them try on their first clerical collars, purchase their vestments, and order their ordination invitations. The moment of truth had come: we would be graduated together, but *they* would be ordained. I remember feeling wistful— even vaguely disappointed—yet determined that no one should know. "Who needs ordination?" I said almost too casually. "There's enough to be done in the parish church without worrying about whether or not I'm ordained." Perhaps I really believed that then— or wanted to. Or maybe I was making a statement I knew to be nonthreatening both to my classmates and to the church at large.

"You have a vocation to the priesthood." Although I had more job interviews than I could handle in the months before commencement, no one saw my servanthood in those terms. Instead they were looking for a director of Christian education who'd been to seminary and would therefore be "exceptionally well qualified." I was a natural for such a post, having brought to seminary ten years' experience in high school and college classrooms. Originally I had even expected to return to the schoolroom. But clinical training and seminary field work had broadened my experience: chaplaincy in a mental hospital and a woman's prison, family case work with the Episcopal City Mission, a student ministry within an innercity parish—all these had prepared me to pursue Christian education, and more. I now had my heart set on serving in the inner city—I had fallen in love with the people there—but I discovered that ordination was critical in such settings. Rarely could an inner-city mission afford a multiple staff that included a salaried lay person. I was more employable in affluent suburbia.

With each new interview I began to realize that the men and women, the clergy and laity, who talked with me had no other conception of how a woman might serve within a parish than that she "work with the Sunday school." It was not that I actually wanted to avoid that area of parish life—I simply didn't want to get boxed into it. At last a parish emerged that liked the idea of having a "parish assistant"—a term that managed a compromise between the parish's expectations that a full-time director of Christian education be hired and my negotiations with rector and wardens for a role that would allow me to minister more widely.

"You have a vocation to the priesthood." That thought was always there—insidious, nagging, dogging my consciousness—but I trusted that I must be mistaken; God didn't call people to what was clearly unheard of! In the early years of my parish ministry I worked hard to prove that ordination—at least for a woman—was neither necessary nor desirable. I didn't need to be a parish priest in order to pursue a vocation within the church. In fact, lay status might even be preferable. There would be fewer barriers between myself and the people I hoped to serve; I would be more approachable, more accessible. In those early years I made some interesting discoveries. No, I didn't need ordination in order to function well in the sphere of education. People understood me and what I was about as long as I directed, coordinated, or administered the parish education program, especially as it concerned the young. The training of church school teachers, the teaching of courses in Bible study, an occasional sermon on Christian education or the Bible—these met the expectations of a parish which had, in effect, employed a director of Christian education. I found that there was also some latitude for me to be a quiet catalyst in the development of prayer groups and the nurturing of the parish's spiritual life. I might occasionally be invited to meet with the women's groups to explain the current mission thrust of the national church or to let them know what the Sunday school was doing. Parish folks knew who I was when I carried out such duties.

But seminary had prepared me for more than Christian education. As I got to know the parish and its wider needs, my own emerging sense of vocation took me to a church school family in crisis, to parishioners in hospitals and nursing homes, to the housebound and the shut-ins, to the families of alcoholics, to mental health, welfare, and social service agencies. Sometimes I went by specific invitation;

just as often I went because the concerns of the people of the parish
had become my concerns. It was at this point, however, that we *all*
experienced some confusion: staff members in various community
facilities, members of the parish, I, myself. Who was I? Why was I
calling at the hospital before visiting hours? What was my business
at the juvenile session of the court? Why was I calling on a lonely
widower or a housebound older couple who faced eviction? Was I a
minister? A social worker? A nun in secular clothes? The confusion
sometimes inhibited the effectiveness of my ministry and the ease
with which I could come and go without tedious explanation. I persisted, hardly realizing then what the real trouble was, and in time
my commitment to people in need throughout the parish and the
community developed its own authority.

I'll never forget the day, years later, when I was first able to say to
a recovery room nurse, "May I see Mrs. Jones? I'm her parish minister." No fuss, no queries, no barriers—just instant communication
and response. The doors were opened as one member of the helping
profession acknowledged the authority of another and allowed her to
take her place on the helping team. Was the difference *only* one of
semantics? I think not. Ordination to the diaconate had given me not
only a new way to describe myself but a newly confirmed identity.
At last I knew who I was, and I could proceed with conviction.

"You have a vocation to the priesthood." They would not have put
it that way, but from time to time in those early parish years the
people whom I'd come to know through hospital and home visits
began to seek me out for counseling or to send to their family,
friends, and neighbors. Parents came to talk about their children.
Lonely young people came looking for someone to listen and to care.
Young adults shared anxieties about their sexuality. Mothers
dropped in with their toddlers just for a chat. Couples explored the
advisability of getting married or staying married. The families of
alcoholics opened to me a whole new dimension of ministry, and the
members of AA and Alanon equipped me with ready resources and
their own expertise. Singles, the divorced, the widowed, the aging—
especially depressed, middle-aged women, frightened and hopelessly alone, some experiencing periodic psychotic breaks—came to
ask in his or her own way: Have I offended God? Is there any hope?
How can I go on? It was a high privilege to become for so many
human beings a friend—even a physician—of the soul. Pastoral care
and spiritual direction were areas in which I discovered I had innate
sensitivities, and I quickly took steps to get more training and super-
vision. But to be entrusted with people's lives demanded a kind of
stewardship of my own gifts that brought me often to my knees to ask

for guidance and for strength. My own disciplines of prayer and meditation were quickened and deepened by a new sense of vocation. Was it blasphemous to pray, "For their sake I consecrate myself"?

"You have a vocation to the priesthood." How much longer would I pretend that this was not so? How much longer would I shrink from facing up to the implications of my ministry? As a pastoral relationship deepens, one eventually recognizes that whoever offers pastoral care must necessarily be a minister, not only of the Gospel but of the sacraments. This is probably most clear with respect to the sacrament of penance. One simply can't hear someone's confession and then call in another to give absolution. To be a pastor yet not a priest is to offer a ministry severely truncated: at a critical moment in that pastoral relationship both parties are deprived of the action that enables God to be sacramentally present and that makes it possible for the gift of God's grace to be outwardly and visibly manifest. How often did I hear, especially in the years before I became a deacon: "But why can't *you* bring me communion?" "Why can't you marry us?" "Why can't you baptize our children?" Occasionally such questions came from lifelong Episcopalians who knew "the rules" but suddenly doubted their wisdom. Sometimes a new or would-be Episcopalian reached by the ministry of a woman discovered that her ministrations were inhibited by centuries of tradition. It was always possible, of course, to call in a priest, but—especially in relationships with the sick and the dying—*who* that priest *was* was important to the meaning of the sacrament for them. "*You* have brought me back to God. I want communion at your hand." "*You* have been with me through it all. Please bring me the sacrament before I die." "Why can't you . . .?"

My work in the parish taught me that the ministry of reconciliation requires as its sacramentalist, not a male *ikon* but a *reconciling person*—one through whose day-to-day ministry in the name of Christ the sick and the dying experience God's healing, the estranged and the lost experience God's peace. I was that person because those to whom I ministered called forth and validated my presence as intercessor and mediator: they accepted me as one of the "stewards of the mystery of God." So I found myself standing in that awesome priestly place between God and the people of God.

"You have a vocation to the priesthood." Yes, it was true. For years I had tried to conform to my church's expectations by denying that possibility, but my vocation was tested and tested again. Had I been male I would probably have been ordained to the diaconate at graduation from seminary and priested within a year. But a woman who senses that God is calling her is deeply perplexed. "Surely I'm delud-

ing myself. How can this be?" In the years since the first intimation
that priesthood was indeed my vocation, I have talked with many
women who were willing to admit that they too had experienced
such a calling. Some had known it since childhood. But it could not
be! God could not be calling them to something that was not possible! Sadly, wistfully, most of them sought other ways to honor
God's claim upon their lives. Yet some of us persisted. ("With God
all things are possible"!) Our vocations have since been tested, not
only in the fire of actual ministry but through the requirements prescribed by canon law: medical and psychological screening, ordination exams administered years after the completion of seminary
studies, parish vestry certification, diocesan standing committee
testimonials—all routine steps in the process of obtaining candidacy.
At length we have been ordained to the diaconate—and the process
continues.

"You have a vocation to the priesthood." My ordination to the
diaconate in February 1972 was hardly the first step in my saying yes
to God's claim upon my life, but at last my yes had sacramental
dimensions. Like so many other women—some of them yet to discover who they are—mine was not a "late" but a "delayed" vocation.
At last I dared to acknowledge how God was acting in my life. At last
my church dared to listen to the God of the prophets saying, "Be-
hold, I am doing a new thing!"

These have been exciting but trying times. Those of us who
"walked by faith" as a result of the action of the General Convention
in Houston in 1970 returned from the Louisville Convention in 1973
feeling deeply betrayed. While God had entrusted us with a *calling*,
our church viewed it only as a *cause*. Much was made of the male
imagery of the president of the Eucharist: women could not represent our Lord in this role. Yet few questioned women's ability to
represent our Lord's *servanthood* within the diaconate.

As it happens, women in the diaconate today don't necessarily
believe that a General Convention is the place where our vocation to
the priesthood can actually be authenticated. Isn't it the function of
the people whom we serve, once they are convinced of our calling
and qualifications, to call for our ordination? A year ago the people of
my own diocese did just that for me, and in response the diocesan
Standing Committee unanimously recommended me for priesthood.
My vocation was confirmed! In October 1974 I was ready to be
ordained. A year later I am still ready. Only one thing really prevents
my bishop from ordaining me, despite his own recognition of my
calling and his approval of my candidacy. I am a woman.

"You have a vocation to the priesthood." It has been a vocation I have wrestled with now for a long time—like Jacob at Jabbok wrestling all night with the angel. It's almost as if my sisters and I have been saying to our church during the long, dark night, "I will not let you go unless you bless me!" Our wounds in the struggle are nothing compared to the new wholeness that will be ours—and our church's —once we know that we too can take our rightful place at the sacramental heart of the living body of our Lord.

chapter 11

SEX AND THE LAW

Frank Patton, Jr.

I

While lawyers are not much praised these days, the law itself enjoys remarkable popularity. There are some who would saddle it with responsibility for curing the inequities of our society, establishing morals and manners, and generally elevating the tone of our existence. Law schools are bursting with students, and applicants often see the law as *the* vehicle for social change.

The success of new agencies—such as the federal Equal Employment Opportunity Commission—in righting social wrongs, the willingness of the courts to identify and extend personal rights emanating from the Constitution, these add fuel to the notion that the law is "where it is."

Very much related to the affirmative use of the law in achieving needed social change is the increasing importance of the right to privacy—as Mr. Justice Brandeis called it, "The right to be let alone." We are now noticing that the law has long been tinkering with private habits through its legacy of "morality regulation." The right to an abortion and the right to a private sexual life of one's choosing are now aspects of the right to privacy. That crimes without victims—such as gambling, prostitution, and consensual homosexual acts—may not be crimes at all is gaining acceptance, and reflects a current sense that we must preserve our private world in the face of growing government interest.

With this in mind, I contend that the law is an enabler, a reflection of society's sense of direction and sense of fairness; that the law does not fashion a moral code or manners, style or habits, but for better or for worse echoes what is generally accepted; that the law can be an early register of our best aspirations—for example, those in our Bill of Rights—but it cannot create those aspirations; and that if people and their institutions concerned with goals and values fail to articulate these aspirations or to take them seriously, then the law will mirror that failure.

We must remember that the law is not unitary but is an array of often conflicting legislation, administrative procedures, court decisions, and enforcement practices. I propose that the law must be seen in its fairly modest role, and that goal-setting institutions—the churches, for example—must move up and assume their proper functions.

Accordingly, through a consideration of sex and the law I seek to illuminate the function of the law and the role of goals; and I will focus primarily on women's rights, homosexuality, and obscenity within their constitutional framework.

II

THE RIGHT TO PRIVACY

A right of privacy is not mentioned in our Constitution, in the Bill of Rights, or in other amendments, but over the years the right of privacy has been recognized in varying degrees by our courts. In 1964 the Supreme Court substantially broadened the expression of this right by holding that the state's "compelling" interest in public decency and social order did not entitle it to impair the woman's right of marital privacy by forbidding the use of contraceptives.[1] The Court held that "zones of privacy" immune from government control were derived from the Bill of Rights and were "formed by emanations from those guarantees that help give them life and substance." That the Supreme Court thus elevated the right of privacy to constitutional status has had great effect on the regulation of sexual practices.

It was not a long next step for the courts to hold that the right of privacy encompassed the general sexual behavior of married couples. A federal court in 1968 ruled that an Indiana sodomy statute could not be applied to make consensual sodomy between married persons a crime without a clear showing that the state had an overriding interest in preventing that behavior.[2] In Texas, a federal court determined that society's disapproval was not sufficient grounds for the state to regulate the acts of married persons in their private conduct.[3]

As the right to privacy became a legitimate and increasingly successful mechanism to test the state's interest in modifying personal behavior, the Supreme Court faced the question of abortion. In 1973 the Court handed down two landmark decisions, *Roe* v. *Wade*[4] and *Doe* v. *Bolton*,[5] establishing the woman's right to an abortion. The Court based both decisions squarely on the right of privacy.

Courts have disagreed as to the precise source of the right of privacy: some jurists, like Justice Douglas, contend that it "emanated" from the Bill of Rights; others, that it was incorporated in the Bill of Rights by implication of the Fourteenth Amendment. Although the right seems, therefore, to float in the "penumbra" or shadow of our specifically guaranteed constitutional rights, the 1973 abortion decisions resoundingly reconfirmed it as a "fundamental" right.

But as we said, the law is not unitary or single-minded, and what is fundamental to one case is not fundamental to another, as illustrated by Justice Rehnquist's dissent in *Roe* v. *Wade:*

The fact that a majority of the States reflecting, after all, the majority sentiment in those States, have had restrictions on abortions for at least a century is a strong indication, it seems to me, that the asserted right to an abortion is not 'so rooted in the traditions and conscience of our people as to be ranked as fundamental' . . .[6]

The tortuous development of the right of privacy, barely touched on here; the diversity of the courts' conceptions of what is or is not a "fundamental" right; the differing ideas among individuals, regions, classes, races, as to their rights; all begin to suggest that "the law" is at best an umbrella description of an exquisitely complex, multifarious nonsystem of law-making, law-interpreting, and law-enforcing.

III

THE STATE'S COMPELLING INTEREST

The right to privacy is not an unrestricted right, any more than any constitutional right is absolute. Indeed, the niceties of judicial line-drawing arise in determining just what limits impinge on fundamental rights. A classic illustration is the limitation on the First Amendment right of free speech: one may not endanger the public by falsely yelling "Fire!" in a crowded theater; the state has a compelling interest in protecting its members against being trampled as they rush to the exits.

Does the state's interest in public decency and order entitle it to prohibit sexual relations between people who are married to each other? Since the right of privacy is now generally understood to extend to the private sexual practices of married couples, the fact that a man and woman are not married to each other does not make their behavior any less private. Here and there courts are recognizing this. A federal court in Virginia recently said:

It is not marriage vows which made intimate and highly personal the sexual behavior of human beings. It is, instead, the nature of sexuality itself or something intensely private to the individual that calls forth constitutional protection. While the condition of marriage would doubtless make more difficult an attempt by government to justify an intrusion upon sexual behavior, this condition is not a prerequisite to the operation of the right to privacy.[7]

The question of whether a compelling state interest overrides a fundamental right is one of balancing and testing, a process which the courts perform fairly well. In the 1973 abortion decisions, the Supreme Court recognized that the state has an interest in protecting maternal health and preserving the life of the fetus. It balanced those interests against the woman's fundamental right of privacy, and found the state's interest insufficient to justify a complete prohibition against abortions. But the Court's role required it to draw a line at the point where the state's compelling need with respect to maternal health became sufficient to justify regulation; it ruled that because of the safety of early abortions this point arrived at the end of the first trimester of pregnancy.

The state, of course, has a "compelling need" to protect life, and the Supreme Court had to meet the question of whether the fetus was a "life" entitled to protection. The Court observed that neither doctors, philosophers, nor theologians could agree on the moment life begins. Therefore, said the Court, the state could not simply adopt "one theory of life" and override the woman's right to privacy by declaring that life begins at conception.

Drawing a line, the Supreme Court ruled that the state's interest in the unborn fetus only begins when the fetus is viable. Consequently, the Court's decision was a neat balancing of interests in light of current medical knowledge and led with inexorable logic to the conclusion: the states may not regulate abortions during the first trimester. Thereafter, the states may regulate in ways reasonably related to maternal health; and after viability the states may protect the life of the fetus even by forbidding abortions except where necessary to preserve the life or health of the mother.

In theory at least, the Supreme Court ruling becomes the law of the land, although not everyone may recognize it as such. Shortly after the abortion decisions, the Rhode Island legislature grasped at the Court's claim that doctors, philosophers, and theologians did not know when life begins. The legislature declared that life began at conception and that no abortion could be performed at any time, except to save the mother's life. Suit was promptly brought, and the law was held unconstitutional on the basis of *Roe* v. *Wade*.[8]

It is profoundly significant to the law that the Supreme Court and other courts are, essentially, interpretive bodies, not lawmakers. In spite of evidently definitive pronouncements, such as *Roe* v. *Wade* on abortions, diversity of state laws will still remain. There is no automatic procedure for reviewing laws and declaring them constitutional or unconstitutional, and a multitude of laws that are very possibly unconstitutional remain on the books. And when Hugh Hefner, the energetic proprietor of the Playboy clubs, wrote a scholarly and substantial article in the *Colorado Law Review*[9] documenting the wildly divergent state laws on sex, he seemed to blame it all on the Victorian insensitivity of the law, forgetting that the system, so-called, is not designed to achieve uniformity but to allow each state to do as it pleases, within constitutional limitations.

IV

THE LAW AND HOMOSEXUALITY

The Supreme Court has yet to test directly the right of privacy against the many state criminal statutes forbidding homosexual acts, but there is every reason to expect that it will do so unless state laws continue to give way to new social understandings that private consensual sexual acts among adults are not the concern of the state. Although many ancient peoples treated homosexuality with respect and perhaps reverence, Anglo-American law has reflected our own culture's view of homosexuality as an offense against society. During the reign of Henry VIII, Parliament enacted the governing English statute, and the courts assumed jurisdiction over the "vice of buggery." The penalty was death. This statute has served as the legal foundation for American laws proscribing homosexual conduct.[10]

As an example, in 1837 North Carolina enacted the English statute but changed the "vice of buggery" to the "crime against nature, not to be named by Christians." In 1854 the legislature deleted the last phrase but retained the death penalty; and in 1869 North Carolina dropped the death penalty and imposed a sixty-year maximum sentence. Not until 1964 did the state reduce the penalty, imposing the present maximum of ten years.[11] Many other states have followed this pattern, but the United States remains, in its statutes and administrative procedures, more intolerant of homosexuality than almost any other nation.

While reductions in maximum sentences are being legislated, the process moves by fits and starts and is pervaded by inconsistencies along the way. California, for example, provides that anyone participating in an act of fellatio is subject to imprisonment for fifteen years.[12] California's statute makes no distinction between private and public acts, between acts performed by a married or unmarried couple, or between heterosexual or homosexual acts.

Illinois, on the other hand, has repealed its prohibition against consensual sodomy and is identified as a leading light in the move toward rational sex laws. However, Illinois still carries its criminal laws forbidding "open and notorious" fornication and adultery; it thereby authorizes so-called irregular sex while forbidding the sexually conventional "living in sin."[13] Arkansas, still mired in the past, punishes sodomy or "buggery" with a maximum of twenty-one years in prison.[14]

Strangely, pressure for change is coming from church-watchers who are alert to supposed breaches of our so-called separation of church and state. It is true that homosexuality is forbidden by the Bible,[15] but courts have begun to suggest that since these religious injunctions are the sole source of our archaic sex laws and our enduring distinction between "natural" and "unnatural" sex, they are, in effect, unconstitutional. As urged by a dissenting judge in a 1972 New Mexico decision:

The sodomy statute reflects a Judaeo-Christian principle. . . . Neither the legislature nor the courts have the power to impose with ecclesiastical fury religious principles upon ordinary innocent adults.[16]

And when the Alaska Supreme Court in 1969 declared Alaska's "crime against nature" void for vagueness, it suggested a constitutional attack could be made because of the alleged religious derivation of the crime, on the ground of violation of the First Amendment's establishment of religion clause.[17]

It is absurd to charge the church with the full burden of our complex heritage of sexual intolerance, and ridiculous to imply that it somehow masterminded our potpourri of sex laws. Nonetheless, our increasing sensitivity to "separation of church and state" may well fuel the move toward de-criminalization of consensual private sex acts.

That the prejudices are deep-seated is plain from the evidently desperate effort of older state statutes to avoid words of direct sexual reference. One court said:

The subjects of "sodomy" and "crime against nature" are said by many to be so loathsome that they should be discussed only in language which is enigmatic to the point of obscurantism.[18]

The state's predisposition in favor of preserving "decency" and "public morals" by punishing or penalizing homosexual behavior is interwoven into administrative rules and economic activities as well as criminal laws. Immigration laws still categorize homosexuality as "psychopathic personality" and use it as a basis for deporting homosexuals who enter this country. The military establishment continues to expel homosexuals, generally stigmatizing them with less than honorable discharges. There is some prospect that the military will slowly follow the state pattern and eventually remove this patent discrimination.[19]

School systems, aided by occasional court decisions, are beginning to drop the traditional ban on homosexual teachers. A few big corporations have declared their willingness to hire homosexuals, and the federal Civil Service Commission, long of the position that homosexuals were not suited for federal employment, reversed this stance in July 1975. But discrimination on the basis of sexual preference is not currently protected by the Equal Employment Opportunity Commission or state commissions on human rights.

In spite of greater concern that here is a wrong to be righted, the fictions about homosexuality are slow to die. One still hears that the homosexual is a security risk because of his vulnerability to blackmail; that he is too unstable to function in the military; and that he is constantly on the prowl for young boys. There is no question, at least in my mind, that the states should continue to treat a homosexual assault as a crime and that the law should protect children from homosexual encounters with adults. But the bulk of our laws on homosexuality are an anachronistic attempt to regulate the privacy of the bedroom, and what goes on in the bedroom is none of the state's business.

It is high time the community recognized these laws for what they are and pressed the legislatures and courts for change. It is high time such holdovers as our immigration prohibitions against homosexuals were held up to the light. The pressure for these changes must come from the community; the judges and courts alone cannot do it for them.

The courts, however, are pushing harder these days, and the direction is fairly clear. In July 1975, the New Mexico Court of Appeals held that state's sodomy statute unconstitutional, ruling that the protected zones of privacy extended to the sexual acts of consenting adults as well as married couples.[20] It seems clear that a crescendo of pressure for change is upon us, as the courts respond to the community's growing sense that the consensual sexual activity of adults is constitutionally immune from prosecution.

V

WOMEN'S RIGHTS

As declared by Sarah Grimké, the nineteenth-century abolitionist and advocate of equal rights:

I ask no favors for my sex. All I ask of our brothers is that they take their feet off our necks.[21]

Sarah Grimké was calling for equal protection of the laws, a constitutional vehicle which together with the right to privacy and general due process is now aiding in vast changes in the legal status of women.

We have discussed the importance of the 1973 abortion decisions to the current understanding of the right to privacy. *Roe* v. *Wade* and *Doe* v. *Bolton* did not, however, answer all or most of the questions about a woman's right to abortion; but they opened the door to new issues raised by the rapid advances of women's rights. Without analyzing them, these are now some of the questions that must be met:

Should the father's consent be required before the mother can have an abortion? What are the father's interests in the unborn fetus?

May the state deter abortions by preventing advertising, barring Medicaid reimbursement for abortions, or maintaining public records of abortions and causing the woman to fear publicity?

Can the state deter abortions by overregulating abortion clinics or by refusing hospital facilities to doctors who perform abortions?

Can hospitals run by religious bodies which oppose abortions refuse to perform abortions?

Does the receipt of federal building funds require that a hospital permit or provide abortions?

May people other than doctors now perform abortions?[22]

Very much linked with the right to privacy issues of the abortion decisions are the issues of equal protection of the laws and general due process. Is a father denied equal protection if he has no say in the mother's abortion decision? Is the abortion-performing doctor denied due process or equal protection if the hospital refuses him facilities granted to other doctors?

"Equal protection of the laws" under the Fifth and Fourteenth amendments seems to say that we are all entitled to the same protection and benefits, that we may not be legally "classified" into special groups—women, blacks, foreigners, farmers, or Episcopalians—and denied the protection or rights given to those not so classified. Increasingly the courts hold such statutory classifications to be "suspect," and subject them to close judicial scrutiny. Again, the courts test such classifications against the so-called compelling interest of the state. In a 1972 federal court case in New Jersey, Stephen Wiesenfeld sued for Social Security survivor's benefits after his wife, the principal wage earner, died. The statute, however, limited those benefits only to the "widow" or "mother." The court held sex to be an "inherently suspect" classification, found no justification for the provision, and invalidated it as denying equal protection to the man.[23]

But as we have seen, the law is not single-minded. A court in Pennsylvania expressly declined to follow the *Wiesenfeld* decision, and in 1974 the Supreme Court held that a $500 Florida real estate tax exemption for widows was not unconstitutional, since the benefit reflected a reasonable distinction in the earnings history of men and women.[24]

The present state of the law seems to be that a statutory distinction between men and women may well be upheld by the Supreme Court if it is fairly designed to relieve the obvious economic disadvantages of women; however, distinctions based purely on sex, without any reasonable reference to economic or social history, will probably be held invalid.

I would contend, nevertheless, that one way toward changing the economic disadvantages of women is to remove from our statutes the protectionist laws designed to favor women at the expense of men; real "equal protection" is certainly a prerequisite to a just relationship between the sexes.

But in contrast to the relatively straightforward public issues raised by criminal statutes forbidding homosexual acts, the statutory and regulatory web affecting the rights and roles of women is exceedingly complex. Further, it seems to me that a coherent public sense of the precise nature of needed change is absent, although there is indeed a strong sense that change of some kind is necessary. Sexual role-playing permeates our society, and many would contend it is central to the maintenance of family life. I find myself urging liberal directions while often feeling privately conservative and strongly anxious to preserve the family role. I suspect courts and legislators find themselves in this position also, and there is no certainty that courts or state legislatures can be convinced that all "protectionist" legislation must fall.

I would argue that if we recognize the limits of the law, particularly that the law cannot establish and maintain sexual roles, we will all be freer to confirm such family and sexual role patterns as are healthy and stable.

The protectionist attitude is at the root of much of our legacy of miscellaneous legislation distinguishing between men and women, but notions of "proper" sexual roles also play a substantial part. While the Equal Rights Amendment, if adopted,[25] may hasten change, there are still major areas of the law where the protectionist attitude and sexual role presumption have life. These include the following:

Child custody. Increasingly, courts are abandoning the presumption that only the mother may have custody. Parents assert that custody can be a burden as well as a privilege and should be shared equally. Courts also are willing to balance the welfare of the child in such difficult situations as an overstrict father and a lesbian mother, and may well give custody to the lesbian mother.

Support. States are beginning to provide that either spouse may receive alimony from the other, depending on circumstances. Nonetheless, the husband generally has the primary legal obligation of support.

Marriageable age. Most states permit women to marry two to three years earlier than men. The Uniform Marriage and Divorce Act (a model law proposed for adoption by states) equalizes the requirements for men and women at 16 with parental consent, and at 18 without it.

Inheritance statutes. State laws often make substantial distinctions between husband and wife in the distribution of property on the death of a spouse.

Employment. Slowly the ponderous administrative, federal, and state statutory machinery is recognizing that women and men are entitled to equal treatment in employment. Only in 1973 was the Fair Labor Standards Act amended to cover women executives, administrators, outside salespeople, and professionals. The human rights commissions in various states and the federal Equal Employment Opportunity Commission are moving us toward the ideal of equal pay for equal work, and the more elusive goal of equal access to preferred employment.

Jury duty. In early 1975 the Supreme Court reversed a history of the exclusion or exemption of women from juries by holding that a Louisiana statute exempting women was unconstitutional in the case of a criminal defendant, in denying him a fair jury list or panel.[26] The Louisiana law did not exclude women, but permitted them to serve only if they filed advance declarations. The effect, of course, was that very few women served on Louisiana juries. The state contended that "woman is still regarded as the center of home and family life," and claimed that jury service would interfere with that role. The Court said:

It is untenable to suggest these days that it would be a special hardship for each and every woman to perform jury service or that society cannot spare any women from their present duties.

The Court's decision does not prevent the states from drawing statutes which make reasonable distinctions—such as, perhaps, the provision submitted to the New York legislature exempting women with children under 12. But why not a statute which simply exempts a parent, male or female, who is primarily responsible for the care of a child under 12?

Women and credit. In order to eliminate long-standing discrimination against women in obtaining commercial credit, Congress recently passed the Equal Credit Opportunity Act. However, the regulations issued by the Board of Governors of the Federal Reserve System to implement the new law have been strongly criticized for very possibly permitting lenders to slip around the intent of the statute by indirect means and perpetuate past discriminatory practices.

Women have long suffered in obtaining credit because of the wide discretion of the lender in deciding whether to make a loan. Under the often used "point system," a lender would typically assign fewer points to a woman, often by discounting her salary on the theory she may have children and stop working. In the past, some lenders have required a "baby letter" whereby the woman and her doctor state she is on a program of birth control with no plans of pregnancy.

With scrupulous application of the new law, and attention by the courts to abuses, these practices can be eliminated.

The marriage relation.

Family law remains one of the greatest strongholds of sex-based generalizations and resultant sex discrimination.[27]

Current state laws of support are heavily oriented toward the man as the earning head of the household and the woman as the house-keeper and babysitter. States have not yet arrived at the "functional" approach envisioned by the Senate Judiciary Committee's final report on the Equal Rights Amendment:

... when a spouse is the primary wage earner and the other runs the home, the wage earner would have a duty to support the spouse who stays at home in compensation for the performance of her or his duties.[28]

Many legal authorities are not optimistic that the Equal Rights Amendment will alter the real facts of the woman's subservient role in the home. Two writers urge enactment of the "partnership family model" to provide specifically that husband and wife owe to their family equal obligations of service, that they share equally in the management and assets of the family, that "family" property and "separate" property are fairly identified, and that husband's and wife's rights and obligations can be altered by contract between them and are enforceable in a court of law.[29]

The preceding recitation of "sexual presumptions" is by no means complete, but it does make evident that laws affecting women are ripe for change. Although the Equal Rights Amendment will not, in my opinion, add to the equal protection concepts beginning to be applied to women, it seems to me that it will add to the momentum for change, invite more cases to be brought before the courts, and emphasize that women are indeed entitled to equal protection of the laws.

VI

OBSCENITY AND THE LAW

Freedom of speech, under the First Amendment, and the right to privacy guarantee us the right to say and write what we wish. The courts, however, have recognized that the state's interest in the protection of public decency and order permits a state to limit the publication and sale of obscene materials. Until 1973 the courts, led by a series of Supreme Court decisions, were approaching the position that any publication which was not "pandered,"[30] was not sold to a minor, and did not invade another's privacy, was constitutionally protected. But on June 21, 1973, the Supreme Court considerably changed the rules by its decision in *Miller* v. *California*.[31] *Miller* established the following standards for state regulation of obscenity:

(a) Would the average person, applying "community standards," find the work "prurient"? (b) Does the material depict or describe, in a patently offensive way, sexual conduct which is specifically defined by state law (impliedly, so-called "hard-core" conduct)? (c) Does the work, as a whole, lack serious literary, artistic, political, or scientific value?

The effect of *Miller* and a series of related decisions was substantially to improve the likelihood that a state could limit obscene publications, provided its statute were carefully drawn. Some states, including Arizona and Hawaii, have entirely abandoned censorship of adult sexual materials. Other states may try to remake their statutes to conform with *Miller*. But the direction of state regulation is not at all clear. In spite of the conclusion of the President's Commission on Obscenity and Pornography that sexual materials do not cause antisocial actions, the Supreme Court held:

Although there is no conclusive proof of a connection between antisocial behavior and obscene material, the legislature of Georgia could quite reasonably determine that such a connection does or might exist.[32]

Those who contend that the state has no business trying to regulate what the public evidently wants to see or read, expected dire consequences from *Miller*. They assumed that redoubled efforts would be made by police to crack down on newsstands selling "girlie" magazines or theaters showing pornographic films. Yet the taste and temper of the times are such that there may well be more patently sexual material freely available to the public now than before *Miller*.

Why must we be confronted with obscenity, with newsstands displaying debasing photographs and drawings of sexual conduct which insult us, our families, and our communities? Such materials are sold to make money—rarely as a serious art form—and there is a major market for these materials. The sellers of pornography are beneficiaries of our tradition of free speech, a tradition central to our open form of government. If I could, I would wish away all such vulgar displays, but that cannot be done without denying free speech and equal protection to a segment of the American people. *Miller* allows the state to apply "contemporary community standards" in defining and regulating obscenity, surely a broad authority. What is the state to do with that authority?

From my point of view the answer is again one of balancing. Can we really afford to nibble away at free speech in order to sweeten our walk past newsstands and "porno" theaters? I agree with those who consider any incursion on free speech a dangerous step toward restriction of political expression, and I would balance in this case in favor of preserving open freedom of speech, even if it means I hear and see some things I do not like. For these reasons, withdrawal of censorship of so-called obscenity seems to me desirable.

The community, however, may disagree; it is the community which decides, and the legislature which enacts the community's sentiment. Where are the people's voices coherently and intelligently telling the legislature what to do?

CONCLUSION

Sex and the law are very much shaped today by constitutional concepts of the right of privacy, equal protection of the laws, and due process. But these principles are themselves reflections of community goals and values. The law—that is, the courts, legislatures, police departments, district attorneys—cannot and will not *direct* the community to justice and fairness; and it may well be fortunate that the law is so diverse and unsystematized that it cannot do so. It seems to me far healthier that the people themselves provide direction and that the law be responsive to the urgings of the society.

NOTES

1. *Griswold* v. *Connecticut*, 381 U.S. 479 (1965)
2. *Cotner* v. *Henry*, 394 F.2d 873 (7th Cir. 1968)
3. *Buchanan* v. *Batchelor*, 308 F.Supp. 729 (N.D. Tex. 1970); judgment vacated on other grounds, 401 U.S. 989 (1971)
4. 410 U.S. 113
5. 410 U.S. 179
6. 410 U.S. at 174
7. *Lovisi* v. *Slayton*, 363 F.Supp. 620 at 625 (E.D.Va. 1973)
8. *Doe* v. *Israel*, 482 F.2d 156 (1st Cir. 1973)
9. Hefner, "The Legal Enforcement of Morality," 40 *Colo. Law Rev.* 199 (1968)
10. See "The Homosexual's Legal Dilemma," 27 *Ark. Law Rev.* 687 at 688–9 (1973)
11. *Ibid.*, p. 690
12. Cal. Penal Code, sec. 288(a)
13. Ill. Rev. Stat., ch. 38, secs. 11–7, 11–8 (1973)
14. Ark. Stat. Ann., sec. 41–813 (1955)
15. Among the biblical references are "Thou shalt not lie with a male as with a woman; it is an abomination." Leviticus 18:22
16. *State* v. *Terjo*, 494 P.2d 173 (N.M. 1972)

17. *Harris* v. *State*, 457 P.2d 638 (Alaska 1969) Cf. *People* v. *Baldwin*, 37 Cal. App. 385 (Cal. 1974), where the court rejected the "establishment of religion" argument as to the California sodomy statute, noting that there are many acts, prohibited by religious tenets, which remain as secular prohibitions long after their "religious sanctions and justifications are gone."

18. *Harris* v. *State*, 457 P.2d 638 (Alaska 1969)

19. See *Time Magazine*, Sept. 8, 1975, pp. 32–43

20. *People* v. *Elliot*, 44 *U.S. Law Week* 2044 (N.M. Ct. App. 1975). The statute has now been repealed.

21. Grimké, Letters on the Equality of the Sexes and the Condition of Women, addressed to Mary Parker, President of the Boston Female Anti-Slavery Society 10 (1838), as quoted in "Why Can't a Woman Be More Like a Man, or Vice Versa?" 35 *The Alabama Lawyer* 409 at 411 (1974)

22. See "Implications of the Abortion Decisions: Post *Roe* and *Doe* Litigation and Legislation," 74 *Columbia Law Review* 237 (1974) for a discussion of the direction of court decisions and legislation on these issues.

23. *Wiesenfeld* v. *Secretary of HEW*, 367 F.Supp. 981 (D.N.J. 1973)

24. *Kahn* v. *Shevin*, 416 U.S. 351 (1974)

25. At this writing, approval by four more states is required before 1979 to reach the necessary total of 38.

26. *Taylor* v. *Louisiana*, 419 U.S. 522 (1975)

27. Krauskopf and Thomas, "Partnership Marriage: The Solution to an Ineffective and Inequitable Law of Support," 35 *Ohio State Law Journ.* 558 at 584 (1974)

28. Senate Report No. 92-687, 92nd Cong. 2nd Sess. (1972) *Op. cit.* at 584

29. Krauskopf and Thomas, *op. cit.*, p. 589

30. The court-cited epitome of sexual pandering is, to date, Ralph Ginzburg, who boasted in advertisements about the sexual content of his publications, sought mailing privileges for his magazines from the postmasters of Intercourse and Blue Ball, Pa., and thereafter deposited his materials with the postmaster of Middlesex, N.J. "The Rise and Fall of *Roth:* A Critique of the Recent Supreme Court Obscenity Decisions," 10 *Crim. Law Bulletin* 785 at 788 (1974)

31. 413 U.S. 15 (1973)

32. *Paris Adult Theatre I* v. *Slaton*, 413 U.S. 49 at 60–61 (1973)

chapter 12

HOMOSEXUALITY
An Overview

Alan Bell

Probably the most important point I'd like to make here is that there is no such thing as homosexuality. I mean by this that the homosexual experience is so diverse, the variety of psychological and social and sexual correlates so enormous, that the word "homosexuality," used as a kind of umbrella term, is both meaningless and misleading.

We shall, therefore, begin speaking in terms of "the homosexualities," and when we speak about a particular individual who is erotically aroused by a person of the same sex and/or who engages in sexual behaviors with a person of the same sex, we try to specify the type of homosexual he or she happens to be. No longer should we ask the question, "What causes homosexuality?" but rather, "What causes this or that particular kind of homosexuality?" No longer should we ask, in our naïveté, such a question as: "Are homosexuals less well adjusted, more creative, or less intelligent than heterosexuals?" Obviously, the answer to this kind of question will depend upon the types of persons—both homosexual and heterosexual—who are being compared. And even when we do find significant differences between a given homosexual and heterosexual sample, we must not use these differences to construct a stereotype of homosexuality which hides important intra-group differences among homosexuals themselves, and which may not begin to do justice to large numbers of homosexuals whose lives and personal characteristics are quite different from the rest of the sample.

In fact—and this is not usually spelled out very clearly to the small number of people who actually read research reports in this and

other areas—significant differences between homosexuals and heterosexuals on a given variable often do not obtain for the majority of the
homosexual sample. For example, more homosexuals than heterosexuals may not have lived continuously with both parents until the age
of seventeen, and thus a statistically significant difference between
the two groups might be reported on this variable. At the same time,
however, it is still possible that most homosexuals live continuously
with both parents until the age of seventeen. Or again, a particular
homosexual sample may, as a group, score higher on creativity than
a comparison group of heterosexuals, and yet the majority of both
groups might still be classified as "klutzy." Or, in the same vein, a
higher percentage of homosexuals than heterosexuals may engage in
cross-sex dressing, and yet it may well be true that a distinct minority
of homosexuals engages in this activity and, because there are more
of them, that most cross-sex dressers are heterosexual.

I have one more example of this kind of thing in mind. From
Bieber's famous study of homosexuality, a great deal has been made
of the association between having a detached father and being a
male homosexual.[1] The fact is, whereas Bieber and his associates
found a higher percentage of male homosexuals than male heterosexuals with detached fathers, the majority of both groups had fathers
who could be defined in this way. The problem is that so much is
made of statistically significant differences that people will take one
or any number of them to construct a stereotype of the homosexual
which does not fit even the majority of homosexuals, much less a
given individual.

Of course, the problem goes deeper than this. There are many
reasons for various persons to maintain simplistic views of homosexuality, to resist the notion that there is a range of experience which the
singular terms "homosexuality" and "homosexual" do not do justice to. The "man on the street" is put off by complexity of any kind.
He tends to take himself and others at face value, to draw all kinds
of conclusions about his own and others' behaviors without being
aware of the quite different sets of motivations which could prompt
the particular behaviors in question. He seeks single reasons for
everything, sometimes "putting himself in another person's shoes"
and imagining what it would be like for him to act in a certain way,
or what the psychological or social outcomes of a given behavior
would be like for him. He tends to identify "across the board" with
those whose behaviors are similar to his own and to conclude that
those who behave differently in a certain way must be quite unlike
himself in every other regard. His conceptual world is full of dichotomies of every kind, beginning with me/not me, male/female, mascu-

line/feminine, and including good/bad, smart/stupid, healthy/ill, right/wrong, and, for the purposes of our present discussion, homosexual/heterosexual. His uneasy sense of unity is easily threatened by whatever upsets his dichotomized existence. His fragile identity is based upon a renunciation of ambiguity.

Above everything else, he wants closure, even if it is premature. And when he doesn't get it, he is apt to become impatient and confused. Usually he wants evidence that everything he has supposed about himself and others is justified; that his old answers to complex questions are true; that his old notions about what leads to what and why, based upon a common-sense theory or any other theory of human behavior, still hold water. Perhaps nowhere is his desperation more evident than in the views he holds of his own and others' sexuality. His pigeonholes and stereotypes amount to denials of the complexity of human life, discourage the fulfillment of human potential, promote a sense of alienation in and between people, and diminish the quality of our common life.

The man-on-the-street mentality with regard to homosexuality can be found in a variety of quarters. There is the newspaper reporter who wants a story, who comes up to me after I have spent an hour explaining that there is no such thing as *the* homosexual and continues to ask questions about *the* homosexual as though he'd not heard a word I'd said. There is also this mentality in the sex educator who wants facile answers to students' questions, who believes that answers that satisfy his students and that might reflect his own level of expertise are more important or appropriate than the additional questions that must be raised, the host of qualifications that should be introduced. The same mentality can be found in the clinician whose theoretical orientations preclude surprise, who would like to see his former mentors' views about homosexuality upheld, who wants to know exactly how to proceed when a homosexual comes for treatment, and whose therapeutic strategies are more impressive than his ability to deal with his patients or clients as utterly unique human beings. The "man on the street" may be the lesbian or male homosexual who thinks that he or she knows exactly what homosexuality is all about—"I'm homosexual and I should know what I'm talking about"—and who then proceeds to tell you that all homosexuals feel oppressed or are psychologically maladjusted or whatever on the basis of his or her own experience of what it means to be homosexual. Frequently, their outrage or political goals will not tolerate the notion that a homosexual is not a homosexual is not a homosexual. They become threatened by whatever might destroy their sense of cohesiveness or group identification. They prefer to think that a homosexual is a homosexual, no matter what the person's age or sex or race or generation or geographical location or manner of employment.

There are still other reasons for viewing homosexuality and heterosexuality as a simple dichotomy, not the least of which has to do with the way in which research has been conducted in this area. If you go through the literature, as we have in connection with our annotated bibliography of homosexuality,[2] you will all too often find research based on small, biased samples, frequently involving no control groups, and usually with an insufficient number of variables. Many of the reports are based upon patient or prison samples where one would expect, for example, to find a good deal of pathology as well as a relatively narrow range of homosexual experience. In this regard, Schofield's study is most enlightening.[3] He found homosexuals and heterosexuals in prison to be more like each other—developmentally and psychologically—than they were like those who happened to share the same sexual orientation but who had never been in prison. In the same vein, he found homosexuals and heterosexuals in therapy to be more similar and quite different from their counterparts who had never been in treatment. Apparently, not sexual orientation but being in prison or in treatment were the chief distinguishing variables.

This leads me to another aspect of research which deserves attention. It is terribly important that subjects be delineated as precisely as possible and over a large number of meaningful variables. In this particular instance, when one is comparing homosexuals and heterosexuals, one should employ whatever statistical controls are necessary in order to be sure that whatever differences are found aren't explained by something other than the differences in their sexual orientation. For example, a researcher might find that homosexuals are more maladjusted—psychologically or socially—than heterosexuals but that when he sets up a control, say for having a detached father, the differences "wash out"; in other words, he finds that persons who report having had a father who had no interest in them or who spent little time with them are more maladjusted than those whose fathers were warm and accepting, and that it has nothing to do with their being homosexual or heterosexual. There are a million other examples I could give, but the point I am making is that throughout the literature you will find either the absence of a control group or, when there is one, such small samples or such a small number of distinguishing variables that a proper multivariate statistical analysis becomes impossible.

In the San Francisco study of the Institute for Sex Research—involving homosexuals and heterosexuals, blacks and whites, males and females—we recruited subjects from all kinds of sources: through public advertising of various kinds; in public and private bars and restaurants, where approximately 1000 hours were spent recruiting potential subjects; at small gatherings in private homes; or through contacts made on a one-to-one basis in an effort to get at the most covert individuals. We sent information about the study to almost 6,000 individuals, using the mailing lists of various homophile organizations, bars, and bookstores. We recruited in eight different steam baths; at the meetings and social activities of twenty-three different homophile organizations in the Bay Area; in men's rooms, theater lobbies and balconies, parks and beaches, the streets and public squares. Needless to say, it would have been much easier to rely entirely on the bars or the homophile organizations for our subjects, but we wanted to make sure that we included as many different kinds of homosexuals as possible in our samples. Otherwise, the incredible range of homosexual experience would have been missing. In addition, we wanted to include a large number of variables, to delineate as precisely as possible our homosexual and heterosexual samples with a view toward exercising the most rigorous kinds of statistical controls in our analysis. In this connection, a 175-page questionnaire was devised for use in a three-to-four hour face-to-face interview with approximately 1500 persons. Since 1968, when the study was first funded by the National Institute for Mental Health, literally hundreds of people have been involved on the project: ethnographers, recruiters, interviewers, literature searchers, coders, field staff members, filers, judges of open-ended responses, consultants, secretarial assistants. Time and attention had to be given to such matters as test-retest reliability and to the construction of various composite measures.

We have in our offices at the University of Indiana seven very large marginal books containing the number and percentages of each of the eight samples who responded in different ways to all the questions. Out of this huge mass of data will probably come two volumes, the first on the development and the second on the management of homosexuality. Since we are just at the point where we can begin to do the kinds of comparisons we plan to make, which involve relatively sophisticated analytic strategies, I am not in a position to offer a final conclusion on the basis of this data.

What I would like to do, however, is illustrate what I have in mind regarding the need to speak of "the homosexualities" and not simply of "homosexuality." For this I'll be making reference to some of the data generated by our white male homosexual sample. These data will show that there simply is no such thing as *the* homosexual, that homosexuals are as different from each other as heterosexuals are from each other, that even after it has been decided that a given person is "homosexual" there is almost nothing that could be said about the person on the basis of that label.

First of all, the label is somewhat arbitrary. There are females who are multiorgastic with a variety of male sexual partners but who define themselves as "homosexual" because they find it easier to become emotionally involved with a sexual partner of the same sex. Some adolescents think of themselves as "homosexual" because of sexual explorations involving members of the same sex, because they have no particular or exaggerated interest in persons of the opposite sex, or because others have labeled them "queer" or "homosexual" on the basis of a lack of interest in sports (if they are male) or an interest in track (if they are female). On the other hand, we know of some male adolescents who will accept pay from older homosexuals for fellatio but do not define themselves as homosexual. There are other males who can be engaged in a variety of homosexual behaviors but who do not define themselves as "homosexual" as long as they do the inserting. Probably a growing number of females, very much into women's liberation and full of resentment over their female status, can be found defining themselves as "homosexual," a definition which amounts to more of a political statement than a true indication of their sexual orientation.

In our own study, we asked respondents to rate themselves on the so-called Kinsey scale, first with regard to their behaviors and then with regard to their feelings. The scale goes from zero (exclusively heterosexual) to six (exclusively homosexual). Although we *suspect* that approximately four or five percent of American males—and half that percentage of females—are exclusively homosexual in their behaviors throughout their lives, much larger numbers are exclusively homosexual in their behaviors at any given time, and even larger numbers engage in both homosexual and heterosexual acts from time to time. For a given individual, ratings on this homosexual-heterosexual continuum may go up or down depending upon the person's age, life circumstances, and the culture in which he or she lives.

Another assumption we made in our study is that there is not necessarily a perfect fit between one's behavior rating and feelings rating on the Kinsey scale. For example, theoretically it is possible for a person to be exclusively heterosexual in behavior but exclusively homosexual in feeling. Such a person might be married and sexually engaged only with his wife, all the while fantasizing a male partner. The fact that one has less control over one's thoughts and feelings than over one's behaviors may be why behavior ratings tend to crowd around the ends of the homosexual-heterosexual continuum while feelings ratings are spread out more along the scale. In our study we quite arbitrarily defined a person as "homosexual" whose scores on both scales—behavior *and* feelings—added up to four. Although the majority of the white male subjects rated themselves as exclusively homosexual in terms of their behaviors and feelings, many did not. The white females and the blacks of both sexes were less inclined to give themselves an exclusively homosexual rating.

In this regard, very clearly a homosexual is *not* a homosexual is *not* a homosexual. With a particular individual, we have to ask ourselves (and him or her) at least the following questions: Where do you think you stand on these two scales, and on what basis? What is the disparity between the two ratings? How frequently have these ratings changed since puberty? Have you ever been heterosexually aroused? At what age, and how much before or after the first homosexual arousal? What proportions of your sexual dreams or masturbatory fantasies involve members of the same versus the opposite sex? In other words, homosexuals differ from each other in terms of the extensiveness of their homosexuality, and they should not simply be lumped together on the basis of an umbrella term, either in research or in the mind of a clinician.

Another area in which homosexuals differ is with regard to the *levels* of their sexual interest. A minority (forty percent) of our white male sample reported that sex was a very important aspect of their lives. Thirteen percent considered sex relatively unimportant. Thirty-seven percent thought quite a bit about sexual things during the course of a day; eighteen percent hardly thought about them at all.

Homosexuals also differ with regard to the kinds of stimuli they find sexually arousing. The largest number (sixty-seven percent) reported that they would be very much attracted by a good-looking male stranger in a social situation; smaller numbers by seeing the buttocks or genitals of a male in photos. Some preferred a masculine-appearing partner, a smaller number a feminine-appearing partner. Only twelve percent of our white male sample expressed a preference for a large penis in the sexual partner. The question, " 'What does she see in him?' said the man as he kissed the cow" applies to homosexuals as well as heterosexuals, and for as large a number of interesting psychological reasons.

With regard to their sexual repertoire, again we find that homosexuals can be differentiated with regard to how locked in they are to certain roles and techniques. Some males insist on being the inserters, others on being the insertees, but clearly this kind of rigidity is

not characteristic of most homosexuals, and only the most naive re-
searchers or clinicians attempt to classify homosexuals on the basis of
such dichotomies as active-passive or inserter-insertee. To be sure,
there are preferences, but they are often modified on the basis of the
partner's expectations or the individual's sexual interest or arousal.
The largest number of our white male sample preferred performing
fellatio on their partners, and a slightly smaller number preferred
performing anal intercourse.

In addition to differences in technical preferences, homosexuals
differ in the *degree* of their sexual activity. For example, sixteen
percent of our white males reported that they had engaged in sexual
activity of some kind with a partner four or more times a week; the
same percentage reported having had sex once a month or less. I
would guess that the range of a person's sexual repertoire, as well as
the frequency of sexual activity, is related to age, to how long a
person has been involved in a homosexual life style, the extent to
which a person has been exposed to various sexual techniques or is
involved with persons who represent a wide range of sexual life
styles. Much would depend upon the extent to which the person has
broken through stereotypical roles and behaviors—most often found
in the young homosexual—and has managed to fashion a more realistic and viable identity.

Homosexuality itself has been viewed as a *problem* for such a long
time that little thought has been given to the fact that homosexuals
differ in the extent to which they experience sexual problems within
the homosexual orientation. Even less attention has been given to
the ways in which these problems can be treated or alleviated. Many
report that finding a suitable sexual partner is a problem for them,
and for a variety of reasons: their age, their physical attractiveness,
their social inhibitions. Some have difficulty maintaining affection
for their partners or are concerned about their sexual adequacy or
have problems with impotence. In a homoerotophobic culture such
as ours, which discourages anything more than surreptitious sociosexual encounters between homosexual males, the kinds of problems
some report are not at all surprising. On the other hand, I would
suspect that homosexuals whose sexual lives are lived out in less
stressful circumstances, who are enjoying a relatively permanent relationship with a sexual partner, and who are generally relaxed about
their homosexuality would report far fewer difficulties than those not
in such circumstances.

Among our white males we find seventeen percent reporting that
having a permanent living arrangement with a sexual partner is the
most important thing in life; twenty percent do not consider it impor-

tant at all. Nine percent report never having had a relatively steady relationship or "affair" with another male, while fifty-seven percent were currently involved in such a relationship at the time they were interviewed. Only thirty-nine percent were currently living with a roommate, and of these, two-thirds were having sex with him. Sexual partnerships are an exceedingly important variable within the homosexual experience. A modal view of the white male homosexual, based on our findings, would be that of a person reporting 1,000 or more sexual partners throughout his lifetime, most of whom were strangers prior to their sexual meeting and with whom sexual activity occurred only once. Only a few of these partners were persons for whom there was much care or affection or were ever seen socially again. During the past year, twenty-eight percent reported having had more than fifty partners; however, thirty-one percent claimed to have had ten partners or less. While there has been a lot of speculation about those factors responsible for the large numbers of partners which many homosexuals report—some suppose that it reflects an inability to integrate one's affectional and sexual needs—we must always remember the kinds of social circumstances under which male homosexuals pursue their sexual interests. We must also be aware of the differences in the sexual transactions that occur between males, as compared to those between males and females.

Female homosexuals present quite a different picture. The homosexual female appears to be far more interested in an ongoing relationship with a partner than she is in more casual sexual encounters. To a large extent, the female scene is a "couples" scene, and many of those involved do all they can to avoid situations that could disrupt an ongoing partnership. Many live together, share their incomes, and enjoy a relatively enduring relationship.

The female couple is apt to do little if any "cruising," a term denoting going out and looking for a sexual partner. Males are quite different in this regard, although again we find important differences between them. While forty-three percent of our white males reported cruising once a week or more, more than one-third went out looking for a sexual partner once a month or less. Not only do they differ in the amount of cruising they do but also in where they do it. The greatest number of our white male sample cruised at least once in a gay bar and, in decreasing order of frequency, in steam baths, streets, private parties, parks and beaches, public toilets, and movie theaters. Where, how, and how often one cruises is related to the extent to which a sexual encounter is casual and anonymous, the likelihood of negative social consequences, the ease with which a person can interact socially with others, the extent of a person's involvement in the

gay community, and, of course, a person's age. Clearly, the homosexual experience can mean quite different things to different people.

Another important way in which homosexuals differ is in the feelings and attitudes they have toward their own and others' homosexuality. Males tend to view their own homosexuality more negatively
than females, but even among males there is a large variation. Something less than thirty percent tended to regret being homosexual and
wished they had been entirely heterosexual from birth. A similar
percentage had seriously considered discontinuing their homosexuality at one time or other. Differing views of their homosexuality may
be related to the extent to which they have suffered socially as a
result of their homosexual status or behaviors, how successful they
have been in fashioning their own personal moral value system—
which amounts to more than a parental hand-me-down—and the extent of their acculturation in the homosexual community. In some
persons, negative feelings about their homosexuality may represent
phobic reactions to sex in general and/or a more pervasive lack of
self-esteem. Needless to say, the extent to which homosexuality is
ego-alien to a homosexual will powerfully affect the core feeling
state he or she brings to a sexual encounter.

Finally, an important dimension to the management of homosexuality has to do with the extent to which one is overt or covert. Some
remain "in the closet," a term used to denote those who lead highly
secretive lives. Others reveal their homosexuality only to their clos-
est friends. Some homosexuals' parents know, others only suspect,
while still others are totally ignorant of their child's sexual orientation. A growing number of homosexuals are becoming politicized in
consciousness-raising groups sponsored by various gay liberation organizations, and they find themselves on picket lines, "zapping" politicians, or at various meetings of the American Psychiatric Association. Needless to say, where one stands on the continuum, which
extends from the so-called "closet queen" to the "gay radical," will
have a profound effect upon one's experience of homosexuality.

In addition to the various parameters associated with homosexuality per se in which we find differences among homosexuals, there
is a host of psychological and social correlates as well as developmental experiences which are hardly the same for homosexuals
across the board. I shall address these matters very briefly.

For a long time and for a variety of reasons, many people have
supposed that homosexuality is *ipso facto* pathological. The fact is
that, almost without exception, whenever samples of homosexuals
not in treatment are compared with heterosexuals not in treatment,

very few if any differences are found in their psychological functioning. With regard to their feeling states or self-esteem or various personality characteristics, whether one happens to be predominantly homosexual or heterosexual does not appear to be the crucial variable, and whenever differences are found, they usually do not stand up in other studies. Or, as I have already indicated, the kinds of analyses that are done make it difficult to conclude that the differences are a function of one's sexual orientation per se.

Perhaps more homosexuals than heterosexuals seek professional help, and probably more homosexuals have attempted suicide, but it is as easy to interpret these behaviors as the consequence of being homosexual in a society which is hostile to homosexuality as it is to conclude that homosexuality necessarily involves or is caused by psychological maladjustment. On the basis of the evidence, I would have to conclude that homosexuality—unlike pedophilia or child molestation, or unlike the extreme forms of fetishism, voyeurism, exhibitionism, or sadomasochism—is a sexual variation well within the normal range of psychological functioning.

Like heterosexuals, some homosexuals are better adjusted psychologically than others. For example, fifty-eight percent of the white male homosexuals in our sample had gone to a professional because of what they or others had construed as an emotional problem; forty-two percent had not. Twenty-six percent had never imagined committing suicide; thirty-seven percent had thought about it but had never considered it seriously; nineteen percent did consider it seriously but never attempted it; and eighteen percent reported that they had actually attempted suicide one or more times. Similar differences were found with regard to their current feeling states and psychosomatic symptoms.

With regard to their social adjustment, again we find differences in their occupations (not all homosexuals are dressing hair or writing symphonies), in their religiosity, in their political involvement, in how and with whom they spend their leisure time, in the number of friends (homosexual and/or heterosexual) they have, in where they live and how involved they are in the gay subculture. While some homosexuals may be rolled or robbed or arrested or fired from their jobs, an even larger number of homosexuals lead social lives that do not even remotely resemble a masochistic enterprise. Many describe a way of life replete with positive reinforcements quite apart from whatever sexual satisfactions they enjoy.

Finally, with regard to etiology, a preliminary view of our own data leads me to suppose that just as there is such a diversity of adult homosexuality, so there are multiple routes into this orientation, routes which may well account for differences in the way particular persons experience and express their homosexuality as well as the nature of their psychological makeup and social adjustment. For some, certain kinds of parental relationships and identifications may loom large. For others, negative same-sex peer relationships may be paramount. For still others, early satisfactions associated with homosexual behavior or negative heterosexual experiences during adolescence may stand out.

When we asked our subjects to enumerate the factors *they* thought were responsible for their homosexuality, the majority of the white males did not mention parental influence at all. Of those who did, the largest numbers mentioned an absent or distant father and/or a dominating or suffocating and overprotective mother. Of those who mentioned nonparental factors, sixteen percent thought that their early homosexual experiences were responsible for their becoming homosexual; fifteen percent thought they had simply been born that way; ten percent spoke of factors which resulted in an opposite sex gender identification. Differences in these perceptions, regardless of their relationship to reality, may prompt or reflect an abiding sense of what one thinks one's homosexuality amounts to and the degree to which a person's perceptions correspond to conventional notions of what homosexuality involves.

By way of summary, our data appear to indicate that homosexuality involves a large number of widely divergent experiences—developmental, sexual, social, and psychological—and that even after a person has been labeled "homosexual" on the basis of his or her preferred sexual object choice, there is little that can be predicted about the person on the basis of that label. One's experience of homosexuality differs according to one's age, social status, sex, race, and geographical residence. It differs according to the time and culture in which it is expressed. In addition, the homosexual experience must be delineated much more precisely than has been done in the past and on the basis of parameters shared in common with heterosexuals.

Perhaps it is not enough even to explore relationships between a much larger number of variables than are found in past investigations or to develop a typology of homosexual experience based upon a variety of commonly held experiences on the part of one type versus another. It may be that, for a given homosexual, an additional differentiation must be made on the basis of what is *figure* (what in my environment or experience stands out for me) and what is *ground* (what in my environment or experience does *not* stand out for me). For example, it is possible that for some homosexuals the most prominent feature of their homosexuality is their attempt to deal with the guilt they experience over their behaviors; for others it may be the management of the tension they experience between the gay and straight worlds; for still others it might be experienced primarily as a social protest, the search for a long-lasting relationship, or as an attempt to overcome sexual inhibitions. What is *figure* for some is *ground* for others; and for all, what is *figure* at one point in their lives may become *ground* at another.

Clearly, where a person *is* homosexually reflects and is accounted for by a wide range of experiences and motivations. And it is this wider view of the matter which, we hope, will come to characterize whatever research addresses itself to the incredible variety of human sexual experience.

NOTES

1. Irving Bieber, et al., *Homosexuality: A Psychoanalytic Study of Male Homosexuals* (New York: Basic Books, 1962)
2. Alan Bell and Martin Weinberg, eds., *Homosexuality: An annotated bibliography* (New York: Harper & Row, 1971)
3. Michael Schofield, *Sociological Aspects of Homosexuality* (Boston: Little Brown, 1966)

chapter 13

HOMOSEXUALITY IS NOT JUST AN ALTERNATIVE LIFE STYLE

Charles W. Socarides, M.D.

This is a time of great turmoil in the understanding of human sexual behavior. Concepts of marriage, family, and sexual patterns are currently being reexamined in the light of a less conventionally moralistic era. Just as there is less prejudice against individuals suffering from mental illness in general, as a consequence of improved public health education, so there is a decrease in the persecutory laws attached to homosexuality.

Removing the stigma from homosexuality does not mean, however, that we should diminish our responsibility as behavioral scientists to understand it, but rather the opposite. To designate homosexuality as a "normal" form of sexual behavior is to abdicate our proper role as psychodynamically trained physicians.

Homosexuality can be defined as a pattern of sexual behavior wherein individuals repeatedly and out of inner necessity engage in sexual acts with partners of the same sex. Contrary to popular belief, this is not a sexual *preference* as there is *no choice*. This desire is determined by unconscious mental processes. If a homosexual engages in heterosexual activity (bisexual behavior), he does so with very little or no pleasure. Despite apparently marked individual personality differences among homosexuals, the factors in the above definition apply to all those who are truly homosexual. For example, one homosexual may appear well integrated and may function well in the vocational and social areas, while another may obviously be undergoing severe anxiety and threats of disorganization to his entire personality. Both, however, are the victims of the same deep inner conflicts which gave rise to homosexuality. The seemingly well-

144

integrated homosexual individual, when subject to any excessive stress, may often rapidly decompensate to the level of the other.

Regarding the homosexual and his condition, there is no substitute for the information gathered from the in-depth clinical situation. Study of a large number of psychoanalytic references demonstrates through numerous clinical examples and case histories that homosexuality is a form of arrested psychosexual development whose etiology is childhood fear (anxiety). This developmental failure results in disturbed gender identity, produces associated infantile fears, and becomes the basis for the later development of homosexuality. The sexual arousal pattern in homosexuality is fear-based, unconscious, and very often completely beyond the awareness of those so afflicted. The repetitive quest for homosexual contacts is thus not motivated solely by the desire for sexual pleasure; relief from and avoidance of anxiety is of paramount importance. In some homosexuals the anxiety is chronic, sometimes conscious and other times unconscious. It is this anxiety which the homosexual attempts to neutralize through homosexual activities. This clinically validated construct forms an important basis for the understanding of homosexuality. Any attempt at approaching a female sexually results in an increase in anxiety due to the fact that his basic conflict is inextricably tied to the fear of women. Consequently, even if a marriage has been attempted, these individuals will be unable to initiate or sustain a loving, tender attachment to the female partner without therapy. These two considerations—fear-based homosexual arousal patterns, and an inability to form an emotionally meaningful and gratifying attachment to the opposite sex—are but two of the criteria which clearly place homosexuality in the category of a pathological sexual adaptation.

Although there are a variety of theories as to the causation of the early developmental failure, they all have in common severe disturbances in the early child-parent relationship when critical maturational changes are taking place. All the data suggest that a binding and psychologically crushing relationship between a mother and son leads to a later concept of women as potentially dangerous and destructive. The outcome of this type of relationship between a young male child and his mother may result in an excessive clinging to her, anxiety upon attempting emotional separation from her, and a consequent disturbance in masculine identity. Similar and corresponding dynamics are present in female homosexuality. Homosexuals consistently describe the father either as a weak, shadowy, and distant figure or an angry, cold, or brutalizing one.

In the light of clinical research, the homosexual symptom can be seen as an intricately designed defense whose purpose is to maintain the equilibrium of a disturbed individual. Tampering with his psyche by unqualified persons is to be condemned, as he may become seriously disorganized if a premature attempt is made to interrupt his homosexual activities. Conversely, an individual who has refrained from homosexual activities, however impelled toward them, may be tragically pushed into them by unwise guidance.

At this point we must make certain definitive statements gained from our clinical research and accumulated knowledge of the human psyche in health and in illness. The claim that homosexuality is simply a variant of normal sexual behavior and exists alongside heterosexuality as an equivalent expression of adult sexual maturation is utterly false:

1. True obligatory homosexuality is a form of psychiatric or emotional disturbance. After detailed exploration, the Committee on Public Health of the New York Academy of Medicine reported its findings that homosexuality is a mental disorder whose only effective treatment is psychotherapy.

2. Homosexual object choice is not innate or instinctual, nor is heterosexual object choice, since both are learned behavior. The choice of a sexual object is not predetermined by chromosomal tagging. Heterosexual object choice is determined from birth due to cultural and environmental indoctrination. It is supported by universal human concepts of mating and by the family unit with its complementariness and contrast between the two sexes. It is further determined by two and one-half billion years of human evolution and is a product of sexual differentiation, at first solely based on reproduction but later widened to include sexual gratification: for example, from one-celled nonsexual fission, to the development of two-celled sexual reproduction, to separate entire organ differentiation, and finally to the development of separate individuals reciprocally adapted to each other anatomically, endocrinologically, psychologically, and in many other ways.

Only massive childhood fears can damage and disrupt the standard male-female pattern. Such early unconscious fears are responsible for the later development of homosexuality.

3. Homosexual behavior which is nonobligatory (episodic) may be practiced by individuals through choice for a variety of motivations and should not be confused with true homosexuality. The motivations are as complex as any other motivations which influence human behavior: personal gain, power, self-defeating behavior, search for a variational experience (an extra sexual thrill), preferred status,

and position. This form is not caused by unconscious fears and ensuing guilt but is due to conscious, deliberate choice. One must carefully differentiate between the obligatory type and the nonobligatory, as the former would like to mask as the latter in order to save pride and justify its occurrence. ("It is not true that I am driven to this, I choose to do it.") This nonobligatory form is not the true sexual deviation, but the incidence of this form of aberrant sexual behavior will no doubt increase as societal, religious, and legal disapproval decreases.

4. Since the obligatory homosexual is suffering from a psychosexual disorder, it is obvious that he should not be penalized for the consequent activities carried out in private and in partnership with a consenting adult. He should not be made to suffer special penalties because of the manifestation of this condition as long as it is not accompanied by antisocial or criminal behavior.

One argument about homosexuality that has confused and confounded us is: "How can such a condition, existing in many competent men, even those of undeniable genius—a condition which seems a part of life itself and goes back to antiquity—be a form of arrested psychosexual development?" It is indeed clear now why homosexuality is prevalent, has existed since the beginning of recorded history, and numbers among its victims those from all sociocultural levels. It knows no distinction among its sufferers as to economic bracket, intellectual endowment, or proved achievement. The answer indubitably lies in the fact that we were all once children; we all had to face the challenge of passing through the most difficult period of separation-individuation (from birth to age three) into separate and independent entities from our mothers. This earliest phase, like the oedipal phase (age three to five), is a universal phenomenon.

Those who urge the acceptance of homosexuality as simply a normal form of sexuality rather than a behavioral disorder, developmental arrest or failure, or a clinical illness, reflect the blurred boundaries of social behavior which currently impair our communal health in many ways.

In man, due to the tremendous development of the cerebral cortex, motivation—both conscious and unconscious—plays the crucial role in the selection of individuals and/or objects that will produce sexual arousal and orgastic release. Where massive childhood fears have damaged and disrupted the standard male-female design, the roundabout method of achieving orgastic release is through instituting male-male or female-female patterns (homosexuality).

Pathology, organically and psychologically, is defined as a failure of function with concomitant pain and/or suffering. It is this failure, its significance, and its manifold consequences that are so obvious in obligatory homosexuality—a failure in functioning which, if carried to its extreme, would mean the death of the species. Beneath this obvious failure of function lies the agony, sorrow, tragedy, fear, and guilt of a both unconscious and conscious nature which pervade the homosexual's life. Psychiatrists who treat such individuals in depth know this very well. Those who do not practice in-depth psychotherapy often do not observe or may tend to minimize the degree of suffering the homosexual endures, inasmuch as the homosexual behavior also provides temporary relief from severe anxiety.

Furthermore, obligatory homosexuality may cause such grave disruption to the equilibrium of the individual that all meaningful relationships in life are damaged from the outset and peculiarly susceptible to breakdown. Attitudes toward the opposite sex are so often filled with profound distrust, abhorrence, and revulsion as to render them impossible of any relationship at all except on the most superficial and brittle basis, if then. The obligatory homosexual is unable to function in the most meaningful relationship in life: the male-female sexual union and the affective state of love, tenderness, and joy with a partner of the opposite sex.

Although psychosis and neurosis exist, of course, in heterosexuality, the heterosexual orientation is not of itself an indication of pathological condition, while obligatory homosexuality always is. The male's inability to function heterosexually and his extreme hostility toward women have produced a wholesale flight from all females. The compromise adaptation is to choose a male partner for sexual gratification in order to save the self from the intolerable anxiety which would ensue were he to approach the female. In this way he also attains a temporary state of equilibrium which can be so misleading, not only to the public but to any investigator who accepts the facade without deep probing. The ability of the homosexual symptom to neutralize anxiety motivates the homosexual to use this as a face-saving rationalization—that is, that he is not ill at all, especially if he is convinced that there is no help for changing his condition.

Despite the appearance at any given time of an adequate life performance, there is always extreme conflict present which threatens to disrupt this fragile adjustment.

It has been shown clinically that all male homosexuals suffer, paradoxically, from the yearning to be a man, not a woman as commonly assumed. They hope to achieve a "shot" of masculinity in the homosexual act through the mechanism of identification with their male partner, his body, and his penis.

There are some who argue that if homosexuality could achieve complete social acceptance, homosexuals would then be able to lead fulfilled and happy lives, free from any problems. In this light, psychiatrists who regard homosexuality as other than normal are attacked as tools of the antihomosexual establishment and become targets of abuse by homosexual organizations, the homosexual press, and even homosexual psychiatrists. We can only agree that the social rejection and discrimination that homosexuals suffer is unjustified. But if discrimination against homosexuals stopped tomorrow, as indeed it should, it still would not relieve their conflicts, anxiety, and susceptibility to frequent breakdown and depression. Society as a whole does not produce the homosexual condition, nor can it mitigate the psychological pain inherent in it. The etiology lies much earlier in life, and the anxiety, depression, and conflict stem primarily from *intrapsychic* conflicts, with only a portion derived from the shame and guilt arising from societal attitudes.

THE SEXUAL UNREASON

On December 14, 1973, the Board of Trustees of the American Psychiatric Association, meeting in Washington, D.C., eliminated homosexuality from its official Diagnostic and Statistical Manual. In essence and by direct implication this action officially declared homosexuality a normal form of sexual life. Henceforth, the only "disturbed homosexual" would be one who was disturbed because he *was* homosexual. He would be considered neurotic only if "unhappy."

It seemed clear to many of us who had worked with homosexuals for years that this was obviously a political-social maneuver and not a reasoned scientific judgment. This stand was taken by psychiatrists, most of whom had never seriously studied homosexuality or the other sexual perversions. Some of the leaders of this movement were of the belief that "social activism" was the best way to help the emotionally disturbed or mentally ill. But psychoanalysis itself, beginning with Freud, had begun to rescue the homosexual from being buried both by society and psychiatry. He was about to be buried again by being called "normal." This pronouncement as to the normalcy of one of psychiatry's most severe examples of sexual pathology is all the more remarkable, brash, and outrageous when one considers that it involved the out of hand and peremptory disregard and dismissal, not only of hundreds of psychiatric and psychoanalytic research papers and reports but of a number of other serious studies by groups of psychiatrists, psychologists, and educators over the past seventy years; for example, the Group for the Advancement of Psychiatry Report, 1955; New York Academy of Medicine Report, 1964; Task Force Report, New York County District Branch, A.P.A., 1970–72 (C. W. Socarides, Chairman). The latter report, commissioned by the New York County District Branch and prepared by an eleven-member group of psychiatric experts in this field, was disavowed by its parent body, the issue being deemed "too controversial." It was later published as a "Group Study Report" in 1973.

Then, at the December 15th Board of Trustees meeting before the final deliberations and vote on the issue, Dr. Irving Bieber, clinical professor of New York Medical College; Dr. Robert J. McDevitt, clinical professor of the University of Cincinnati, and chairman of the Department of Psychiatry at the Good Samaritan Hospital in Cincinnati; and myself complained that colleagues well versed in the area of homosexuality had never been consulted personally or in writing by the A.P.A. before this action was taken. We stressed that we had all along been and would continue to be in the vanguard of the movement for decriminalization of consensual adult homosexual acts in private; our opposition was built on the false and pseudoscientific basis for eliminating homosexuality as a psychosexual disorder. We argued that there was no legitimate scientific reason given for this change in basic fundamental psychiatry and psychiatric theory.

The board of trustees vote was nearly unanimous against our position, with two abstentions. It is interesting to note, however, that only two-thirds of the members of the board of trustees were present to vote on this crucial issue. The only course left open to us was a referendum. Within two weeks our Ad Hoc Committee Against the Deletion of Homosexuality secured the necessary 200 names of members and fellows of the A.P.A. to petition that the new change, brought about in what we considered to be such an undemocratic fashion, be undone. The Ad Hoc Committee was later erroneously criticized for bringing a scientific issue to a "vote." It was the board of trustees, however, who first brought this issue to a vote, and our committee was left with no choice but to call for a referendum which would show the board of trustees that their vote was not a valid representation of the views of the general membership. The referendum lost by 2004 votes and over fifty-eight percent of the membership had voted. However, we believed that this vote may have been more a response to a "letter of embarrassment" which was sent to the entire A.P.A. membership between February 28 and March 3, 1974, rather than an expression of views on the basic nomenclature issue. In a complaint procedure officially filed with the A.P.A., we stated that the sending of this letter without acknowledging that it was largely written by, and paid for, by the National Gay Task Force, may have indeed constituted unfair and hidden lobbying with certain of our members and was a violation of the ethical and fair voting procedures of our organization.

On Monday April 8, 1974, the results of the referendum were announced to the nation:

Reporter: "This is the CBS Morning News. The results of the referendum were disclosed at a meeting of the Psychiatric Association's board of trustees. About 5800 of those responding favored the trustees' decision to no longer classify homosexuality as an illness. About 3800 opposed the change. What does this mean? Does this mean that homosexuals should be considered normal?

Dr. Alfred Freedman, President, American Psychiatric Association, and Presiding Officer of the Board of Trustees: "The action of the American Psychiatric Association doesn't state it as normal. It merely states that it is not a mental illness."

Reporter: "Where does that leave it?"

Dr. Freedman: "That leaves it as a condition. It's a difference, let us say, from the prevailing model, but yet is not a mental illness."

Reporter: "What other things might be considered a condition?"

Dr. Freedman: "Well, for example, is spinsterhood a mental illness . . . is vegetarianism?" (4/9/74 CBS News—B. Sarafin, Reporter)

Thus a movement within the American Psychiatric Association accomplished what every other society, with rare exceptions—ancient Greece for a short period during an individual's life, pre-Meiji Japan, certain top echelons of the Nazi party, and special status groups such as the Berdaches, Nata slaves, and Chukchee shamans—would have trembled to tamper with, the revision of a basic code and concept of life and biology: that men and women normally mate with the opposite sex and not with each other.

The Ad Hoc Committee pressed a demand that a board of inquiry be set up to study whether or not illegal voting procedures had taken place. Persistence prevailed and six months later a committee was formed to study this matter (the Redlich committee). Although this committee concluded that the actions of the leaders of our association in allowing their names to be used on a letter written by and paid for by the National Gay Task Force was "unwise," no action was recommended by the Redlich committee either to nullify the referendum, notify the entire membership of all the facts in the matter, or ask the membership if a new referendum was desired in view of these "unwise" actions. The Ad Hoc Committee Against the Deletion of Homosexuality is at present asking for a critical review of the Board's findings.

AFTERMATH

Over 3700 psychiatrists believe there are no legitimate scientific reasons for the A.P.A.'s change in fundamental psychiatric theory. Indeed our organization's position on homosexuality may have serious consequences both for individual homosexuals and the nation as a whole.

Karlen, one of our leading historians in the area of sexual customs and behavior, comments that some scientists, psychologists, and psychiatrists ransack literature for bits of fact and theory that can be pieced together into a prohomosexual or bisexual concept of nature, man, and society. These individuals end up by saying that they are healthy, that society is sick, and that scientists should cure society. They raise false or outdated scientific issues in their war with traditional values. Many of our values could use change but polemical pseudo-science is not the way. No society has accepted adult preferential homosexuality. Nowhere is homosexuality or bisexuality a desired end in itself. Nowhere do parents say: "It is all the same to me if my child is heterosexual or homosexual." Nowhere are homosexuals more than a small minority. Nowhere does homosexuality per se place one in an enviable social position. The myth that ancient Greece was completely accepting of homosexuality has been exploded by writers such as Lacey and Opler.

Heterosexuality has self-evident adaptive value; and decades and even centuries of cultural change are not likely to undo thousands of years of evolutionary selection and programing. Homosexuality is not a means of birth control, as suggested by those who would declare homosexuality normal—a chemical is simpler.

Man is not only a sexual animal but a care-bonding, group-bonding and child-rearing animal. His sexual behavior cannot be unrelated to his broader sociosexual nature. Many prohomosexual proponents state that mental illness is simply a product of social definition and that sexual behavior considered normal in one society may be deviant in another. Examination of the facts shows that this is not true of all illness and all behaviors. Some behaviors are universally deviant and every society thinks them disruptive. Incest, rape, psychopathic (apparently unmotivated) violence are considered deviant everywhere. So is predominant or exclusive homosexuality or even bisexuality. There are exceptions to these sanctions. Incest, rape, homosexual acts, and random violence are permitted in some societies at certain times on occasions, at certain ages, or with certain partners. No known society however accepts preferential homosexuality.

The militant homosexual has already demanded homosexual marriage and the right to adopt and raise children, and in some instances this has been accomplished. This raises the crucial question as to whether one has a "right" to something which may well prove to be inimical to the rest of society, especially if accepted generally and raised to the level of a sexual and social institution. A society governs the behavior of its members from birth to death, through its laws, mores, and other institutions. The facts are that a human individual is born with responses which constitute his mammalian heritage (a product of evolution). He is born into a web of social institutions which are a result of cumulative traditions constituting his cultural heritage. The two, mammalian heritage and cultural heritage, lead man to his sexual pattern—heterosexuality. Heterosexuality has a biological and social usefulness. It protects the species and the evolution of man. It creates the family unit and allows men and women to live together under conditions where there is likely to be the least amount of fear, rage, and/or hate. It furthermore regulates this relationship through a system of laws, penalties, punishments, or rewards.

With the normalization of homosexuality, men and women experiencing potency disorders may misinterpret them to be expressions of "bisexual potential" or "homosexual naturalness." This may well lead to homosexual *behavior* and resultant loss of pride, self-esteem, and an eroding of the male-female sexual identity.

Above all, let us not forget another member of the disturbed heterosexual family—the individual homosexual, who has to cope with what early unfortunate childhood upbringing has so cruelly forced upon him. He can only feel despair that psychiatry, behavioral scientists, the law, and even the clergy have forsaken him. This psychiatric nonsense and social recklessness may well bring social and individual tragedy.

Men and women who no longer care for their appropriate sexual roles will create confusion in the very young in decades to come. There may well be a rise in homosexuality of the nonobligatory type at first, but ultimately profound gender identity disturbances may well increase and more true homosexual perversions will result as parents distort the maleness or femaleness of their infants and children.

As regards psychiatric theory, an alteration of theoretical concepts of healthy versus unhealthy sexual development will "logically" occur. The individual homosexual will despair at the psychiatrically abetted forfeiture of his mammalian heritage—the ability and opportunity to engage in male-female sexual conduct. Homosexuals in therapy will develop tremendous resistances which will retard their progress, while others may be unwisely dissuaded from seeking appropriate therapy at necessary times. Suicide may well increase among persons with gender identity confusion. Where will such persons get help if they cannot turn to psychiatrists? Other medical specialists, such as pediatricians and internists will be baffled by psychiatry's faulty reasoning. Men and women, homosexual and heterosexual, will be increasingly disturbed by homosexuals continuing to lecture in our public schools and colleges on the value of homosexuality as simply an alternative sexual life style. Sex education courses already include homosexual sex education as a valid life style in some schools. Residents in psychiatry may well have little interest in going into an area of psychiatric research where they will be attacked, belittled, and demeaned, and their knowledge of sexual development will cease to grow. In time, as has been suggested by the homosexual militants, those who treat homosexuals may be subject to legal pressures not to treat those who wish to become heterosexual. Above all, the individual homosexual wishing to change will suffer the most.

Anyone whose task is the alleviation of distress in man can only be saddened by the scientific unreason that has brought this to pass. Young men and women with relatively minor sexual fears may be led with equanimity by psychiatrists and nonmedical counselors into a self-despising pattern and life style. Adolescents, nearly all of whom experience some degree of uncertainty as to sexual identity, will be discouraged from assuming that one form of gender identity is preferable to another. Those persons who already have a homosexual problem will be discouraged from finding their way out of a self-destructive fantasy, discouraged from learning to accept themselves as male or female, discouraged from all of those often painful but necessary courses that allow us all to function as reasonable and participating individuals in a cooperating society.

To paraphrase Dr. Abram Kardiner, Professor Emeritus of Psychiatry at Columbia University, homosexuality cannot make a society or keep ours going for very long. It operates against the cohesive elements of society. It drives the sexes in opposite directions and no society can long endure when either the child is neglected or when the sexes war upon each other. Those who reinforce the disintegrative elements in our society will get no thanks from future generations. The family becomes the ultimate victim in homosexuality, which any society can tolerate within certain limits.

The following quotation from *Measure for Measure* epitomizes our current dilemma. I was recently reminded of it by a patient on the analytic couch—a homosexual and a distinguished scholar, who had begun to learn of the roots and dynamic forces behind his homosexuality and gradually to gain control of them.

But man, proud man,
Drest in a little brief authority,
most ignorant of what he's most assur'd,
his glassy essence like an angry ape,
plays such fantastic tricks before high heaven,
as make the angels weep.

SUGGESTED READING

Freud, A. "Some Clinical Remarks Concerning the Treatment of Cases of Male Homosexuality," *Int. J. Psa.* 30 (1949).

Freud, A. "Homosexuality," *Bull. Amer. Psa. Assn.*, 7 (1951) 117–118.

Bieber, I., *et al.*, *Homosexuality: A Psychoanalytic Study of Male Homosexuals*. New York: Basic Books, 1962.

G.A.P. Report: Committee on Cooperation with Governmental (Federal) Agencies of the Group for the Advancement of Psychiatry. Report on Homosexuality with Particular Emphasis on the Problem in Governmental Agencies. Rep. no. 30, Jan. 1955. Topeka, Kansas.

Glover, E. *The Roots of Crime: Selected Papers on Psychoanalysis.* vol. 2. London: Imago Publishing, 1960.

Karlen, A. *Sexuality and Homosexuality.* New York: Norton, 1971.

Lacey, W. K. *The Family in Classical Greece.* New York: Cornell University Press, 1968.

Opler, M. K. "Anthropological and Cross Cultural Aspects of Homosexuality," in J. Marmor, ed., *Sexual Inversion: The Multiple Roots of Homosexuality.* New York: Basic Books, 1965.

Mahler, M. M. Discussion of "Healthy Parental Influences on the Earliest Development of Masculinity in Baby Boys" by Stoller, R. J., in *The Psychoanalytic Forum,* vol. 5, 244–247. New York: International Universities Press, 1975.

Rado, S. "A Critical Examination of the Concept of Bisexuality," *Psychoanalytic Medicine,* 2 (1940), 459–467.

Rado, S. "An Adaptational View of Sexual Behavior," in P. H. Hoch and J. Zubin, eds., *Psychosexual Development in Health and Disease.* New York: Grune & Stratton, 1949.

Rado, S. "Evolutionary Basis of Sexual Adaptation," *J. of Nerv. and Mental Disease,* 121 (1955), 389–401.

Redlich Committee Report: Report of the A.P.A. Ad Hoc Committee on the Conduct of the Referendum to the A.P.A. Board of Trustees, Dec. 13–14, 1974. A.P.A., Washington, D.C.

Socarides, C. W. *The Overt Homosexual.* New York: Grune & Stratton, 1968.

Reissued by Jason Aronson 1974. also *L'Homosexualite* Paris: Payot, 1970; and *Der Offen Homosexuelle*, Suhrkamp Verlag, 1970.

Socarides, C. W. "Theoretical and Clinical Aspects of Overt Female Homosexuality" (Panel Report). *J. Amer. Psa. Assn.*, 10 (1962), 579–592.

Socarides, C. W. "The Historical Development of Theoretical and Clinical Concepts of Overt Female Homosexuality," *J. Amer. Psa. Assn.*, 11 (1963), 386–414.

Socarides, C. W. *et al.* "Homosexuality in the Male: A Report of a Psychiatric Study Group," *Int. J. of Psychiatry*, vol. 11, no. 4, 1973, pp. 460–479. (Task Force Report, New York County District Branch, A.P.A.)

Socarides, C. W. "Homosexuality," in Arieti, S., *American Handbook of Psychiatry* (Rev. ed), vol. 3, 1974, pp. 291–316. New York: Basic Books, 1974.

Socarides, C. W. "The Sexual Unreason," *Book Forum: Special Issue, Psychotherapy and Social Structure*. 1:2. New York: Hudson River Press, 1974.

Socarides, C. W. *Beyond Sexual Freedom*. New York: Quadrangle/New York Times, 1975.

chapter 14

A THEOLOGICAL APPROACH TO UNDERSTANDING HOMOSEXUALITY*

Norman Pittenger

Not long ago a young man was ordained to the ministry of the United Church of Christ in the United States although he had publicly announced himself to be homosexual. Shortly afterward a Methodist minister was disciplined for blessing the union of two homosexuals. Several Christian denominations in the United States have issued statements in which they welcomed homosexuals as church members and urged others to adopt a charitable and understanding attitude toward them. Some states of the American union have altered their laws about sexual offenses in such a fashion that no longer are homosexual relations put among the criminal acts which are subject to police action and court proceedings. And in Britain, since the mid-sixties, the law has explicitly stated that homosexual contacts between consenting adults are no longer illegal.

A great many Christian people consider the positive steps toward accepting homosexuality and homosexual persons as noncriminal and acceptable by society to be a shocking and ominous departure from the moral standards for which Christians ought to stand. They think that any minister who will bless a homosexual union should indeed be disciplined; they feel that no active homosexual should be admitted to membership in the Christian community; and they believe that at best a homosexual man or woman is a sick person and at worst an abnormal and sinful one.

* Reprinted from *Religion and Life,* copyright © 1973 by Abingdon Press. Used with permission.

Now most of the discussion of this question of homosexuality has been undertaken from a psychological, sociological, or ethical stance. The discussion has had to do with whether or not homosexual desire and activity are deviations from a supposed norm of sound and healthy psychological development; whether or not they are damaging to the social patterns which preserve order, decency, and right communal living; and whether or not they can be reconciled with what are taken to be the explicit teachings of the Bible about moral behavior or the standards of the Christian ethical tradition in respect to sexual expression. Very infrequently, if at all, has the matter been approached from the specifically theological side.

To some of us this seems very strange. Whatever may be our conclusions in respect to the normality or abnormality of homosexual desires and activities, we believe that this issue, like all other basic issues about man, can only rightly be handled when basic theological questions have been taken into consideration. I am speaking here, of course, as a Christian and from within the Christian community of faith. In a pluralistic society, like that with which nowadays we are all familiar enough and in which willy-nilly we are participants, it is impossible to dictate to non-Christians the position they should take. But for a Christian, in any and every question concerning man, the world, and whatever else has to do with human existence and life, the theological background is essential. By theology I do not mean recondite or pedantic discussion of speculative issues, although often enough theology has seemed to be just that. What I am talking about is the thoughtful and faithful development of the consequences of the Christian faith about God and man and the world in the light of, and as the inevitable result of, acceptance of Jesus Christ as the disclosure in act of what God does in the world and hence what God is as creator and redeemer and enabler of that world in its ongoing movement—or, as most of us would say nowadays, the evolutionary process.

It is in that context and against that background that the question of homosexuality should be seen. And this paper is an attempt to provide for the reader some material which will be of assistance to him in engaging in this enterprise. Ever since my book *Time for Consent* (SCM Press, 1967) was published, I have been astounded and dismayed at the way in which just such an approach has been dismissed or disregarded by so many who have read it. In that book, as also in *Making Sexuality Human* (United Church Press, 1970), I sought to base my argument for acceptance of the homosexual man or woman on theological considerations, from a Christian understanding of the meaning of human sexuality in all its various expressions.

Much of the negative comment on the argument has entirely over-looked this primary theological concern and has contented itself with falling back on supposed psychological deviance, societal damage, and moral indignation at what was taken to be a denial of "what Christians have always believed and what the Bible clearly teaches." Hence in this paper I wish to begin again and to outline fairly briefly the specifically theological points that to my mind are not only rele-vant but essential in any Christian view of the question.

I begin, then, by affirming as a matter of Christian faith the follow-ing very simple conviction: whatever else God may be, he is above all the cosmic lover whose scope is indeed cosmic but whose love is applied particularly and specially to each of his human children. When we say that God is omnipotent, therefore, we can only mean (if we do in fact accept the conviction that he is pure unbounded love, in Wesley's grand words) that this cosmic lover and his love are the strongest and most enduring of all powers, despite the appearance that force or coercion is more effective than love. When we call God omniscient we can only mean that cosmic love is all wise and unto such a lover "all hearts are open, all desires are known, and from him no secrets are hid." When we speak of God as omnipresent, we assert the availability of that cosmic love always, everywhere, and to everyone. When we say that God is eternal, we are talking about the unfailing and constant reality of that cosmic love; and when we men-tion immutability we are indicating, not some supposed impassibility or entire unchangeableness in the divine way of working, but the conviction that God as lover is always precisely *that:* he is indefatig-able and indefeasible in his loving and in that respect never changes, although in his adaptation of his loving to the exigencies of the world and the needs of the creation he is open to and ready for an illimit-able variety of modes and ways of acting. His "nature and his name is Love," as Wesley said; and this is the ultimate criterion by which everything else said or thought about him is to be judged as true or false, adequate or inadequate, proper or erroneous.

In the second place, God not merely *is* love; he is ceaselessly and unfailingly in action *as* love. That is, he relates himself to, partici-pates in, and works through the creation at every point in it; and he does this always as the lover of the creation. Of that divine activity, Jesus Christ—with what went before to prepare for his appearance, what happened during his days in Palestine in response to his pres-ence, and what has followed afterward as his impact has been ploughed into history—is the classical instance. He is not the su-preme anomaly, utterly different from whatever else God has been doing; he is that point and place where what God is *always* up to receives focal and decisive expression. This does not mean that in Jesus there is only a disclosure of God to a supreme degree. Rather, precisely because there was such a disclosure in concrete human existence, the way the world goes has been changed and those who respond to him are enabled to realize and make actual their own God-given potentialities and live in wholeness of life, good and abundant now and so good and so abundant that nothing (not even death) can destroy it.

What then is God's abiding purpose or will for his human children? The answer is that he is creating them through his subtle operation upon them and in them as they make their own free decisions and accept the consequences that follow, creating them so that they may become creaturely or finite lovers. To be truly human is to be a human lover, nothing more and nothing less. As men move in that direction they are moving toward the fulfillment of the divine purpose for them—as Paul Lehmann has put it, God's purpose for men is "to make and keep them human." There is nothing esoteric or superhuman about man's intended destiny; on the contrary, it is all of a piece with his potentiality to become more completely and responsibly the man God intends him to be. The Scriptures tell us that man is made "in the image of God"; in an evolutionary perspective we can phrase this better with a slight change of words: *toward* the image of God. Jesus Christ himself is the image humanly expressed; other men are to move in that direction, so that the cosmic love which in Jesus is "en-manned" in human loving is known as both the "master-light of all their seeing" and the drive which impels them onward and the goal toward which they tend when they are rightly and truly using all their powers in the fashion God wants for them.

And again, among these preliminary theological considerations, finite loving such as men can know, and toward which they are meant to move, requires community with others of their kind. They are to love God, to be sure; but their loving God is expressed practically and immediately in a loving relationship with other human beings. I John 4 is the great reference for this truth; the man who loves God *must* love his brethren, and conversely the man who genuinely loves his brethren is truly loving God. Why is this? Because God *is* love and (in Tolstoy's words) "where love is, there God is"—or, in the lovely Latin of one of the ancient liturgies, *ubi amor et caritas, ibi Deus est:* "where loving, out-going concern and care are present, there God is present and working."

But how are finite men and women to love and to learn to love? Here we have another theological consideration, following upon the primary ones with which we have concerned ourselves so far.

In the scriptural and central Christian understanding, man is not a soul who happens to inhabit a body. That would be more Hellenistic than Christian, however much some Christian teaching has approximated it. The main drive of the Christian view, however, has been quite different. For the Bible and for the central Christian tradition, both Catholic and Reformed, man is what we call a psychosomatic being—he is a complex unity of matter and mind, stuff and spirit, body and soul. He is a body, just as he is a mind or spirit. Therefore, man's bodyness is as much his manhood as his rationality or his spiritual capacity. And in consequence, his loving and learning to love involves his body quite as much as his spirit.

This means, to my mind, that the only way to understand what human sexuality is all about is through seeing it as the bodily, physiological-psychological-emotional base or ground for his capacity to love and his way of loving. With angels, if they exist, it might be otherwise; they are supposed to be "disembodied pure intelligences," in the classical definition. But man is not disembodied, neither here and now nor in whatever existence may be his beyond the grave. Do we not affirm, with all its difficulties and problems, the resurrection of the body as well as the immortality of the soul? In any existence beyond mortal death, Paul tells us there will be a spiritual body. This is inadequate English for the idea which in Greek suggests a genuine embodiment, continuous with our present physical one but changed (as the apostle says) into one that is appropriate for life in and with God—not a matter of chemistry, so to speak, but none the less a real body.

Human sexuality is continuous with the sexuality of the animal order in that sexual organs and drives are present in us as in the so-called lower creation. But there is also a difference. At the animal level, the biological purpose of sexuality is dominant. The sexual apparatus, in all its complexity, is for the animal a reproductive system. A specific type of union between two dogs or cats or horses—or whatever else you wish to suggest—has for its biological end the production of another individual of that species; and the high degree of pleasure attached to such a type of union is obviously intended to drive the animal to engage in that act. For man, however, the sexual apparatus which is in a general way identical with that of the animals has changed in its primary purpose. For man the sexual desires and acts have acquired the new possibility of expressing and sharing a total personal relationship, a union of life with life which is all-inclusive and all-enriching. Love is the meaning of human sexuality; and the procreation of offspring is the consequence of heterosexual love given and received—which is why on the basis of Christian theological understanding it is not only proper but essential that procreation should be responsibly planned and intended, rather than an accidental consequence of a highly pleasurable act. To put it simply, what in animals is the reproductive system in man has become (as part of this emergence, under God's overruling activity, *as* man) the conjunctive or unifying system.

And incidentally, this point makes very clear the fallacy of that sort of rejection of "planned parenthood" or "contraception" which rests upon the idea that man is *just like* the animals sexually speaking and that no responsible planning of offspring is licit. Such teaching reduces man to the level of the animals precisely in the moment when it claims to be exalting him and his sexual existence. God has given his human children both the freedom to act and the responsibility for acting through decisions that are taken in genuine human ways for genuine human ends. God respects that freedom and uses it; hence procreation.

What has all this to do with homosexuality? Have we not wandered off into general theological considerations of the meaning of sexuality and forgotten our major topic in this paper? Far from it, I urge, and for the following reasons.

In the first place, sexual expression of some sort is inevitable in human beings, provided that we do not confine sex to explicitly genital contexts. If my argument is sound—that sexuality is the pervasive quality, inclusive of sexual apparatus physiologically speaking, which makes relationships between persons possible—then in all our activity we are active as sexual beings. In friendships there is a sexual element; some people might be shocked at the very thought, but that indicates a certain pruriency in their way of thinking. In any and every contact of any and every sort, *all* of a man or woman is included, not least when that person assumes that the contact is merely mental or spiritual. If this is true, as a little attention will confirm, then the homosexual male or female is naturally expressing his or her sexuality in whatever relationships are known and enjoyed.

Secondly, the majority of people (perhaps some eighty-five to ninety percent, if sociological surveys are to be trusted) will find their sexual desire and drive (in a more explicit genital sense) directed toward persons of the other gender. Boy meets girl, boy falls in love with girl, boy wishes sexual contacts with girl—and vice versa. The institution of marriage, developing through a long history and in Christian thought blessed by God to be a faithful monogamous union of man and wife, is the means by which this heterosexual drive is provided a setting and through which it receives social (and for Christians and others, also a religious) approval. On the other hand, for somewhere between ten and fifteen percent of the race, we are told, the experienced sexual drive is not toward somebody of the opposite gender but toward somebody of the same gender (hence homosexuality, which is a combination of two words, one Greek and the other Latin: *homos,* Greek for "same," and *sexus,* Latin for "gender"). For that minority, which is by no means a tiny number (it would mean perhaps twenty to twenty-five million Americans, for example, or five to eight million Britons), the natural tendency is toward another man or boy, girl or woman. Hence whatever we say theologically about human sexuality must have its relevance for these people, as well as for the majority who are heterosexually built.

But—and here we come to a very controversial question—are not people like that, these homosexually inclined men and women, really abnormal or deviant? Obviously, if by norm we mean what the majority prefer, and by deviance mean a departure from that majority preference, homosexuals are abnormal and deviant. But this is a grave misuse of terms. Who is to establish what is truly normal for men and women? In my own view, it is normal for them to express their sexuality in a desire to love another of their species through mutual giving and receiving, through as much personal relationship as is possible, and through a concern for others in every area of their personhood. And it is abnormal to hate, to be cruel and hurtful, to treat persons as things, to act irresponsibly toward them and with them. To act in this latter fashion is indeed deviant; it is to act subhumanly and to violate the very nature of the love toward which men are meant to be moving. But that is not the same as saying that love for persons of the same gender, sexual interest in them, and desire for sexual contacts with them, is abnormal or deviant.

We do not know the origins of homosexuality; but neither do we know those of heterosexuality. The basic issue is not there in any event, but rather in the origin of our loving at all, and in the kind of development of loving which makes us whole and real humans. And the basis for that, I have urged, is our sexual apparatus, with equipment, desires, drives, and emotions. To discover that some genetic patterning, some family influence, some response to external pressure, brings this man to be heterosexual and that man to be homosexual is only to discover how such capacity for any sort of love has come to be; it is not to be determined that this way is inhuman and that way is human, this normal and that abnormal. People are to be taken for what they are, not judged good or bad on the mere grounds of direction of their loving, homosexual or heterosexual.

But then we shall be asked about the biblical passages which are taken to condemn homosexual contacts as inherently sinful. I can only reply here that we must read the biblical material in the light of its context, with regard for the conditions prevailing at the time of speaking or writing, and in due recognition of the particular ideas of sexuality prevalent then and there. If we do that—and unless we are biblical literalists we must so do—it is patent that the Old Testament passages (relatively few, by the way) have to do with the general notion that anything that "spilled the seed" without producing more Jews was wrong, since it was the duty of the chosen people (so they thought anyway) to multiply their numbers, while the association of homosexuality with idolatrous Canaanitish worship made this particular kind of sexual activity abhorrent to the strict monotheistic worshiper of Jahweh. In the New Testament, again, St. Paul is plainly a representative of the tradition he inherited as a faithful Jew; he is also shocked by the licentiousness of the Greco-Roman world, as were many Gentiles too—for sheer vituperative attack Juvenal in his *Satires* is more violent than St. Paul at his worst. Nor does St. Paul dwell on homosexual practices more than on other instances of what he considered wrong; as many commentators have noted, he uses this particular matter as *an* example, not as *the* example, of what he takes to be human wrongdoing.

Was Paul right about this? So far as I know, nobody but a biblical fundamentalist would claim that every word of the apostle is divinely inspired and hence authoritative for all time. He was the child of his age in many ways; he was also the child of his Jewish background. If he condemned women to an inferior place in church worship, that does not mean that *God* takes the same view. If he thought demons dwelt in long hair, that does not mean that we should think so. What Paul said on this matter of homosexuality, like the long Christian moral tradition on the subject, is not *ipso facto* divinely given and divinely imposed. In all such teaching, on many more things than sexual issues, new occasions teach new duties. Our ancestors were not fools, but they were not all-wise either. We need to look at such statements in the light of new knowledge, new understanding, new awareness, deeper Christian perception. Some of us are convinced that such an enterprise will result in an openness to homosexuality as an equally licit way of sexual genital expression as heterosexuality. We shall not pity nor condemn the homosexual man or woman; we shall try to understand him or her, help him or her to be the best sort of person possible, just as we should try to do for the heterosexual.

I diverge slightly from the theological consideration of the matter to make one point. Thanks to the publication of the books to which

I referred earlier, I have come to know well several hundred men and women who are admittedly homosexual in their desires and drives. I have found them for the most part to be in every way as decent, honorable, and splendid as their heterosexual brothers and sisters, sometimes (I confess) rather more so, since they do not have the heterophobia which is the opposite of the homophobia often found in the heterosexual. They have been generous and friendly, seeking a moral pattern which is appropriate to their particular kind of personality, and often enough deeply religious in feeling. Furthermore, I can think at this moment of some fifteen male couples who have lived together, in the complete sense of that word, from five to twenty-five years in utter happiness, genuine love, and remarkable generosity of spirit. To call them abnormal or deviant specimens of humanity would be a scandalous misuse of words. According to the possibilities which are theirs, they are entirely normal; they are not deviant, but obviously they are different. And I venture to speak of *that* difference in the same fashion as did the Frenchman in the story who said of the difference between man and woman, *"Vive la différence!* That is, I should rejoice in the fact that there are people who thus love persons of their own sex, just as I rejoice in the fact that there are people who love persons of the other gender—it adds variety, color, and spice to the common life, if only we will accept and help rather than reject and condemn.

For it comes down to the theological conviction that God has worked in his creation to produce men and women of different kinds and interests, including sexual kinds and interest. Why should we not agree with this? I can think of no reason for failing to do so, except for inherited prejudice, dislike of what is not "our own thing," and failure in insight and charity.

The homosexual cannot be creative in the sense that he or she will produce offspring. That is granted. But human sexuality is not primarily for that purpose at all. As I have urged, it is essentially a matter of conjunction or union of lives; where procreation takes place, it is to be decided upon and responsibly made possible. Otherwise such reproduction is more like animal rutting than human loving. But if the homosexual is not creative in the reproductive sense, he or she can most certainly be creative in the deeper and truer sense of sensitivity, capacity to contribute to life's enrichment in art and science, in culture and social amelioration, in the beautifying of relationships and the deepening of human existence through sharing and mutual sympathy. Above all, homosexuals can be creative in their religious awareness—among the hundreds I have met since 1967, a great many have been so deeply Christian that they have shamed the ordinary churchgoing respectable heterosexual. And they have included some of the finest priests or ministers I can ever hope to know; although alas, if their homosexuality were published abroad they would doubtless be shunned or their ministry brought to an end by official action.

Every homosexual man or woman with whom I have talked has confessed that what was really wanted by each of them was to love and be loved. The frequent promiscuity and "one night stand" type of contact are more a substitute for the deep relationship they desire than the main intention of their lives. As the famous English Quaker report on the subject said so plainly, society (and the church) drives people into such behavior because it refuses to treat them as God's dear children and fails to help them become the best persons they have it in them to become. Not least, it frowns on their efforts to set up permanent or quasi-permanent relations with another of their own gender, the sort that so many so earnestly desire, and then treats them as dirt because they act in less desirable fashion. It is very strange; to my mind, it is un-Christian and immoral.

In speaking on this subject recently in London, I remarked that everybody knows that sex is always fun. Of course it is; why not, since God made it and presumably esteems it? But only when sex is put in the context of genuine sharing of life in every aspect, as it may be in true heterosexual marriage, is it given its richest significance. For if sex is fun, "making love" is unutterable joy. That is as true for the homosexual as for the heterosexual. To my mind, the church has enough theological assurance to move forward in helping the homosexual in his or her kind of union to live as faithfully and in intention as permanently as the heterosexual. That ought to be the purpose of our Christian counseling and our Christian dealing with the homosexual—not to call him a greater sinner than others, which he is not, but to assist him to become a great lover. I am convinced that a sound theological approach will do a good deal to bring about this day of acceptance, welcome, and support.

chapter 15

SOME WORDS OF CAUTION

William Muehl

We know very little about the causes and nature of homosexuality. Some psychotherapists treat it as an illness. Others refuse to do so. There appear to be people who are born into a physiological sexual ambiguity. And there are obviously many who adopt it either in response to abnormal social isolation such as imprisonment, or to provide outré thrills and stimulate a jaded appetite. There are homosexuals who long to become heterosexuals, while others profess to be quite content with their lot. As a psychological phenomenon homosexuality still seems to be a profound mystery.

There is nothing unclear, however, about the attitude of the Christian community toward sexual relations between persons of the same gender. They have been consistently proscribed and their practitioners often cruelly persecuted by ecclesiastical authorities. Both Old and New Testaments condemn homosexuality. Any effort to make a case to the contrary involves the kind of torturing of Scripture by which racists seek to defend segregation, and martial spirits to justify preemptive strikes. Whether the motives of those who want to blur the hard edges of the truth are compassionate or self-serving, the facts of history cannot be disputed. Genital homosexuality has been regarded as immoral by responsible Christians. Any discussion of the subject which begins with another basic assumption is doomed to futility.

To make the statements I have just made about the past and present attitude of Christians, even to propose that this attitude is right and ought to be perpetuated within the community of faith, does not imply any justification for the way in which homosexual people are treated by secular society today. Our society has encouraged the most flagrant exploitation of sexuality. It has allowed our appetites to be titillated in a great variety of ways by experts in the business; and the relevant moral standards of the past are being abandoned with shouts of liberation by those who first reflect and then shape the prevailing mood of Western society.

Statesmen and politicians are only mildly embarrassed when they are reported accurately to be womanizers. Business enterprises use commercial lovemaking to lure customers and clinch deals. Colleges virtually subsidize fornication by their dormitory arrangements. And those newspaper columnists who have become the arbiters of ethics urge prudent parents to put their teen-age daughters on the pill.

It is both hypocritical and grossly unjust, therefore, for secular institutions to persecute and prosecute those whose sexual irresponsibility is somewhat more adventurous than average. A society cannot make free sex the national hobby and then penalize those who show creative imagination in the way they play the game.

It seems clear to me, as to many others, that when they act as citizens, Christians have a serious obligation to support basic civil rights for homosexuals. It is unthinkable that men and women should lose jobs, be denied housing, and suffer police harassment for refusing to be bound by rules which most of their neighbors have for all practical purposes abandoned long since. If we argue that what happens in bedrooms is not the public business, we cannot in good conscience keep peeking through keyholes. If we hold that what happens in bedrooms *is* the public business, we have far more pressing problems to solve than those presented by Gay Liberation.

Does the logic of this position require that Christians abandon their historic stand on homosexuality and declare to be good what they have in the past condemned? Obviously not. What is required is a firm reassertion of the time-honored distinction between toleration on the one hand and approval on the other. Or to put it in more familiar religious terms, adherence to the principle that one must love the sinner while hating the sin.

The appropriate Christian answer to the increase of sexual irresponsibility in society is neither to adopt that irresponsibility as its own mode of behavior nor to expel from its midst those who fall victim to it. It is, rather, to see all abuses of human sexuality as manifestations of that sinfulness which plagues our common existence; and to define homosexuality as one more symptom of a general problem rather than the outward and visible sign of a special depravity.

This is not an easy thing to do; partly because homosexuality has been so consistently condemned by religion that it has come to be regarded with special distaste. But more important for this discussion is the fact that homosexuals themselves show so little interest in being tolerated and seem determined to equate *acceptance* of themselves as persons with *approval* of their peculiar life style. As one informed colleague puts it, "The gays don't really want the right to privacy in their sexual activities. They want to act out their fantasies in public and force the rest of us to applaud."

The demand of militant homosexuals today is for social and religious endorsement of gay relationships, the recognition of same-gender sex as an appropriate expression of Christian love, the accrediting of gay persons as instructors, interpreters, and exemplars of the faith, and the solemnization of their unions by the church. They are asking, in short, that the religious community reverse its strongly held position on genital homosexuality and declare it to be fully consistent with a viable Christian commitment. And when anyone presumes to suggest that this proposal requires careful examination and the review of a number of substantive theological issues, he or she is very likely to be accused of loveless bigotry and charged with causing great pain to some very sensitive people.

A central feature of Gay Liberation strategy in the churches is to call attention to the unhappiness of homosexual men and women in our society and to demand that, as an expression of acceptance and love, compassionate Christians redefine homosexuality and call it good. You cannot really love us, they argue, unless you love our sexual preferences. And they have had an amazing success in getting otherwise intelligent human beings to accept this fallacy.

Yet if anything is central to Christian ethics it is the need always to distinguish between the doer and the deed. One need not embrace Marxism in order to acknowledge the humanity of Communists or adopt the social statics of Herbert Spencer out of regard for Republicans. If an alcoholic were to declare that we could not accept him as a person unless we endorsed alcoholism as a desirable life style, we should suppose him to be well into his cups. When the Christian community is faithful to its calling, its doors and hearts will be open to all people. But it cannot be expected to deny its convictions and consecrate what it has steadfastly condemned in order to make any of us sinners feel more at home in the pews.

In a recent panel discussion of this topic I used the analogy with alcoholism and was immediately and angrily pounced upon by one of the other panelists. "What a cheap shot," he declared, "to compare homosexuality with alcoholism. Alcoholism prevents one from functioning as a viable human being. Homosexuality doesn't."

Well, that is precisely the issue involved in the Christian consideration of homosexuality, is it not? Does genital homosexuality impair one's ability to function in truly human fashion? Obviously it does not interfere with basic physical activity, any more than most alcoholism does. Thousands of alcoholics perform their daily jobs adequately, even impressively, then go home and drink themselves into a stupor. Undoubtedly an equal number of gay persons, perhaps many more, play out their economic and social roles efficiently all around us from nine to five.

The viability with which the Christian must be concerned, however, has far deeper and more complex dimensions than can be measured by a well-earned pay check. It is with this profound viability that moral statements are intended to deal. The panelist who wanted to make a qualitative distinction between homosexuality and alcoholism was guilty of a classic form of question-begging. He *defined* the gay life as "viable," and therefore good, and he casually brushed aside the great weight of Christian opinion to the contrary.

This is a problem which cannot be solved by definition. One must bore in relentlessly in a search for some responsible answer to the question which my fellow panelist sought to beg. Do homosexual relationships harm the persons involved in them?

Those who reply in the negative tend to rely on relatively gross standards in measuring the damage done to human beings by particular modes of behavior. (And they delight in finding damaging contrasts between the position of the church on homosexuality on the one hand and war on the other.) Homosexual activity does not kill, cripple, or shed blood; it probably causes no more incidental pain than heterosexual coupling. Ergo, it does no damage to those who participate in it.

There is only a superficial plausibility to such reasoning. And in any other area of debate those who champion the gay cause would be among the first to point this out. The human psyche is a very fragile thing and can be wounded in ways that leave no obvious scars. There is something called "dignity" that can wither and die without ever uttering a cry of pain or shedding a drop of blood. Why do Christians oppose the treatment of criminals by brain surgery or electrode implants? Surely such remedies are more humane than lifelong imprisonment. Why do we waste the bodies of our dead on cemetery grass when their decaying flesh could be used as fertilizer to ease the world food shortage? They are beyond the reach of pain and embarrassment, and the living would be greatly served by such a policy. Why do we prevent people from exposing themselves in school playgrounds? There is some reason to suppose that the kiddies find the performance highly amusing.

The answer to such questions cannot be given in measurable units of harm to personality. We can only affirm that there are ways of hurting people which break no bones and may even provide the victim with a moment of pleasure. And there seems to have been a clear consensus among Christian thinkers over the ages that genital homosexuality assaults human dignity in some such subtle fashion. That view may be in error. But it cannot be defined away or refuted by the absence of scars on homosexual partners.

Even if one were to grant the unsubstantiated premise that gay relationships do no damage to those individuals most immediately engaged in them, questions inevitably arise about the social consequences of giving religious sanction to genital homosexuality. What will happen to the concept of the Christian family in a society which *endorses* same-gender sexual coupling? Will the painful sexual ambivalences of adolescence be made more difficult and more likely to be resolved in favor of a homosexual orientation if the local rectory is occupied by the pastor and his or her "lover?" Can the battered institution of Christian marriage stand the sight of gay unions being solemnized at the altar? What will be the effect upon all sexual relationships of the consecration of what are essentially sterile unions characterized by a very high degree of instability?

It is the multitude of such legitimate questions and the scarcity of persuasive answers which argues strongly that the Christian attitude toward gay relationships be one of toleration rather than approval. Centuries of ruthless repression—one indication of how strongly the traditional opinion has been held—have forced gay people to live their lives furtively and have made it almost impossible even for sophisticated analysts to evaluate the impact of homosexuality upon persons and society. It is altogether possible that much of what seems essentially destructive in the gay life style is really the neurotic consequence of a hostile environment. Once legal bans on same-gender sex have been removed and its practitioners allowed to live without harassment, we shall be in a far better position to see the implications and consequences of any change in the basic position of the churches on this difficult subject.

I wish it were possible to stop at this point and assume that I have made the case for great caution in responding to the demands of gay militants for full approval of their way of life by the Christian community. Some experience in this area, however, has convinced me that those who wish to give serious thought to the place of homosexuals in the churches will find themselves under considerable pressure to throw caution to the winds in the name of something loosely called "love."

"God is love"—so runs the argument. Anything that is an expression of love is good. Since same-gender sex is an expression of love, it should be blessed by the church. This is another classic example of question-begging, an effort to define homosexuality into a state of grace. As such it needs very careful examination.

One of the most popular errors in the realm of Christian ethics has been the effort to make love an omnipotent spiritual quality which has the power to sanctify anything that is done in its name. The Inquisition tortured people's bodies in order to save their souls and sought to justify this action in the name of love. For centuries white Christians imposed patterns of paternalism upon blacks as an expression of their love for the sons of Ham. Employers once professed to love their employees too much to let them fall into the evil clutches of labor organizers. Parents tend to dominate their children's lives in the name of this same love. And generations of male chauvinists have counseled their sisters, wives, and daughters to eschew power and find their dignity and security in the love of their menfolk.

It is fashionable to interpret all such claims as sheer hypocrisy, as many of them were. But far more often than we care to admit, acts of exploitation and even brutality have been committed by people who honestly believed they were expressing disinterested love for their victims. It was the recognition of this hard fact of life which led Reinhold Niebuhr to say that we human beings are "never as dangerous as when we act in love." When we are motivated by anger or aggression, he pointed out, we arm our own consciences, alert our critics, and put our intended victims on their guard. But when we act in love, we disarm conscience, critic, and victim in one act and can do our worst unimpeded.

This was Niebuhr's characteristically dramatic way of saying that love does not empower anyone to transcend fully the structures of responsibility in human relating, and must always be expressed in ways that are appropriate to particular historical contexts and specific human associations. Love does not hallow the inquisitor's cruelty; the white's oppression; the employer's, parent's, and male's domination of others. It condemns such inhumanity and bids it cease. Love *establishes* the modes of interpersonal relating. It does not simply consecrate those that we find pleasant or profitable.

Thus, love does not always justify sexual union. It frequently makes it clear that sexual union is grossly inappropriate to a relationship. It is wrong for fathers to act out their love for their daughters in coition, for mothers to take their sons to bed, for brothers and sisters to copulate. Only the sickest minds would hold otherwise. And once we have established that fact the argument that homosexual union is good simply because it is motivated by love falls of its own weight.

It is every bit as likely that the love of man for man or woman for woman bids them refrain from sexual intercourse as that it urges them into it.

For the purpose of making such statements about the argument that same-gender sex is an expression, however inappropriate, of love, I have assumed that some form of affection is, indeed, the driving force in gay relationships. This is by no means incontrovertibly established. A number of authorities in the field argue that the dynamic of homosexuality is not love for the same sex but hatred of the opposite sex. Men who take other men to bed, they suggest, may be less interested in expressing affection for their partners than in displaying contempt for women. And the same would be true, *mutatis mutandis*, for lesbians.

Still other psychologists hold that homosexuality is the result of a less sexually focused anger and reflects a more general aggression against people of both sexes. And there are obviously additional interpretations of the phenomenon for which there is no space here. While I am not qualified to evaluate such analyses, their net effect is to cast even more doubt upon the proposition that Christians ought to reverse their historic position against genital homosexuality and accept it as a manifestation of interpersonal affection. One needs to be very cautious about sacramentalizing what may well be a ritual of hatred or aggression.

In all discussions of this topic it seems crucially important to insist upon adequate time for full consideration of what is at stake. Too rapid a rate of change in critical areas of human relating can be dehumanizing in itself. But the Christian community has an understandably uneasy conscience on this point. It has often dragged its feet when it should have been leading the parade. And in consequence its leadership is somewhat inclined to suppose that in any proposal for change the burden of proof rests upon those supporting the status quo.

Some of the more militant gay leaders have been quick to seize the opportunity which this guilt syndrome offers. No more delays!—they cry. And link their cause with crusades on behalf of blacks, poor people, antiwar programs, and women. But there is a very important distinction between the proposals of Gay Liberation and such other appeals for changes in the attitudes of Christian churches. Most of the confrontations with which Christians are being called upon to deal these days reflect the demand that they bring their practice into line with their principles, that they more fully live up to what they have long been preaching.

The appeals of Gay Liberation, on the other hand, represent a proposal that the churches reverse their position on a moral issue of great importance to both themselves and society. This is not a question of bringing practice up to the level of principle but of revising principle in order to accommodate a particular and somewhat exotic practice. It is critical that Christians bear this distinction in mind and not allow their guilt feelings to push them into premature and ill-advised responses toward homosexuality. To allow themselves to be stampeded on this issue by emotional appeals and the fear of hurting someone's feelings will set a precedent which cannot help returning to haunt the churches often in the years ahead.

Let us end where we began. Homosexuality ought not to be treated as the manifestation of some special depravity whose practitioners should be driven from the church and harassed at law. But neither can it be defined as an appropriate expression of Christian love in interpersonal terms. The gay relationship is one form of sexual irresponsibility among many and no more reprehensible than most. Those involved in it have as much place in the pews as all the rest of us sinners. And as long as they recognize it as a problem and are prepared to seek help in dealing with it, there should be no arbitrary limits placed upon their full participation as leaders in the Christian fellowship.

When gay people claim, however, that their way of life is a morally healthy one, insist upon their intention to affirm it publicly, and ask that it be consecrated in some way by the church, they put themselves in contempt of Christian conscience. Under such circumstances it is not only the right but the duty of other Christians to express grave misgivings about the seriousness of their faith and to challenge the wisdom of admitting homosexuals to positions of leadership in the churches.

PART IV

Psychological Perspectives

chapter 16

ADOLESCENT SEXUALITY

Raymond C. Yerkes
Robin B. Yerkes

Exploring all the ramifications of adolescent sexuality would be an impossible task in the scope of one article. What we have observed from common experience, from everyday contacts with young people as patients, friends, and family members, must serve as the basis of our approach to the subject. It is on this basis that we shall examine the most common patterns of sexual behavior among adolescents.

The pros and cons of such specifics as contraception, sexual freedom, living together, and the accessibility of abortion are openly argued and weighed daily by both the popular and the professional media. But to skip over or ignore the basics of adolescent development is a serious mistake which we would like to correct.

Any attempt to examine and understand adolescent development, sexual as well as all other kinds, must recognize the universal stages that the young person goes through on the way to maturity and adulthood. These have been more or less arbitrarily divided into early, middle, and late adolescence, each with its own special physical and psychological changes, and the interpersonal involvement with peers, parents, parent surrogates, and other authority figures. Certain steps for growth take place throughout these stages, varying with social class, ethnic group, and cultural background. This paper will not take up value systems per se, but will point out the important steps in all stages. It will describe patterns of growth and some of the pitfalls intrinsic to certain developmental crises. We shall be concerned with the average adolescent, not with seriously disturbed young people or those with any markedly distorted patterns of development.

Ever since Aristotle's impassioned cry that young people were becoming worse and worse, the same judgment has been visited upon each succeeding generation. This is a recurring theme and is one aspect of the way adults continue to view the young. Adolescence is, indeed, an anxious time, fraught with rapid changes, mounting self-doubt, and painful insecurities. We should like to point out at the start, however, that in spite of all the prophecies of doom and despair, the majority of adolescents do, in fact, grow up, reach a stable maturity, and assume their places in society and the world.

EARLY ADOLESCENCE

The first stirring of change begins to occur toward the end of the grade-school period, that phase we call preadolescence. Early adolescence begins with the onset of puberty, commonly defined as starting in girls with the first menstrual period, and in boys with the first experience of ejaculation. One may observe, in this phase, increased bodily awareness, the turning of attention inward, mounting sensitivity to the opinions of others about oneself, and the pressure of striving to assert independence. In this period, vacillation between maturity and immaturity occurs from hour to hour and day to day; and emotional instability and supersensitivity tend to increase. Each child's developmental level may vary markedly at the onset of early adolescence, giving the overall group an appearance of wide variation which, in turn, has a profound effect upon grouping and the development of peer relationships.

Grade-school children, engrossed as they are in mastery, learning, and dealing with concrete reality, are relatively stable, flexible, and social beings. Sexuality is very much present through this so-called latency period, but it is private, separated from the adult world, and largely secondary to other concerns. Changes in subjective body feeling are followed by early physical changes in secondary sexual characteristics and rapid physical growth, changes that are very disconcerting to the young person. As one young girl put it: "Sometimes my body seems all filled with electricity." The body image is disrupted by changes in size and shape. Boys may be disturbed by frequent and easy occurrence of erections, even with nonerotic stimuli and often in the most inconvenient situations. The frequency of such erections probably accounts for the earlier masturbatory activity in boys as compared to girls of the same age.

At this stage masturbation seems to arouse intense feelings of anxiety even when it is not prohibited or punished, and it is a time when young people need the help of frank and open discussion of sexual matters. Having learned long ago where babies came from, and later how they got there, preadolescents are faced for the first time with the disturbing fact that sexuality is a real and immanent matter. They need proper information on this new subject, but even more they need the emotional support that can only come from the acceptance and understanding of an adult who acknowledges their maturing processes as natural and good. Without this support they experience a deep loneliness, high vulnerability to feelings of guilt, and wild concerns about bodily harm to themselves. All these painful experiences are intensified by the bizarre misinformation they are almost certain to hear from others.

Although there is good instructive literature available, it is no substitute for open discussion with a trusted adult—a parent or an older sibling or friend. This sort of discussion can begin with information about menstrual periods for girls and wet dreams or masturbation for boys. It will soon broaden into dialogues about relationships with others, about one's own personal conduct and behavior; and it may be the start of a relationship that can be the foundation for communication throughout adolescence. It is most important that the adult be sympathetic and, so that the young person feels free to ask simple, even foolish questions, be ready to listen and respond.

It often happens with surprising suddenness that a previously orderly and predictable child becomes tense, erratic, and preoccupied with self. Many families, caught unprepared for this occurrence, unwisely decide to ignore the changes in their child. This forces the young person to try to attract attention by rebellious acts, or worse, to retire to lonely isolation and alienation from the family. There is clearly a need for a reexamination of the family role in such circumstances.

Fluctuation of the level of maturity can be expected at this time, and the family must deal with adolescents at whatever level they are in at any moment or hour or day. It is possible, for example, that on one day a punishment more appropriate for a much younger child may be accepted by the adolescent as normal; and yet on the very next day the same punishment for the same individual may be experienced as humiliating and demeaning. Assertion of independence is a real necessity at this stage, but judgment is still not mature and must yet be developed through experience. For this reason the setting of limits is most critical, and they should be clear, concise, and directly connected to real substantial issues. Parents should not decide to abandon the young teen-ager to his resources, but they should also take care not to be so restrictive that they deprive him of the opportunity to take responsibility for his behavior.

No adolescent can learn responsibility without a certain amount of failure in the effort to live up to expectations. Each step in the young person's attempts to assume responsibility should be kept separate from the previous step, and comparisons or reminders of past failures should not be made. Minor infractions should be commented on at the time they are made, but no more should be made of them than is warranted by the degree of infraction. Failures in taking responsibility ought to be dealt with for the purpose of finding out what went wrong, *not* in a way that diminishes the self-esteem of the young person. It is important to support self-esteem even while offering criticism, especially with one whose self-esteem is so constantly on trial.

One particular developmental pitfall that can impede progress in taking responsibility is that of "mutual undermining." The young teen-ager demands freedom to do or act in a certain way, but once that freedom is attained, he may be unconsciously frightened of it and may fail to behave responsibly. This makes the parents lose confidence in their child and accuse him of being irresponsible when he is only suffering, unconsciously, from anxiety and fear. Being worried about him, they are overrestrictive, thus weakening the chance that he will try to take responsibility another time. He is angry and protests the punishment, which is a way of avoiding the anxiety that the freedom and responsibility evoke. Parents and adolescent accuse each other angrily, each having effectively cooperated to avoid taking any new steps.

Another common developmental situation comes from the fact that young teen-agers are very stimulating, both consciously and unconsciously, to the adults around them. Unresolved or poorly resolved issues of the parents' own adolescence can be reawakened by the family teen-ager. Overidentification or projection of one's own conflicts onto the behavior of the adolescent is a serious failing among adults. An example that has special application in the area of sexuality is the father who had a premature, sexually active adolescence himself and who overreacts to his teenage daughter's basically innocent flirtatiousness as if it were a sexual come-on of an older person. He may see each boy friend as an embodiment of his own teen-age sexual wishes. A mother can also overidentify, treat her daughter as a peer, invade her privacy, and never really be aware of her own vicarious gratification. This may even provoke the teen-ager to live out the adult's sexual wishes, particularly if they are outwardly forbidden. These matters can be even more difficult when there are unresolved problems in the family. The teen-ager can then become an unaware partner to matters not even of his or her making.

Aggressive impulses can be lived out by an adult through a teen-ager. For example, the father who chuckles at his son's aggressive behavior and justifies it by citing his own adolescent adventures is supporting unsocial or antisocial actions. Rivalries between the mother with fading beauty and her daughter in blossoming youth are seen all around us. In dealing with a teen-ager, particularly in early adolescence, adults must be very much aware of their own feelings, conflicts, and boundaries. The intensity of the relationships that occur in the family with a teen-age child can effectively reopen issues that had not come to the surface in many years. These family issues can strongly affect the developing teen-ager. It does, however, often give the adults another opportunity to settle old issues between themselves if they do not take the rigid stand that being adults automatically makes them right. Even though teen-agers expect perfect parents, they will usually settle for reasonable human beings.

At about the age for junior high school is the time of the clique and of shifting, capricious, and fickle relationships. Bitter hurts are felt over who is the favorite of what group. Girl-to-girl friendships can result in rivalries when a third girl tries to interfere with the relationship. Innuendo, cold ignoring, or starting unpleasant rumors can be the weapons in popularity contests. The boys often become loud and exhibitionistic. The art of the put-down, and calling "fags" those boys who tend to be less aggressive, operate to support the shaky self-esteem of the young teen-age boy. In most cases, young people somehow survive these tribulations, but sometimes the wounds to one's self-image can leave scars. Occasionally, the rigid roles that teen-agers are cast in by their peers live with them through their whole school career.

The other side of the junior-high syndrome, however, is a sensitive and compassionate mutual support of each other. With so many new things in life, with moving a step away from the support of the family, the young teen-agers seek each other out to fill dependent needs, ask advice, and find a sense of themselves as one among others of their kind. This is when the "uniform" of the age becomes important. Whether it is the bobby sox and saddle shoes of the forties or the tattered dungarees and long hair of the seventies, the uniform becomes the badge of membership in yet another generation of young people.

Here the early relationships are usually of the same gender. The young teen-ager seeks to find himself or herself in the image and person of another, and this can reach a degree of intense infatuation. Teen-agers occasionally become involved in sexual activity, usually of an innocent nature, which often generates strong feelings of anxiety and guilt. These adventures must be kept in perspective for the young person. Transient sexual acts at this time should not be confused with concretized homosexual choice; they are much more likely to be merely extensions of self-love. We often find that young people who have a transient homosexual experience are precipitated into the fear that they may be homosexual, when it is sexuality itself that is responsible for the panic. Often the primary motivational factors are unmet dependent longings, with sex as the subsequent result.

Both boys and girls have concerns about sexuality. Girls seem more oriented to where they stand in the eyes of others. Boys have their own variety of concern: anxiety about adequacy and capability, whether they will be found desirable or not. At this age, with a sexual organ that is frequently aroused, masturbation becomes an expectable sexual outlet. It appears to offer an opportunity to master in fantasy future sexual behavior. Even in these apparently enlightened times, when masturbation is no longer considered an act that will sap one's vital essence and lead to insanity, it is amazing that the anxiety and guilt still arise in young people, and they must be given reassurance that everything will turn out all right.

This phase of same-sex relationships leads to a friend acting as the go-between for heterosexual friendships. Thus, same-sex grouping grows into mixed male-female friendship groups, and this process of establishing gender identity is the key to the next step in adolescence.

Somewhat unique to the present generation of young people is the trend away from paired dating toward the mixed group, which has allowed boys and girls to have genuine friendships with each other before involving themselves sexually. It appears advantageous, particularly in the development of judgment about a relationship with someone of the opposite sex before the erotic interests weigh so heavily. Commonly, when later pairing up begins, the couple leave the activities of the "family of peers" for greater privacy and individuality.

Early adolescent heterosexual involvement must be of some measure of concern. Excluding those young people who actually have matured earlier and more rapidly, it is often a sign of trouble. The girl who has been rejected by her female peers and is shut off from dependent support may seek for it from a boy, with the result that the intensity of the relationship will shut off the peer involvement that is necessary for more genuine independence. And the boy who is forcing his independence through sexual prowess instead of through competence in living is equally kidding himself. The use of sexuality to fight out dependence issues or to escape the lonely adolescent blues can impair the social and personality development that should be taking place.

MIDDLE ADOLESCENCE

The period from about fifteen to seventeen years is usually considered middle adolescence. There is less of a sense of newness about life at this time and teen-agers turn more to the world around them. They have come through many of the early issues of independence and have a more secure sense of self, some identity with their gender role, and as a rule have moved toward interest in the opposite sex. Personal identity is now the most important issue to be settled.

At this age young people become very concerned and discerning about values, not accepting those of the past on authority but having the immediate need of developing principles upon which to live everyday life. They are idealistic and at the same time skeptical. As they leave the last of childhood and turn anxiously to the new responsibilities of adulthood, they tend to go through periods of vague anxiety and dis-ease. The peer group and the mixed male and female group of friends become increasingly important in social development: for a sense of individual identity, as a source of values, and for mutual support. Often the first actual heterosexual experience occurs as an isolated experiment. Adolescents at this age experience varying degrees of sexual activity from very little or infrequent to more regular sexual relationships.

As the adolescent moves from centering fully upon self to establishing relationships with other individuals, the development of relationships of intimacy, consideration, and caring tends to predominate. The special best friend changes to confidant and consultant about life. Much time is spent just hanging around with others, which is not sheer idleness but a necessary interchange of self with others.

During this period, a trusted adult other than a parent is often sought out to fulfill many parental roles. This helps the adolescent develop a capacity to relate to others older than himself, but without the strong feelings associated with parents. From this other adult, the adolescent can accept advice that might not be accepted from parents, and the adult may offer a variety of alternatives for the modeling of roles and the development of positive ideals—suggestions that might not be available in the parental home. The teen-ager expects his parents to be perfect, but at the same time he makes them constantly aware of their imperfections, almost as though he wished to diminish them so that they will not be so difficult to leave.

With the combination of peers, significant adults, and parental family, teen-agers establish some sense of themselves as male or female, as individuals with a sense of place in the world; and they develop a value system that takes into account past values as well as present practical circumstances. They know how to be a friend and they can establish closer relationships that are something more than just parent and child.

It is in the middle and late adolescent stage that the young person begins to develop greater independence, a growth factor that is concurrent with the adolescent's reluctance to accept emotional support from the parents. Paradoxically, this is also the age when the young person seems to need more such support. The peer group becomes increasingly important, as do older friends, and there is greater peer pressure to conform to standards of the group about what clothes should be worn, whether and in what way to drink or take drugs, and general standards of behavior.

Emotionally, this growing away from the parents is frequently accompanied by a period of mild depression characterized by petulance, irritability, and dissatisfaction at home. This behavior can be misinterpreted as antagonism toward the parents, but in fact the teenager is looking for reassurance from them that they care about him. Such changes of mood should not be seen as a rejection of parents but as a moving toward a more mature ability to find support from peers.

Parents usually have many concerns for their teen-agers at this stage. They wonder if pressure from peers will result in misbehavior, and they worry that drinking, drugs, and sex are potential dangers to their inexperienced youngster. One of the pitfalls common to this stage is the tendency of parents, out of their anxiety, to dictate behavior to teen-agers instead of helping them determine their own standards. When the young person will not listen or obey, the result is a hurt and bewildered parent. Unthinking punishment at this stage tends, in fact, to reinforce negative behavior, to produce rebellious action as a means of protest, and to miss the real issue in the process.

The parent should negotiate limits with the young person and be able to listen to him or her in turn. From this a bargain can be struck which all parties are expected to live up to, firmly and with responsibility. Appropriate limits provide the adolescent room to grow without the overriding fear of his own impulses. Communication is of the utmost importance and should be kept open even if, at times, it seems like a one-way street.

Adolescents prefer to think of themselves as adult, and they will often practice what they see as adult behavior. Sex and drinking are forms of adult behavior. Parents realize this and worry that their teen-agers are now suddenly exposed to such realities. In fact, the teen-agers have watched the adult world for a long time. They know

what their parents believe, and are quite aware of what is expected
of them.

Trust becomes especially important in middle adolescence; and
within mutually defined limits, parent and young person should trust
each other. As the adolescent grows in ability and responsibility,
these limits should gradually expand. With the experience of being
considered trustworthy, teen-agers develop trust and genuine confidence in themselves; without it the parent-child relationship is seriously jeopardized, perhaps lost.

Ideally, the processes of adolescence result in the formation of a
solid identity. To do this, the young person must question and try
different life styles. In this experimentation with living, parents frequently feel that their values are being negated. Young people often
do question certain of their parents' values, and by examining them
they sometimes stimulate the parents to reexamine them as well.
Parents should be confident in the wisdom that living has brought
them, while, at the same time, remaining flexible and open to the
new perspectives their teen-agers are contributing. If basic differences develop, both young people and parents should remember that
the adult world does not and cannot expect absolute uniformity.
Each member of the family should be able, out of respect for each
other's opinions, to agree to disagree. Most of the time, young adults'
values derive from a synthesis of those of family, friends, and peers,
and from their own personal experience. The family must have faith
in the outcome of these processes.

LATE ADOLESCENCE

In this final stage, the independent strivings of early adolescence,
with the changes brought about by a new and growing body, moves
the young person into his own world of peers. The working out of
gender role within middle adolescence, and a growing sense of identity prepare the young person for those last steps into adult responsibility. These must precede the actual separation from home, living
separately, finding one's place in the world, loving, and working.

In this rapidly changing world, with its increasingly complicated
systems of plural values, to ignore the existing limitations and assets
of human development is to court trouble. Whatever the "system" is,
it must take into account human endurance and human psychological
strength in order to insure its own destiny. To neglect it is either to
waste human resources or destroy the human spirit in the processes
of growing up.

chapter 17

THE FREUDIAN PERSPECTIVE

W. Walter Menninger

It has been observed that few intellectual movements in recent history have had an impact on Western thought comparable to that of psychoanalysis, which evolved from the work and ideas of Sigmund Freud (1856–1939). Particularly influenced by Freudian concepts have been ideas about sexuality.

To sense the Freudian perspective of sexuality, you must start where he started. He was a physician whose clinical practice was ultimately spent in treating anxious, troubled, emotionally ill patients. In trying to get to the bottom of their problems—phobias, anxieties, obsessions, compulsive behaviors—he developed the therapeutic technique of psychoanalysis. A keystone of his technique was encouraging the patient to talk freely about whatever came to mind, the process of "free association," which he developed after one of his women patients urged him to just let her talk without interruption. In the course of his listening to his patients, both male and female, he formulated various ideas about the structure and function of the human mind and its development from the formative stages of infancy to adulthood.

He considered the powerful motivating forces behind the wide range of human behavior, and he concluded that the search for pleasure was extremely powerful. He identified what we commonly think of as sexual behavior as just one manifestation of the larger search for pleasure, yet he felt you could consider much of the pleasureful activity in life as part of sexuality. Thus he broadly defined all pleasureful activity as a manifestation of the sexual drive or libido (Latin for "lust").

In certain respects, Freud might now be understood as looking at human behavior as if it were the result of a computer which was programmed by life experiences at a critical period when it was subject to distorted input; that is, behavior patterns established in infancy and childhood when the individual is not able to fully appreciate and understand what is being experienced. The child, living in the land of giants, thinks in concrete terms and can't appreciate subtleties and abstractions. Events in the life of a child are all personalized, so that what happens must be because of something "I" did or didn't do.

Freud sought to identify the antecedents of the behaviors and ideas which his patients presented to him. He postulated the roots of pathological conditions he encountered by reconstructing the development of the infant and child in the context of a powerful drive for pleasure. He assumed that sexual or pleasure-seeking behavior was always present, prompted by an instinctual force which is both psychological and physiological. He theorized that the individual, in the course of normal development from infancy through childhood to mature adulthood, passes through stages of psychosexual development, learning different ways to achieve pleasure and the relief of tension, utilizing different body zones or areas which are emotionally (and erotically) sensitized. He also identified a progression of object choices which the individual can utilize for the drive to be fully achieved in its expression. He felt that the hang-ups or disorders which people have in their adult sexual behavior result from problems in the early developmental process; and he believed that many of the struggles people have in fulfilling their masculine and feminine sex roles stem from distortions in their perceptions of childhood or infantile experiences.

Freud had a number of limitations in his formulations which are still being reviewed and revised. Indeed, he himself revised several times his initial "Three Essays on the Theory of Sexuality," which was first published in 1905. His formulations of male development were precisely stated, but he acknowledged in his later years that he did not really understand female development. His early viewpoint was patriarchal in orientation, implying that female development was both second best and second rate. Nonetheless, his concepts are of great value in understanding certain commonalities in sexual drive and behavior of both sexes.

INFANTILE SEXUALITY

Freud challenged the prevailing view that sex was absent in childhood and only set in at the time of puberty in connection with the process of coming to maturity. Rather, he outlined infantile sexuality, the early phases of which have no gender specificity. His concepts were most unsettling to the Victorian times in which he lived. He did not consider the infant as a little homunculus with adult lust within. Rather, he saw the infant containing a libidinal drive which is diffuse and labile and free to be expressed or "invested" in different directions. The modes of its expression, however, evolve with the natural physiological maturation of the child through oral, anal, and genital stages. The first three years of life generally comprise the period of the oral and anal, or "pregenital" stages of psychosexual development, essentially the same for both boys and girls.

When the infant is born into the world, he has no interest except to selfishly gratify his own cravings. He has certain instincts and the demand to satisfy these is his essential motive in life. In his early months, he gives nothing to anyone and he makes no attempt to please anyone. He is interested in receiving what he wants. In effect, he follows the path of gaining all the pleasure he can and, insofar as possible, avoiding displeasure and pain in any form. This operational principle has been labeled the "pleasure-pain principle," and may be paraphrased: "I want what I want when I want it. Now!" While the behavior of an infant and young child may obviously reflect the pleasure-pain principle, it remains a powerful motivating force throughout life, a manifestation of the libidinal drive.

During the major part of the first year of life, labeled the oral stage of psychosexual development, the infant primarily relates to the world through and around the mouth, that part of the body where the nerves first mature. Food represents the infant's chief interest and gratification. The infant takes in affection as well as mother's milk through the mouth; through oral motor activity of sucking (breast, pacifier, fingers) and biting, he reduces tension. The later "taking in" or receiving capacities of the individual are affected by the experiences during this period. Of course, the mouth continues to be an avenue of pleasure and tension-reduction throughout life, although in varying ways at different times. There are the direct carryovers of gratification and tension-relief from eating—snacking, overeating, becoming a gourmet. There are the erotic activities of kissing and other oral sexual contacts. There are, in addition, a wide range of tension-reducing activities of the mouth—chewing, sucking, drinking, smoking, talking, gossiping, singing, or blowing musical instruments. These activities all provide gratification through oral activity and are considered "sexual" in Freud's broad definition of sexuality as the search for pleasure.

As the infant grows into the second year, the maturation of the nerve fibers extends into the limbs, permitting increased voluntary control over muscle activity. The child can sit up, stand, walk, and control bowel and bladder function. At this same time, the parents of most infants begin "potty training." For a period of many months, during what is labeled the anal stage of psychosexual development, the child is confronted with his processes of elimination. The myriad of transactions surrounding elimination increases its significance as a pleasureful and tension-reducing activity. There is pleasure in defecation. There is a sense of power over the parent by producing in the potty and thereby gaining admiration and love; or by not producing, retaining the feces, or producing it in the wrong place. There is pride in mastery of the body, with gratification from either expulsion of *his* creation or retention of it; in either case he can rightfully have a sense of omnipotence, a power that no one can take from him. Not only is the process sensed as important to his parents, but the child also has his attention focused on what is produced. The product is literally his first creation. But he is made aware that it is "bad," and he must come to grips with why and how something bad should come out of a "good" child.

A host of adult behaviors can be related to the patterns learned in this anal period, behaviors which may also be identified as sexual in the broad Freudian perspective. Indeed, the adult expressions resulting from this period may be even greater than the oral expressions. There are the direct expressions—the pleasure and relief of having a "good" movement, keeping regular to avoid "irritability," relaxing in the "throne" room. However, because anal activity is a "messy" activity, there is a greater tendency to repress the drive and modify the expression of the libidinal impulse through activities more socially acceptable—collecting or accumulating objects, painting, craftwork. Similarly, related to this period are the capacity to gain pleasure through giving and traits of orderliness, perseverance, persistence, conscientiousness, parsimony, obstinacy. In addition to the struggle of giving or withholding, the sense of "goodness" and "badness" or ambivalence has its roots in the anal stage.

In the process of bowel training, the child becomes keenly aware of the anatomy in the genital area and the fact that it is physically pleasureful. The child comes to realize at some point thereafter that there are differences between people in this body area. Heretofore, the child may ascribe sexual differences to overall size and physique, or hair length, or dress. The interest in the genital area makes the child aware of the anatomical sexual difference, although that may not be immediately appreciated or understood. The direct adult expressions of the libidinal drive in the genital area are obvious, with the ultimate pleasure being sexual intercourse and genital orgasm.

But there are also sublimations—modifications of sexual expression into behavior not traditionally viewed as sexual—such as investigation to satisfy curiosity, exploration, invention, initiative.

SEXUAL IDENTITY: CHILDHOOD STRUGGLES

The genital stage is a critical period in the evolution of sexual identity and sex role development of the individual. During this time, the child must begin a differentiation which was not so obvious in the pregenital stages. And the differentiation is an evolution through childhood and adolescence. As adults, we recognize and accept that there are basically two anatomical types of animal life, one categorized as male and one as female. The essential biological feature of this difference is that procreation and survival of the species depends upon sexual union and interaction between the two types. But the child doesn't know this. Indeed, the child can only think in simplistic and concrete terms; the child responds to what can be seen, not what is unseen. Therefore, as the child identifies the anatomical difference, he or she is faced with a powerful dilemma and has to come to terms with who and what he or she is and what that means, without benefit of abstract understanding.

Freud formulated the struggle in the boy as castration anxiety and the Oedipus complex (after the Greek myth of Oedipus who slew his father and married his mother). The process is postulated in simplistic fashion as follows, with an awareness that it is not something consciously appreciated by the child. At the time the boy has an increasing awareness of his genitals and the pleasure they can provide, he also has an increased interest in and attachment to his mother. Yet he is aware that father has certain privileges and receives certain attentions and affections from mother which he is not permitted to have. Consequently, father is seen as a rival, toward whom resentment and jealousy are felt. The conflict: how can he have mother as his love object and at the same time establish a satisfactory relationship with father? The striving for the mother is not necessarily in terms of adult sexual love; rather it is infantile in nature, a wish to possess mother without a clearly defined aim. Indeed, the small child, when confronted with the "primal scene" of sexual intercourse between mother and father, often misunderstands and misinterprets what is actually going on. He may react much more to the apparent violence of the activity than to the tender or loving aspects, and this distortion may have its own impact in the wish to protect mother and save her from a violent father. And while the child may not be conscious of his objective, he may show its presence by speech and behavior. He may be far more intimate with his mother in physical caresses; expressing the desire to have bodily contact with her, to sleep with her; saying he doesn't care if Daddy doesn't come home, or wishing mother would love him like she does Daddy.

At the same time that he experiences these feelings, the boy becomes aware that there are people without a penis. At this age, between four and six, the boy differentiates not in terms of male or female, but in terms of "with penis" and "without" or "castrated." When he is forced to accept the existence of persons without a penis, then he assumes that they did have one once, but lost it. He does not understand exactly how that happens, though he may actually hear threats about losing his. Certainly, when he is a bad boy, his toys are taken away. Feeling guilty about the resentment and envy he feels toward father, he may expect father to be angry with him and wish to punish him. Consequently, he has a fear, sometimes consciously perceived, often subliminal in awareness, that father might take away his penis. Or further, that father, who is so much bigger and more powerful than he, might totally destroy him. The fear of castration theoretically becomes so threatening that it literally breaks up the attachment to mother. The boy decides "If you can't beat him, join him," and identifies with father, becoming like him. Through the strength from such an identification, he stamps out the sexual interest in his mother and the desire for her. He builds up prohibitions which prevent him from giving further consideration to his own desires to have his mother as a love object and to his resentment and hate for his father. The eventual solution is to find a substitute for his mother in the form of a girl friend and later a wife.

FEMALE DEVELOPMENT

In the case of the girl, the genital phase is likewise highlighted by the development of rich sensations in the genital (clitoral) area which make it a central point of pleasureful activity as well as psychological interest. The little girl, like the boy, initially assumes that everyone is exactly as she is. When she comes to realize this is not true, she too divides people into phallic and castrated. However, for her the knowledge that there are creatures with a penis prompts a reaction of either, "I, too, would like to have that," or "I once did have one but I lost it." It is this process which has been labeled "penis envy." In a hypothetical process paralleling the boy's oedipal struggle, the girl must come to grips both with her identity as a girl and her relationship in the family triangle. She too has an initial attachment to the mother who has nurtured her. With the awareness of the lack of a penis, the girl becomes disillusioned with mother for not giving her a penis. Yet, though mother is also without a penis, she does have access to father's penis. The result is a desire to possess father's penis and a competition with mother for father. Inevitably, there is the realization that mother has the inside track. Anxiety is provoked by mother's ability to destroy the small child who proves to be too great a threat. Therefore, the girl too renounces the interest in father and defers her wishes to a substitute object in adulthood. Again, this process is oversimplified as stated, but nonetheless characterizes the struggle of the developing child.

The girl meanwhile struggles with a host of formulations about her lack of a penis, feeling deficient and disadvantaged, wondering if she is retarded. It may be questioned whether this is simply the result of an anatomical distinction or a reaction to prevailing social experiences that imply girls are inferior. Without question, the problem of accepting the traditional feminine role in life is much more difficult than accepting a masculine role. We might assume that the little child, either boy or girl, does not naturally want to be a passive dependent individual, yet until recently that has been the expectation of most adult femininity. The girl is faced with the fact that she still is born into what is primarily a man's world, where most of the work is done by men, particularly the major discovering, exploring, scientific, and business work. Furthermore, the little girl, whether she wishes or not has to accept the role of being a member of the "weaker" sex because of man's superior physical strength. In this context, the penis may come to symbolize the advantages of masculinity, not only in the ability of the boy to stand up and urinate a steady stream (instead of having it dribble down the leg), but it seems to give the possessor more independence and less frustration. The special problem is that the girl's mind is so focused on the concrete aspects of being a "have not" that it is hard for her to appreciate that she has something else which is equally significant, though internal and not physically apparent. The girl must simply struggle with her envy, perceiving herself to be in a state of "lack," punished, whether deserved or unjust.

Freud developed his concept of "penis envy" while working with adult patients in psychoanalysis. He didn't work with children. Yet, I became a believer from practical life experience as well as through analytic work. When my oldest daughter was about four and a half, she was presenting problems in nursery school. Since that was unusual for her, I decided to see if she could tell me what was bothering her. When we sat down to discuss the situation—and she was remarkably verbal—she told me, "Daddy, I want what Fritz and John [her two older brothers] have." I did a double take, realizing that what she was talking about was their penises. I fumbled with some sort of response, explaining that she did have something which was just not as obvious. I don't think I did very well at the time, although she did settle down. I felt the important thing was that her mother and I appreciated what she was struggling with and allowed that it was a legitimate dilemma in life for her. Interestingly enough, almost exactly two years later, when our next daughter was then four, my wife mentioned to me, "I can't understand what is wrong with Marian. She keeps going up to the boys' rooms and getting their underpants." We recognized that she was at the time struggling with her "penis envy" in a different way, perhaps thinking that there was something special in her brothers' underpants which would rub off and help "hers" to grow.

In any case, one is reminded that the four-year-old child is faced with quite a dilemma. Unable to fully appreciate the abstract concept of two sexes, the child perceives himself/herself as either having or not having some anatomy—a penis—which is not universal. Why do some have it and some not? If you are a boy, you know it feels good to play with; but some have lost theirs. You are aware of your own jealousy when somebody else has something you would like to have. Therefore, you must be careful about this thing called the penis; particularly you must watch out when you deal with the "have nots," for they might take it. If you are a girl, you struggle with why you were left out when they were passing these out. Or how come you are so slow to develop? Are you not as good? Can you make up for being disadvantaged? Can you really compete with a boy who has one? Inevitably, some of the remarkable differences in the later development of both boys and girls stem from the boy's unresolved childish fear of "I may be punished" and the girl's unresolved feeling of "I have been punished."

RELATIONSHIPS: OBJECT CHOICE

To understand the Freudian formulation of the evolution of male-female relationships, one must review the development of object choices which parallel the psychosexual development of the personality. Freud conceptualized a progression of object choices from an object-less phase; to a commitment to oneself as the center of the universe; to relating to other persons most like yourself, that is, of the same sex; to relating to persons of the opposite sex. As with the modes of sexual expression (oral, anal, genital), at different developmental periods in life, one object choice may be primary; but all may be appropriately utilized in achieving pleasure and relief of tension, that is, in the fulfillment of the libidinal drive.

During the first year or two of life, the infant does not really differentiate between "I" and "it." This period of life is essentially object-less, and the mother as well as the immediate environment are all part of the child himself. Gratification is achieved from purely mechanical measures: sucking, biting, defecating, urinating, squirming, kicking, jumping—all activities in which he makes no real object choice. Since the activities concern only himself, the phase has also been labeled an autoerotic stage of object choice.

Around age two, the child learns to differentiate himself from the world, or rather, the world from himself. From this age on, however, "he" or "she" is the most important person in the world and becomes the object of all interest. This period is labeled the "narcissistic" phase (based on the Greek myth of Narcissus who regarded himself as being more beautiful than anyone else and who literally fell in love with himself). The chief characteristic of this age in childhood is self-love. The child may go through the "show-off" period, exhibiting himself in every way he can to create and attract attention. Unless he is abnormally intimidated, his own property and his own interests are all that concern him. The narcissistic phase exists with varying intensity throughout life, being heightened at the beginning of adolescence and generally diminishing with maturity. Every individual needs to develop some sense of self-respect, self-esteem, pride, and interest in oneself. However, in its extreme, such behavior is considered selfish, egotistical, inconsiderate, greedy. And there are a substantial number of people who remain primarily fixed in the narcissistic phase and who are unable to establish effective and continuing relationships with others outside themselves; they are often seen as shallow and manipulating in their relationships.

Around age six, as the child copes with his/her sense of sexual identity, there is the period of the oedipal or parental triangle. The desire of the child for a close and possessive relationship with the parent of the opposite sex is not unrelated to the narcissistic phase. It is interesting to note that Freud was much impressed by reports of his patients that, in childhood, they were seduced sexually by a parent of the opposite sex. He came to realize that these reports of seduction were false memories, wishes of the child given a sense of "reality" by his or her narcissistic infantile desires.

At the point of resolution of the oedipal struggle, there is a period during which the child relates mostly to others of the same sex. It is as if there is a strengthening of identity as a boy or girl by relating primarily to others most like oneself. The transfer from the narcissistic phase is a simple one, because in a sense the child becomes interested in the mirror image. The period is labeled the homosexual phase of object development, evidenced by the tendency to form gangs, clubs, have a "crush," and participate in youth organizations which are all male or all female—scouting, Campfire Girls, etc. Again, the object choice of the same sex persists into adult life, and for some persons, a member of the same sex may be the only gratifying and meaningful relationship one can make for intimate sexual gratification. However, homosexual attachments for most people are generally nonsexual, nonerotic—bridge clubs, lodges, fraternal organizations.

In the usual course of evolution, the individual ultimately shifts in object choice to a person of the opposite sex, a heterosexual choice. In this stage, the sensuality and sexuality of infancy can be expressed directly in the adult partnership. There is a breaking off of the childhood investment in one's parents, along with a coupling which serves not only procreational purposes, but which also satisfies needs for a balance of dependence and independence. Essentially, Freud viewed the relationship of the sexes as mutually satisfying. The male satisfied the oedipal struggle by finding a substitute mother while keeping his penis (masculinity) intact. The female resolved her penis envy by producing a baby (which, if a boy, was literally the creation of a penis by the woman). At the same time each achieves resolution of these infantile struggles, the man and woman mutually gratify their libidinal drive in direct erotic and indirect sublimated ways. Obviously, there can be a multitude of variations in how the male-female relationships are played out; and Freud acknowledged that there is no pure masculinity or femininity, but that every individual has elements of both sexes.

VARIATIONS OF SEXUAL BEHAVIOR

One can outline the normal progression of psychosexual development and object choice, but in reality life events and human development rarely proceed on a smooth, even course. Thus, much of the psychoanalytic literature deals with the variations, and particularly what were considered pathological consequences of "faulty" psychosexual development. As noted earlier, in the Freudian scheme, one can trace personality and emotional problems back to origins in infantile sexuality, the result of some kind of hang-up ("fixation") which reflects a distortion of a childhood or infantile experience. Characteristically, problems are presumed to be the result of needs of a given stage being either insufficiently or excessively gratified.

The result in adult behavior may then be identified as the direct expression of the infantile sexual drive, and as a variation or "perversion" or "deviation" from the normal adult sexual behavior. Or it may be seen as an indirect, covert expression, with the infantile drive repressed; and all that is evident is a symbolic activity or "neurosis." Every stage of psychosexual development (oral, anal, genital) and object choice (autoerotic, narcissistic, homosexual, heterosexual) has potential pathological consequences. For example, a fixation at the oral stage might be evident in excessive preoccupation with food, overeating, obesity which cannot be controlled, or some other type of unmanageable oral gratification. Similarly, a host of personality patterns may result from unresolved oedipal issues, one of which may be an exaggeration of sexual traits—a male who is a seductive, exhibitionistic, narcissistic Don Juan who must repeatedly demonstrate his sexual prowess; or a female who may likewise be seductive and exhibitionistic, but in addition competitive and manipulating, "castrating" men repeatedly by humiliating them.

SUMMARY

In summary, Freud sought to understand why people behaved as they did and why they experienced some of the struggles and inner conflicts they did. He approached these questions by listening to his patients and developing insights and postulates he could check and recheck. He was profoundly impressed with the drive for pleasure and its manifold manifestations, which he subsumed under the sexual drive. He identified antecedents of the varied behaviors in infantile experiences. He did not seek to pass judgment on human behavior, but simply to understand it, and to enable those people who felt hurt and uncomfortable to change.

chapter 18

C. G. JUNG ON MALE AND FEMALE

Ann Belford Ulanov

Sexuality holds a place at the center of Jung's theory of the psyche. It is a principal modality of the human for Jung, a means by which we approach the depths of our own unconscious and relate to life, to other people around us, and to God. The essence of Jung's perception of the meaning of human sexuality is to be found in his theory of contrasexuality. There, a radical reordering of values and a new kind of intellectual comprehension can under certain circumstances come together to initiate nothing less than a revolution within the personality.

BASIC TERMS

Jung believed that within every person there are elements of the opposite sex. This contrasexual core, which Jung calls the *anima* in the male personality and the *animus* in the female, performs the specific psychic function of connecting the conscious male or female ego-identity with the deeper regions of the unconscious which Jung calls the *objective psyche*.[1] Jung calls this deep unconscious layer of the psyche objective because our subjective ego-consciousness gradually emerges out of its prior existence and continues to experience that existence as other than itself, alien to its own subjective ego-territory. In contrast to what Jung calls the personal layer of the unconscious, whose contents consist of repressed memories and traits which can be recalled to consciousness and experienced as belonging to the ego, the contents of the objective psyche, the *archetypes*, are more impersonal and collective in nature and hence harder to integrate into conscious adaptation.[2]

We never meet an archetype directly; it is only Jung's verbal concept to describe the effects of the deep unconscious upon our conscious ego adaptation. When we experience this archetypal level of the psyche, we feel in the grip of some force that is not our own. We feel confronted or borne along by an autonomous energy drive that is not really at our disposal; rather, we are its to deal with. This force invades us like an impersonal "other" that mixes in with our most personal reactions, often forcing them to veer off course. An uncontrollable emotional outburst may, for example, take possession of us, leading us to wonder, after it has passed, what got into us. Accompanying these spontaneous emotional and behavioral reactions are images that have much to tell us about the meaning of what we are experiencing if only we could understand them.[3]

Central among the archetypes of the objective psyche are the contrasexual anima and animus.[4] Our initial experiences of the objective psyche usually come in our more significant confrontations with sexuality, with persons of our own and the opposite sex.

THE STRUCTURE OF THE CONTRASEXUAL ELEMENT

The structure of the contrasexual element in our personalities consists of three factors. The first is biological: composed of the recessive genes of the opposite sex that reside in our bodies. The second is cultural: our images of masculine and feminine, shaped by the influence of significant members of the opposite sex in our own lives and the dominant types of male and female operating in our own culture. The third is psychological: the symbolic images of the masculine and feminine, accumulated over centuries of human experience, that lie dormant in our own unconscious, waiting to be activated by our encounters with the opposite sex. These images exert a shaping but not absolutely determinative influence on our experience of sexuality.

THE FUNCTION OF THE CONTRASEXUAL ELEMENT

The contrasexual archetype functions like any other archetype: it operates unconsciously and autonomously within the psyche. It often seems to have a life of its own which frequently conflicts with our clear intentions and values. Thus, to the conscious ego the anima or animus seems to be an impersonal "other" that confronts the ego from outside itself. Somehow the ego must learn to bring this force into connection with its own personal identity. Jung coined the words "anima" and "animus" as a result of observing in countless

patients split-off sides of the psyche recurrently appearing in personified forms as male or female figures. One common example was the
overly rational male who consistently dreamed of being confronted
by an emotional and sexy female who tempted him into "irrational"
behavior. On awakening, the dreamer still felt possessed by the
mood of this dream anima-figure, invaded by a bittersweet mixture of
excitement and longing. This anima-lure is typical of the way the
unconscious tries to acquaint the one-sided ego with affects and impulses it has excluded from its conscious functioning. This is what
Jung means when he says that the function of the contrasexual factor
is to lead us to the deeper realms of the objective psyche. The anima-
figure points the way, in this example, to the split-off nonrational
side of life.

The animus and the anima take on personified form in dreams or
fantasies when they are not functioning properly in us, not acting to
connect the ego and the objective psyche. One way or another, these
personifications work to bring the unconscious to consciousness in
each of us. When the unconscious is ignored by consciousness, the
animus or anima is unconsciously projected outward onto people of
the opposite sex.[5] It greets us then from outside ourselves, even
though it is in fact part of our inner selves. When we do this—project
a part of us onto other persons—we do not see who others really are.
Our projections present us only with illusory versions of other persons and thus increasingly isolate us from other people, wrapping us
as they do in a cocoon of falsifying images. Caught as we are in our
own autoerotic circle we insist all the more loudly that other persons
do not understand us, as indeed they do not, because we are not
reaching them at all. Moreover, what we are projecting belongs to us
more than to them and really must be understood by us, not by them.

Relationships that endure and grow between the sexes invariably
involve the sorting out of the mutual projections and unconscious
expectations that one partner imposes on the other. If successful, this
is a process of psychological differentiation that promotes an ever
deepening relationship, one that never ceases to be lively and en-
grossing to the partners. Without such psychological differentiation,
most relationships between the sexes fall into well-worn ruts that
lead to stifling boredom or disintegrate into misunderstanding and
suspicion.

DIFFERENTIATION OF THE CONTRASEXUAL: THE BODY

Our efforts to differentiate our egos from unconscious identification with the anima or animus in our personalities take three forms,

in keeping with the biological, cultural, and psychic structure of the contrasexual factor. The first is the biological: we must reflect on how we feel living in our own bodies with their particular male or female structure; on what body-image we have of being a woman or a man; and on whether or not these physical facts of our particular body with its workings (such as, for a woman, menstruation, capacity to give birth, menopause) conflict in any degree with other self-images or with urges for development that would take us in different directions. A familiar example is the conflict for women between wanting a family and a career. A woman needs to be aware of the degree to which her sexual behavior is influenced unconsciously by an instinctive urge on the biological level toward pregnancy. For example, a woman may not consciously want children; but she must take into careful consideration the degree to which she is instinctively urged toward conception, simply on a biological level. The failure of women to do so may account for the great number of consciously unwanted pregnancies in present day society, despite the widespread availability of simple birth-control methods. We are not locked into what our bodies want, but we do live in our bodies and we cannot disregard their effect on us and on our lives. Coming to terms with the contrasexual factor of our personalities means trying to become conscious of images that seem opposed to our sexual anatomy and that seem to want to pull us in directions very different from our familiar procedures. These are directions we may choose to take, but we must do so in full consciousness.

BISEXUALITY

Jung's emphasis on the body gives us a way to understand what is positive and what is negative in the currently popular notion of bisexuality. In its root meaning, bisexuality denotes being of two sexes in one body. The appeal of this notion is that it conveys the fact that none of us is exclusively male or female and that a whole person must develop both aspects of his or her sexuality. But how we do this makes all the difference in the world. If we unconsciously identify with the contrasexual element in our personalities rather than consciously integrating it, we take bisexuality literally rather than symbolically. We live our contrasexual side on the outside, as if our bodies were equipped with exchangeable parts, acting out male and female roles interchangeably with persons of the same and the opposite sex.

In contrast, Jung stresses the facticity of each particular body, with its particular sexual anatomy. Though we may have a contrasexual element in our personality, we still have a dominant sexual identity as male or female. Our body is the fleshly and the spiritual and the psychological place where we live and through which we touch and are touched by others. Hence to live in a body structured as female is to live in a different arrangement of "being in the world" than it is to live in a body-space structured as male. As our ego emerges from the unconscious it comes to conscious self-identity first through the body-ego. Thus our way of differentiating ego-consciousness from the unconscious and of finding a place in the world for ourselves is vastly different as a result of our female or male anatomy.

CULTURE

The second approach in coming to terms with the contrasexual element in our personalities is to gather into consciousness all the relevant sources of cultural conditioning of our images of male and female. First among these is the role our fathers and mothers have played in shaping our picture of the opposite sex. We need to become conscious of how much our notion of "man" or "woman" is a reflection of our parents' personalities. Failing to do so, we may find ourselves endlessly reliving the dynamics of our relationship with the parent of the opposite sex in all our adult relationships with members of the opposite sex. For example, a woman who is unaware that her animus is all but an exact replica of her father will unconsciously choose only those men with whom she can repeat the same problems she had with her father. She may be unable to establish any close relationship to a man because "her heart belongs to Daddy." This aspect of animus entanglement is explored in great imaginative depth in Freud's Oedipus-Electra formulations.

In addition to recognizing parental influence, a person coming to conscious terms with contrasexuality must become aware of other significant members of the opposite sex—siblings, cousins, teachers, public figures—who contribute to his or her dominant images of male or female. Cultural stereotypes vividly condition one's images of men and women, as for example the television and magazine pictures of the strong "masculine" figure alone with his cigarette and horse, or the "feminine" woman almost always portrayed as an infinitely maternal laundress or cook on the one hand or as a dazzling sexual object on the other. Cultural images of male and female do influence and contaminate our relation to sexuality, but Jung's theory of contrasexuality takes sharp exception to those culturalists who assert that sexual identity is a product *only* of cultural conditioning. Such a view reduces the body and psyche to mere puppets of cultural influence. In trying to change cultural traditions we must respect the unconscious roots of those traditions which grow deep beneath the surface and hold fast despite our declared intentions to alter them. One sees, for example, the man who consciously professes himself an ardent supporter of feminism but who unconsciously exhibits the most flagrant prejudice against women; he is apt to take advantage of young women struggling to throw off the double standard applied to sexual behavior, by accusing them of not *really* being liberated from the stereotype of the "old fashioned" virgin if they resist his sexual advances. Another common example of a man unconsciously dominated by archetypal images of women is the one who really objects to some positions taken by feminists but will not say so because he fears an explosion of female wrath against himself. For him, unconsciously at least, a woman is still surrounded with the magic power of the great mother who must not be defied. As a result, a modern woman is dehumanized for him, unconsciously mythologized instead of met in a vigorous discussion and exchange of viewpoints and dealt with as a human being of individual qualities that are all her own.

ANDROGYNY

Many contemporary persons who argue that all sexual identification is merely the product of cultural conditioning see as the goal of their efforts to change cultural stereotypes the ideal of the androgynous human being. And indeed androgyny is an ideal—an image of the unification of the two sexes which represent symbolically, physically, and culturally two different ways of being human. Where there were two opposites warring against each other, now there is one harmonious being. As an image of human wholeness this has its proper appeal. But to those living concretely in the world of men and women in space and time, and seeking to achieve that unification, the image yields little of practical value. We cannot get beyond sexual identity until we have gotten to it and through it to the other side. If the image of androgyny is taken literally instead of symbolically, we simply try to skip over the concrete human tasks of learning to live as men and women in relation to each other. More often than not we fall into unconscious identity with the presexual stage of personality development, where differentiation of sex has not yet even occurred. Instead of being both male and female in an androgynous wholeness, we are neither male nor female, having regressed to a psychological stage of presexual infantilism. We cannot simply wish or legislate away the centuries of traditional sexual roles. We can change them by building something new, but that means concrete, arduous work, bringing unconscious materials into consciousness.

THE PSYCHOLOGICAL

This brings us to the third way we come to terms with the anima or animus—the psychological approach. Jung makes an important distinction between archetypal symbols of masculine and feminine and concrete male or female persons. Archetypal symbols refer to images and to behavioral and emotional response patterns that invade our personalities and motivate our behavior without our knowing so. These images and patterns are unconscious, autonomous, and impersonal; hence they do not and cannot apply to our consciousness directly, let alone prescriptively to actual men and women. They are pictures of types of female and male behavioral and emotional response, such as those personified in mythological gods—the fiery aspect of male aggression symbolized by Mars and his warlike propensities, or the consuming life-killing destructiveness of feminine wrath symbolized by the Indian goddess Kali who devours her children.

Through his researches into mythology, Eastern and Western religious traditions, and alchemy, Jung found that the symbolism collected around the poles of masculine and feminine has a significance far beyond its obvious relevance to sexual categories. The symbols of masculine and feminine polarity stand for all the central polarities of life, such as spirit-soul, height-depth, conscious-unconscious, light-dark, heaven-earth.[6] In the history of mythologies and religion, these opposites are almost always characterized in terms of the masculine and feminine. The unity and harmony of masculine and feminine, therefore, symbolizes the reconciliation of life's opposites in a workable way. To lose access to either the masculine or feminine pole, then, is to lose access to a large part of one's humanity. The results of the loss of connection to the feminine pole, so common in our time, are far too frequently illustrated in the contemptuous attitudes taken by men against women working to gain equal opportunity for a full life in employment, in politics, in every aspect of their lives and persons. Equally serious is the plight of men·cut off from the grounding in their own depths, which conscious connection with the anima could give them. We see, for example, the frequent splitting off of a man's actions from what he professes to believe, a split that has had tragic consequences for our world.

THE FEMININE IN MEN: THE ANIMA

The concepts of anima and animus are attempts to describe the various ways the wide range of symbolism associated with the opposite sex presents itself to an individual's ego-consciousness. Through the anima, for example, a man experiences his own feminine qualities and constructs his image of the feminine, introjected to consciousness and to his unconscious from significant females in his life. There is also the nonpersonal side of the anima, which, when properly functioning, introduces him to age-old symbols of woman that lie dormant in the male's unconscious. The anima opens the deeper layers of the unconscious to a man's ego through images of the feminine in its typical forms—mother, wise woman, helpmate, maiden in distress, tigress, temptress, amazon, and so forth. Which of these archetypes of the feminine is called into play in a given man's life depends on his circumstances. If he wants to be all of himself, however, he must come to terms with as many aspects of this contrasexual factor as possible, for it symbolizes in its images and instinctive dynamism the other half of being human, the feminine way. Without access to the contrasexual life in him, he is only half a man, standing on one leg in relation to his own unconscious and in his relations to women.

The symbolism attached to the feminine is vast and complicated, pointing to a different tempo from the much more familiar rhythms of the masculine and the accompanying arrangement of the human functions of thinking, acting, and creating.[7] In keeping with its symbolism as earth, deep waters, dark womb, and unfathomable depths, the dynamism of the feminine is represented symbolically as leading downward from conscious to unconscious, from abstractions to concrete realities, from distance to nearness. No wonder there is such clamor for inclusion of the feminine in church hierarchies! Christianity suffers from being too dry, too much removed, too much abstracted from human beings and where they live. It needs the blood and passionate involvement associated with the feminine modality of being human.

No wonder there is such fear of including the feminine! Every archetype has a dual aspect—positive and negative. The positive value of getting right into the midst of things that so characterizes the "eros principle of relatedness," as Jung describes the feminine modality, is countered by the fear aroused in a man of being dragged down beyond his depths, beyond the reach of the counsels of reason and common sense.[8] Another cluster of archetypal images surrounding the feminine is associated with the female as caster of evil spells, a witchlike bringer of madness—lunacy as associated with the dark side of the moon, the symbol *par excellence* of the feminine.

Side by side with the death-dealing images of feminine symbolism, there is her image as bringer of life, as the fleshly mother who gives birth biologically and the spiritual mother to whom we must return if we would be reborn. Thus the symbol of Sophia represents a high form of wisdom in whom are gathered all the opposites of life, a figure tolerating and dissolving all the contradictions in a higher unity. Life is also quickened by the frank sexual symbolism associated with the feminine. The anima is familiar enough in men's dreams as the one who excites a passion so compelling that the dreamers often feel they would give up all in order to follow the passion. Behind this sexual symbolism is a call of the spirit that asks the average man to venture, like a hero of old, to the unknown regions of the unconscious to recover the precious treasure of his soul. Jung calls the anima the "archetype of life itself," behind which stands the wisdom of the unconscious.[9]

THE MASCULINE IN WOMEN: THE ANIMUS

In contrast to the anima, the animus represents in female psychology the masculine as it operates in a woman. Archetypally, the animus represents spirit, not as an intellectual formula but as the attitude by which a woman lives. Over against the instinctive reactions of nature, so strongly associated with all the biological processes of the feminine in its maternal mode, the masculine as spirit points to all those focused and unfocused aspirations for the sake of which we would strive against our natural tendencies. This is spirit as the force that lifts us out of unconscious identification with our bodies and our emotions and yet without excluding them from our lives. As Jung points out, ideally a girl gets a picture from her father of the spirit by which life is lived. From association with him she can draw hints that "may suffice to make clear what kind of spirit it is that the daughter needs. They are the truths which speak to the soul, which are not too loud and do not insist too much, but reach the individual in stillness. . . ."[10]

No wonder so many young women, especially in religious circles, are consumed with anger at what they call the "patriarchs"! They feel—consciously or unconsciously—that their fathers have failed them, their own fathers and the fathers of the church. Instead of a sense of truth to live by, they feel they have been given intellectual formulations that parch the spirit rather than quicken it. Instead of being given a guiding attitude that includes body and soul, with all their privileges and responsibilities, women have been excluded from the full life of the church. The fact that they have not been given the images and examples and offices of the life-guiding spirit is no excuse, however, for their failing to find it for themselves.

Women's outrage, and their blaming of the fathers, too often merely imitates what they wish to repudiate. They are too easily caught in a pseudo-masculinity, living their animus on the outside. Like Adam's cowardly self-justification through accusations directed at Eve, they project the blame outward rather than take up the task of completing the lack in themselves.

The animus, for Jung, is not simply derived from one's biology and personal biography compounded by cultural conditioning. The animus also has a foot in the nonpersonal world of the objective psyche. Through that archetypal side the animus presents a woman's ego with typical images, behavioral and emotional responses associated with the masculine for centuries. Central to this range of symbolism is the masculine as a discriminating force, what Jung calls "the logos principle," that leads upward from dark unconsciousness to clear conscious differentiation.[11] The animus is manifested instinctually in a woman as an urge to penetrate and probe, to poke into things, to search into inner depths, and bring up long buried contents to the light of reflective consciousness. If left unrelated to a woman's ego, this phallic dynamism of the animus runs wild. We see it in such unrelated behavior on a woman's part as her pervasive curiosity that blunders into things that are simply not her business just for the sake of pushing ahead—gossip for example, or her tendency to a persistent and compulsive nagging that pushes and pushes, less for a stated goal than just to see how far she can push.

In its intellectual presentation, the animus drive to discriminate shows itself in a woman's personality as an impetus toward focused differentiation of elements into their proper categories, no matter how minute. If this animus is well related to a woman's ego it often shows itself as a capacity to make remarkably articulate descriptions of the most murky subject matter and to bring clarity where only fuzziness has dwelled before. If insufficiently integrated, however, this capacity for focus and articulation fails to find its proper place. A woman then falls into a volubility about general truths that just does not apply to particular situations. With remarkable insensitivity, such a woman keeps missing the mark of what she wants to say, becoming increasingly and painfully frustrated with her listener for refusing, as she sees it, to hear her and to understand her point.

When the animus functions to help a woman focus on what she cares about, and to bring it up from her deepest feelings to share or display to others, the force of the truth by which she lives is stunning and the most effective silencer of so-called male chauvinism. To this sort of woman a man submits willingly because he senses that she is deeply connected to what is true, or would like to be, and is therefore trustworthy. A symbolic example of such a person and the kind of event she invokes is the parable of the anointing of Christ by the mysterious Mary (whether the Magdalene or Mary of Bethany or some other). She pours out upon Christ sweet-smelling unguent, to the astonishment and disapproval of the disciples. Such a costly oil should have been sold and the money given to the poor, they protest. But Jesus defends her, accepting her love and her intuitive perception of his coming crucifixion. He even says, and its relevance in this context should not be missed, "Why trouble ye the woman? For she hath wrought a good work upon me. For ye have the poor always with you, but me ye have not always. For in that she hath poured this ointment on my body, she did it for my burial" (Matt. 26:10–12).

Thus in the face of hostile criticism, she rests on her own authority and follows what she perceives to be true. As a result she is the first, if not the only, person who prepares Jesus for his death, taking on the awesome task of ministering to Christ. Moreover, she ministers to him a love that includes the sexual dimension rather than excludes it, and reaches beyond it into the dark probings of the spirit.

When the animus functions to connect a woman's ego to her own unconscious, it puts at her disposal the resources of the unconscious. Paradoxically, this helps her to see more clearly what is presented to her consciousness. By being related directly to her unconscious she projects less of it outward. Hence she sees what is really there rather than what she thinks or wishes were there. An example of this clarity of vision, and the durable capacity to contemplate reality that comes with it, is the group of women named Mary in the Gospel. They were the only ones to stay by Jesus at the end. They saw him clearly as Lord when all others turned away. They were able to endure the last stripping away of illusion projected onto him by his followers— accepting that he was not the human version of a mighty conqueror, nor would he or could he be always the famous miracle worker. More intimately, these women were able to endure the stripping away of their own personal illusions that they probably would have liked to project onto him—seeing him as lover, faithful son, fatherly authority who would always remain with them, the always enduring teacher of the new way. These women alone saw him through the worst of his life on earth and were the first to receive the news of his triumph over death.

If the animus is not connected to a woman's ego, but operates only autonomously, in her unconscious, a woman is particularly vulnerable to enslavement to an outside cause or authority upon whom she will unconsciously project her animus. Her authority is now located outside herself in a cause or movement or person she finds irresistible and must follow to the end. How much she is unconsciously animus-dominated can be gauged in terms of how she treats people who do not agree with her cause or ideas. If she is immediately incited to harangue them or icily to dismiss them as enemies, the chances are that she has fallen under the sway of animus-projection.

PERSONS AND TRANSFORMATION

Jung's theory of contrasexuality brings us to the threshold of something new in our understanding of the human—a conception of the whole person as defined by a distinct male or female identity and an integrated contrasexual side. This theory can help guide us through the danger of being caught in stereotyped sex roles on the one hand or in a formless lack of identity on the other. With contrasexual theory, we can understand homosexuality as a variant way of relating to the contrasexual archetype in the personality, in which persons identify with this archetype and act it out on the outside instead of realizing it as a connecting link to the unconscious that dwells unheeded, inside.

The theory of contrasexuality enables us to see the task before us, the ways each of us must work to develop an individual sexual identity, finding it among the factors of physical anatomy, cultural conditioning, and archetypal symbols that are active in our psyches. People who succeed in integrating their contrasexual sides in these ways seem to be more vibrantly female or male, full of a life-force that radiates outward from a deep, inner sufficiency.

In a world that seems all but overpowered by mass-mindedness and bureaucratic red tape, where everyone feels mistreated and no one is responsible, we may find our salvation lies in repersonalizing the world. To do this we need to feel we are persons whose actions in our own lives have an effect on the outer collectivity. This is really possible if as individual persons we come into better personal relationship with the inner collectivity of the objective psyche which the contrasexual side of our personalities opens to us. Without a working relationship to our own unconscious we remain shuttered to our real selves and closed to others, going our own way often at cross purposes to our own conscious needs and desires. In religion, for example, many people want to believe and want to live out their faith, but this is wishing more often than fact. There is no unconscious wellspring for their faith, no living presence that holds all of them at ease and at peace with themselves. Their religion has lost touch with its own unconscious dimension. As a result, what was once numinous has degenerated into sentimentality and a drive for power. They wish the church would somehow revive, but they have nothing to offer toward renewal except ethical maxims, political platitudes, a large rhetoric of commonplaces preached more than lived.

To recognize aspects of one's own contrasexual side, and to venture into the depths of the unconscious that this opens to consciousness, is to be led beyond the concerns of sexual identity. Not only are we changed in our own personalities, but astonishingly enough, it is as if the stuff of the unconscious has also undergone some fundamental transformation. As was said earlier, the symbolism of the masculine-feminine polarity represents all the polarities of life that reach the psyche. To arrive at new mixtures and combinations of the ancient polarities of masculine and feminine through an integration of one's contrasexual side, is to influence the central ways reality is, or will be, perceived in our culture. Jung's theory of contrasexuality promises the fullness of being human, an increase in humanization that must affect unconscious life itself.

NOTES

1. See C. G. Jung, *Two Essays in Analytical Psychology*, trans., R. F. C. Hull (New York: World, 1967), pp. 76ff., 82, 100ff., 120, 150ff., 159, 164, 166ff., 170f., 180, 283ff., 313n. Jung also calls this part of the psyche the "collective psyche."

2. Jung says of archetypes: "Archetypes are, by definition, factors and motifs that arrange the psychic elements into certain images, characterized as archetypal, but in such a way that they can be recognized only from the effects they produce. They exist preconsciously, and presumably they form the structural dominants of the psyche in general. They may be compared to the invisible presence of the crystal lattice in a saturated solution. As *a priori* conditioning factors they represent a special, psychological instance of the biological 'pattern of behavior,' which gives all living organisms their specific qualities. Just as the manifestations of this biological ground plan may change in the course of development, so also can those of the archetype. Empirically considered, however, the archetype did not ever come into existence as a phenomenon of organic life, but entered into the picture with life itself." "A Psychological Approach to the Trinity," in *Collected Works*, vol. XI, trans. R. F. C. Hull (New York: Pantheon, 1958), p. 149n.

3. For a discussion of the behavioral, emotional, and image-like aspects of the archetype, see A. B. Ulanov, *The Feminine: In Jungian Psychology and in Christian Theology* (Evanston: Northwestern University Press, 1971), pp. 45–58.

4. See C. G. Jung, *Two Essays*, pp. 198–224, and C. G. Jung, *Aion: Researches into the Phenomenology of the Self*, in *Collected Works*, vol. 9, II., trans., R. F. C. Hull (New York: Pantheon, 1959), pp. 11–23.

5. For a discussion of projection, see C. G. Jung, *Psychological*

Types, Collected Works, vol. 6, trans. R. F. C. Hull (New York: Pantheon), pp. 457–458.

6. See Ulanov, *op. cit.,* pp. 143–145.

7. See C. G. Jung, *Mysterium Conjunctionis, Collected Works,* vol. 14, trans. R. F. C. Hull (New York: Pantheon, 1963), pp. 106, 108n, 135, 163, 233, 241, 379–380, 426–428.

8. *Ibid.,* pp. 179ff.

9. *Ibid.,* p. 452.

10. *Ibid.,* pp. 182–183.

11. *Ibid.,* pp. 135, 179ff., 428.

PART V

Theological Perspectives

chapter 19

THEOLOGY OF MARRIAGE

Rosemary Haughton

To get a full grasp of what the phrase "theology of marriage" means we have to make a great effort to get away from one kind of notion of theology, which is that it is a ready-made set of ideas and principles, bestowed on mankind at some point in history, and thereafter needing only to be elaborated and elucidated. Theology is a discovery, a perpetually renewed search for understanding of "the ways of God to man." It is under the inspiration of the Spirit, always, but depends for its scope at any given time on the human experience—events, concepts, words—available to bring it within reach of real, historical people. So, although truth itself, the eternal wisdom, is unchanging, the discovery of truth and wisdom by human beings is a long, strange, and unpredictable voyage of exploration, in which new kingdoms are discovered in every era. Old insights are added to new ones, modifying both and enriching the Christian heritage of each generation with new treasure. Yet the search is never over, the full wisdom is always beyond the reach of human language, however inspired.

Theology grows from the relationship of God and man, and man's share of the work is dependent on historical experience. This is true even of such apparently abstract doctrines as that of the Holy Trinity, whose development owed much to the particular kinds of philosophical concepts which were the "language" of theological discussion at the time. This is all the more obviously true of the theology of marriage, whose development has passed through some dramatic changes, as marriage customs shifted through tremendous cultural upheavals.

This essay is too short to permit of even a summary of the history of Christian ideas about marriage, but one or two ideas picked out from the great store of historically acquired wisdom really help in understanding our present situation. One of the most important, for instance, in Christian thinking about the God-relatedness of marriage comes from the pre-Christian inheritance, and acquired special (and unique) character from the paradoxical fact that Hebrew religion, alone among those of neighboring peoples with whom they otherwise shared much of religion and custom, attached no magical or ritual significance to sex. Not only was sex not used in worship of the Hebrews' God, it was kept at a distance, literally and symbolically, from all ritual occasions. This has often been regarded as proof of Old Testament puritanism, but even a cursory reading of Scripture banishes this idea. The Israelites were not prudish, rather their attitudes to sexuality, marriage, and child bearing were based on a sense of human worth in relation to God. Sex was human, not divine. There was one God, Yahweh, Father-Mother, source of all, but not a sexual being such as populated the great pantheons of other nations. Yahweh blessed human fertility, and sanctified that of his own people, so that they might raise up more sons to Israel. For the same reason sex was surrounded with a careful and even fierce hedge of law, to ensure the protection of marriage and its offspring, and to preserve the children of Israel from the danger of involvement with foreign ideas and loyalties through marriage outside the fold of Israel.

So marriage was *both* secular *and* holy to the Lord. Sex had no powers, but it was important and could be holy. Divorce was allowed, but as a regrettable failure; the norm, applauded and honored, was lifelong fidelity and real conjugal love, and these were signs of God's favor and blessing.

At the same time and, as it were, side by side with this very practical view of sexual relationship, the prophets of Israel, as time went on, developed an understanding of the nature of the Lord's covenant with his people which they found it most suitable to express in terms of human love and marriage. The totally transcendent, asexual character of Yahweh was so profoundly rooted at the heart of Hebrew religious culture that it was possible to make such a comparison, and to elaborate and celebrate it without in any way weakening the sense of the divine otherness. In the period of the exile and after, when the covenant relationship could no longer be thought of as a promise of political domination, the bridal relationship of Yahweh and Israel became a way of understanding the vocation of the chosen people. They were the beloved, the one true "wife" among many other peoples, courted and cherished, repeatedly rescued from infidelity, forgiven, reconciled, and brought home to her rightful husband.

The purpose of such meditations was to make sense of the stormy and perplexing history of the people, to give them a conviction of being beloved, of having a purpose in their national existence in spite of all that defeats and disillusion could do. Yet to use such an image shows that the marriage relationship itself appeared to the Jewish people to be one of tremendous value, humanly and divinely. The tenderness, patience, endurance, and generosity which are attributed to this union of God with his people are evidence that such qualities were desired and admired in marriage. Human marriage was being recognized as a *means of holiness,* a way of God's love, not merely of genealogical necessity.

This sense of the human graciousness of the marriage relationship, informed and sanctified for God's purposes while never ceasing to be human, has stamped the Christian theology of marriage. It has suffered from many aberrations, as cultural changes seized on men's minds, but this constant and ordering theme was never wholly lost and reasserted itself steadily. When this theme is sounded, we recognize the Christian mind once more playing over its essential statement, which is incarnational. The word and wisdom of God is expressed in bodies and minds, historically existing in particular places and cultures, loving and begetting in the light of eternity. Yet all this is human and temporal—not eternal, not divine—but the love growing in this bodily life, and *only* in this bodily life, is of the stuff of eternal, divine life.

This delicate sense of the essential polarity of human life illumined by the incarnate wisdom is easy to distort. Over and over again the balance has been lost, and only painfully recovered. Christianity burst into its first self-knowledge with a strong sense of the God-bearing quality of human love. This is reflected not only in Paul's famous bridal metaphor of Christ and his beloved, the church (and this is a direct linear descent from the Jewish prophets on whose words he was reared) but much more importantly in the constant emphasis on the need for the nurturing of love between believers and toward all men, even the persecutors. Down to earth service, loyalty, joy in companionship, and mutual reverence of God's workers for each other; care of the sick, the insecure, and the lonely; hospitality and generous giving—these things were meant to be, and visibly were the marks of the heirs of the kingdom. In this context, married love found its position. It was not singled out but was part of the whole economy of Christian life. It presented moral and religious problems, and it seemed sometimes that it would be better to remain unwed and be without those particular problems—but nobody suggested it was tainted with evil. Yet within a few decades the fear of the flesh, absorbed through contact with gnostic sects and writers, had gained so strong a hold on the spiritual consciousness of Christianity that it became easy to *except* sexual love from other kinds of love, and even to regard it with loathing because it was unequivocally bodily and pleasurable. The Fathers of the Church, though they were often saintly and courageous and loving men, produced a corpus of antisex and antiwoman literature which has provided those who regard Christianity as essentially antilife and joyless with all the ammunition they could possibly want.

Later, the Romance doctrines sought to establish the spiritual value of sexual love in the unpredictable godlike power of passion, especially unsatisfied and illicit passion, holding in contempt the bonds of domestic loyalties. At another extreme, canon law and the mentality it fostered tried to codify and control sex and marriage in terms of purely bodily acts and words, regarding emotions as outside its scope and even as tiresome irrelevancies. At times, procreation was regarded as the punishment laid on woman for being preeminently a "fleshly" creature, a view which made it possible to resist as immoral any attempts to make childbirth less than painful. Indeed, the whole history of Christian attitudes to women does not make pretty reading. To write about this as it deserves would unbalance the shape of this essay, but the reasons behind it, conscious and (above all) unconscious, need to be considered with very great care as we struggle to renew our understanding of Christian marriage.

One could go on listing the aberrations of Christians in relation to sex and marriage, and notice the heavy legacy of legalism that still burdens the Catholic tradition, and the equally harsh and inhuman effects in the Protestant one of a cult of domestic respectability and order as a test of Christian acceptability. To go into all this in a short essay is impossible, but it is important for two reasons to remember how easily and constantly Christians have drastically failed to assert the incarnational balance in the theology of marriage. One reason is that the errors show that we can never come to a "definitive" understanding of God's work in human sexuality, so the Christian mind and heart has constantly to renew its search for the proper balance, realizing the limitations of the human search yet confident that "the full stature of Christ" *is* somehow growing within and through all the failures and fresh starts. The other reason is that, over and over again, the mistakes were necessary, in the curious way in which such things work, because it was only by exaggerating, in good faith, some aspect of human sexuality that the real nature of that aspect could be fully seen, and later properly appreciated. For instance, the Romantic exaggeration of the value of passionate sexual feeling made it possible, much later, to recognize the "converting" power of sexual love in *marriage* to deepen and strengthen the relationship. It also gave a clue to the reason *why* marriage has been regarded by some Christians as a sacrament and by others as a specially "honorable" state in God's eyes, since the spiritual illumination between two people, which can go with the experience of passion, has that cleansing and ennobling power that we recognize, by hindsight, as typical of the converting work of the spirit in mankind.

In the same way, the legalistic emphasis which still affects our attitudes to marital status began in an attempt to protect the institution of marriage from cynical manipulation by power-seeking dynasties and a land-hungry nobility, and to uphold the right of even the humblest to a stable marriage, safe from the lust of a capricious overlord. It protected women from casual abandonment and children from being bastardized when a new wife proved better endowed. The reliance on a "law" of marriage, couched in terms purely of bodily acts and words and leaving feelings out of account, has caused terrible abuses, yet it is now enabling us to realize that we do need this element of objective support for fidelity and continuity in marriage, since we have discovered, to our chagrin, that reliance on unbridled feeling can be even more tyrannical and cruel. The woman deserted in favor of a more "real" love, the children bewildered by loss of parents self-absorbed in search of "fulfillment," the embittered young people caught up in emotions whose strength they had never been taught to recognize until it was too late, are all sufferers from a lack of that sense of "norms" to be observed in sexual matters, which can harm when used alone, yet which are necessary when kept in proper balance.

The theology of marriage has lurched through the centuries, falling to one side or the other, rising to new insights and glories, learning and relearning, repenting and renewing itself. So where are we now?

Certainly not at the end of the road. We have to keep on relearning, but we do not have to go back and begin again. Christian marriage has a history, and it is *part* of us, part of our whole way of thinking and feeling, whether we feel it positively or negatively. And we can consciously learn from that history, indeed if we do not we shall join the ranks of those who "will not learn from history and therefore are destined to repeat it"—a depressing prospect indeed.

The institution of marriage is in a difficult situation, because in the West the old culture is visibly crumbling, and people no longer easily take for granted the institutions it created and maintained. The *moral consent* which makes a way of life generally acceptable has gone, or is under such stress that it cannot long survive. The ideals of fidelity, virginity before marriage, and close family bonds grew to their peak of popular esteem in the last century, when the disruption of other kinds of close-knit communities by the industrial revolution had made family stability more important than ever before. No matter how often people failed to live up to them, the "moral consent" of society supported them in principle, and embodied the principles in law as far as possible.

The effect of a period of comparative affluence and increased state support for the needy has been to make the close-knit family less essential to society. With the collapse of the "moral consent" which gave marriage external support, the internal pressures found little resistance. Many sincere Christians now question, not only the harshness of past treatment of sexual and marital "offenders," but ask whether the ideals are worth anything positive at all. Cannot love be expressed sexually on a temporary basis, or with more than one person over a long period? Must children have just two "parents"? Is fidelity really a form of possessiveness?

These questions are sincerely asked, but very often the people who ask them fail to recognize the essential preconceptions which make it possible for them to talk in this way. For all such questions assume that the marriage relationship is a matter of emotional adjustment and development for the people concerned. This is a very "middle-class liberal" view, only possible for people who take economic and political security for granted and can envisage a life in which a great deal of mental and emotional energy can be spent on sorting out sexual feelings and finding the most satisfying combinations possible. The historical fact is that marriage is an arrangement of sexual and generational relationships which is intended to stabilize this aspect of life in order to allow people to get their living—to *survive*, in fact. There have been many marriage patterns, some including several wives or husbands, and in some cases comparatively easy divorce, but all the regulations of the most disparate forms tend toward creating a stable and accepted arrangement of relationships, within which people know who and what they are, and what is expected of them, thus freeing psychic energy for the labor of farming, ruling, making things, teaching, healing, organizing, and so on. A society which has for several decades deluded itself into assuming that it is *bound* to survive can feel able to ignore this necessity, and concentrate on emotional fulfillment in a way which was previously possible only for a tiny minority of economically privileged people.

It is worth emphasizing this sociological fact, because it helps to "place" some of the discussions at present developing about the Christian notion of marriage. There is no doubt that the institutional forms of marriage are changing, as they often have before, because cultural changes require it. There is no doubt, also, that we are not in a position to direct the outcome of the changes, nor even to predict them with any accuracy. What we can do is to avoid being jostled into false positions based on insufficiently examined premises, and at the same time we can try to understand the essential theological insights by which Christians have to try to understand, interpret, and modify whatever sexual patterns emerge in a particular society.

This is not easy, because there is a natural tendency to mix up essentials with what is familiar and traditional, so that both are treated as equally unalterable or else both are rejected when customs change, the trouble being that no one distinguishes what *is* essential.

Can we ever do so? We can to some extent, provided we can accept the notion that there is no perfect form of marriage, but only better or worse attempts to find, cherish, and develop within the secular reality those limits and images and experiences which belong, here and now, to the kingdom of God. The Jewish religious genius managed to take the marriage customs common to the surrounding tribes and discover and develop in them that sense of the transcendent love within the human which has become an essential Christian insight.

The same thing has to be done with the sexual chaos in which we flounder. It consists of remnants (quite large ones) of inherited forms of marriage; a genuine longing for deeper and more human sexual relationships; a lot of wishful thinking, some experimental pattern of marriage (both quite hopeful-looking ones and totally unrealistic ones); and a large element of uncertainty about *any* kind of overt personal commitment, sometimes amounting to a sort of phobia.

How on earth can we make theological sense of all this? I think we are bound to make many mistakes, but we can avoid the really disastrous ones by trying hard not to treat marriage as an isolated experience. The essential thing seems to be indicated, for instance, by St. Paul's use of the phrase "in the Lord." To him, the living of daily life and relationship, for a Christian, took place "in the Lord." For a generation expecting the imminent return of Christ, the questions of social and political responsibility which plague modern Christians did not arise. The given social order, including its marriage customs, was accepted, unless aspects of it were clearly contrary to the way preached by the apostles. Certain things, such as prostitution, were felt to be incompatible with faith in Jesus, though there were arguments even about these. Other things, it was felt, could be lived in faith; even slavery, for the status of master and slave became, in a sense, irrelevant, since both were brothers "in the Lord."

It was "in the Lord" that men and women must marry and rear

children, buy, sell, labor, and exercise hospitality. How did Paul and others distinguish what could become "in the Lord" and what could not?

I think it was, and is, partly through careful theological reasoning (Paul does plenty of that) and partly through that "communal sense" of the feel of life in the Christian way, to which there are no short cuts. Just as theology cannot be separated from the historical circumstances surrounding its development, so what we might call "Christian sensitivity" can only grow with and on the *actions* of the Christian life. The one defines and reinforces the other. Paul's Christians struggled, not always successfully, to follow Christ in the chaotic social and religious situation of the Roman Mediterranean at a peak of the Empire's political power but when it was already disintegrating from within—a situation not unlike our own. As they struggled, they reflected, and analyzed and applied what they learned. Paul, writing to the Romans, told them to *"prove* what is the will of God, what is good and acceptable and perfect." And they were to do this by giving themselves, body and mind, to God, and so be "not conformed to this world but transformed by the renewal of your minds." And this renewal is to appear in everyday matters and virtues, in brotherly affection, patience in bad times, hospitality, sympathy for the sorrowful or the joyful, obedience to proper authority, paying just debts—all this oddly assorted collection to be done because, ultimately, love demands it.

Thus, living "in the Lord" clarifies the mind and renews the spirit, and again the understanding gained helps to distinguish the right way to live "in the Lord."

This is because Christianity is about incarnation, and man's bodily self is not merely intellectual, but also a mixture of feelings, instincts, inherited customs, economic conditions, physical conditioning, learned motivations, and spiritual aspirations which are always to a great extent inarticulate.

If we are to discover and cherish in our uncertain situation those strong bonds with the incarnate Lord which are the toughness of Christian marriage, we shall have to adopt Paul's methods. It is only by attempting, however clumsily, to live "in the Lord" in *every* aspect of life that our power of spiritual discernment (truly a gift of the spirit) can grow, and can make sense of the apparently conflicting demands in the area of sexuality.

The theology of marriage is about bodies, not only because sex is (among other things) bodily, but because all Christian theology is bodily. For example, there is a tendency among some Christians to feel that if people state an intention of spiritual love and loyalty in a marriage relationship, then what they have stated *is the case,* and what they do with their bodies will fit in with what they have stated. Man is not made like that. The actions of the body *pull* the spiritual, essential person, and commit the person *by those actions,* regardless of what the mind decides and pronounces. St. Paul is quite clear about this, and bases on it his condemnation of prostitution, heavy drinking, service of idols, and so on. The aim is wholeness, not just because that is a beautiful ideal but because to fail to seek integrity is to begin a process of disintegration, which is what we can see happening to many well-intentioned people at present. This is not a merely metaphysical conclusion, anyone can see it who takes a cool look at the state of discussion and experiment in the area of sexual morality.

It cannot be said too often that the Christian revelation is about the whole human person, in both private and communal aspects. What the Christian theology of marriage tries to do is, not impose abstractly formulated precepts but to *discover*—by thought, by faithfulness, by prayer, and by brotherly and sisterly communication—how sexual and family relationships can be seen to reveal the glory of the Lord. Within the pattern of a given society, it is the Christian's task to judge and distinguish by means of that "sensitivity" of faith which I described earlier. It is necessary to reject what impedes the development of the capacity for glory, yet to observe and cherish every sign of grace and truth in however unlikely a setting. We must assist and try to develop it further, yet not necessarily accept that, because when grace flashes out of a given situation, the *whole* situation is sanctified. This nicety of spiritual judgment, this balance of love and humility with a certain toughness of spiritual insight, is necessary for true theological development.

Theology cannot be conducted in an intellectual laboratory. Theology is an intellectual work, but its task is to try to articulate the complexities of God's love affair with human minds and bodies and spirits—all these, and all together. Those who wrestle to make sense of marriage "in the Lord" in this chaotic period of Western history have to begin, perhaps, with the sense of worship, as that word was formerly used in the marriage rite. To worship the glory of God in men and women trying to grow together and to God is to become awe-fully aware of their needs if they are to achieve, not just their fulfillment, now, but their hard, long-term, socially situated growth into full freedom and love. This is inseparable from their social and economic situation, so the theology of marriage can never be concerned purely with individual meanings. The couple finds its Christian meaning within the community, and the community's self-awareness as God's beloved is expressed in the devotion of individual couples—to each other, to their children, and to others—in new attempts to create life styles that make sense for a hard future.

The bedrock of Christian theology is incarnate love, and incarnate means *fleshed*, not just in a particular human body but in humankind —historical, limited, emotional, instinctual *and* rational. It is this whole thing that reaches toward God, by the power of God within it —Emmanuel. Part of this yearning is expressed in sexual relationships and the patterns by which they are stabilized and given a chance to deepen and grow. But all love—sexual love too—is hard and demanding and painful, and only grows that way, as Christ did. This is a hard time in which to love, and those concerned to illumine the ways of God to man have to be very sensitive, very humble, very patient, and sometimes very angry.

chapter 20

IS PATRIARCHY OBSOLETE?

Ruth Tiffany Barnhouse

The principal arguments against the ordination of women to the priesthood are that Jesus was a man, and that since the priest represents him at the Eucharist, the priest must also be a man. Further, Jesus chose only men to be his disciples, which is taken to underline the necessity of an exclusively male priesthood. Some cite further that the old Hebrew priesthood was limited to men. In addition, the New Testament refers to God as Father, and nearly all theological language, particularly in the last few hundred years, speaks to and about God as male. The nearly two thousand years of tradition during which only men have been eligible for the priesthood are also brought in as evidence for this view. While the acceptance of women as deacons on the same footing with men was opposed in some quarters (since in the Roman Catholic Church diaconate, presbyterate, and episcopate are held to be all one sacrament), it seems to be the idea of a woman either celebrating the Eucharist or exercising authority which arouses the most resistance.

Let us begin by considering the symbolism of the Eucharist to see whether there are reasons why women should not celebrate it. Throughout the centuries innumerable meditations and theological treatises have been written on the meaning of the symbolic use of bread and wine. The religious use of these symbols long antedates the Christian era, and occurs outside the Jewish and Christian traditions. Psychological and theological terms are both useful in trying to understand the rich significance of symbols; in fact, when properly understood, those two vocabularies are often difficult to distinguish.

The principal meanings may be summarized as follows: as nature, the bread and wine represent the typical food of humankind, the fruits of the earth. Bread is our physical means of survival; wine represents the spiritual. In order to produce these substances from nature's raw materials, human knowledge and ingenuity have been applied; therefore, the processes and fruits of civilization are also represented. In ancient times the chemistry of leavening and fermentation was unknown, and these mysterious processes, which are essential in the production of bread and wine, were considered specifically heaven-sent. In addition to nature and civilization graced by the divine, humanity itself is included in the meaning of these symbols. Many writers have perceived the wine as masculine and the bread as feminine. This symbolism has roots deep in the history of human consciousness. For example, in ancient times in the West a male deity, Bacchus, presided over wine, while the goddess Ceres presided over grain. In Christian thought, the masculine wine and feminine bread, taken together, represent the whole community of men and women who are Christian believers. Lastly, there is the familiar meaning of bread and wine as the body and blood of Our Lord.

As is typical of such powerful symbols, these various meanings are all simultaneously present. One does not choose among them. The bread and wine are *both* nature *and* humanity; *both* physical *and* spiritual; *both* humanity *and* God. Now this way of thinking is very different from our usual logical mode. In a daily, ordinary situation we would have to evaluate such pairs of opposites as an actual person and a portion of food in the *either/or* pattern of customary rational process. Not to do so would be evidence of having lost our grip on "reality." But the very purpose of religious symbolic thought is to mediate the paradox, to reconcile opposites, to remind us of the larger eternal frame of reference in which, mysteriously, there are no contradictions but all is included in the harmonious consciousness and presence of God. Therefore, when we consider the many levels of meaning which we have managed to extract from such a symbol, we are in error if we single out one meaning and assign to it an importance which takes precedence over the others. To do this is an inappropriate application of the otherwise useful *either/or* mode.

One role of the priest celebrating the Eucharist is to represent the Christian community, and it is on behalf of all believers that the gifts of bread and wine are offered. And (not *or*) the priest also represents God. God is *both* sacrificer *and* victim, and humankind, included in *both* God's human nature through the Incarnation *and* in the gifts, is also present. We are assured that through our participation in these rites we all, men and women alike, are spiritually fed and healed.

As for the issue of God's masculinity, we are specifically told that "God is a spirit, and they that worship him must worship him in spirit and in truth." The scriptural evidence is that while God includes the concept and attributes of masculinity, he is not defined by it or limited to it. On the contrary, we are told that in order to create humanity in his image, he found it necessary to create both the male and the female of the species. Woman as well as man is made in the image of God.

Nevertheless, the ultimate and essentially spiritual nature of the divine does not conflict with our classical understanding of God as personal. While God is not "a person," he manifests to us under a personal analogy, without which we would not be able to communicate with him since we have no basis in experience for understanding a two-way relationship with the nonpersonal. It has been customary in recent centuries to emphasize the ways of speaking to and about God which are mainly masculine, such as Father and King. But while masculine ways of referring to God predominate, there are other ways as well. In the creation story, the spirit of God is the Hebrew word *ruach,* a feminine word. The etymology of names is often difficult to unravel, but many scholars believe that *Elohim,* the name for God used in Genesis 1, is a feminine noun with a masculine plural. In addition, there are many feminine metaphors used throughout Scripture in describing God. During the Middle Ages, the vocabulary of popular piety was replete with feminine language about God, and mystics, who spend the greatest part of their life in prayer and communion with God, often speak about the feminine aspects of deity. When we remember that the full image of God, to become manifest on the physical plane, requires the creation of both men and women, these facts will not surprise us.

At the same time, any specific way of speaking about God is not to be taken literally, but is to be understood as reflecting God's gracious efforts to make it possible for us to think about and communicate with him meaningfully. He is, after all, an ineffable mystery, certainly not to be circumscribed by our anthropomorphic ways of thinking about him. We must recall that there are many completely impersonal references to him, especially in the Old Testament, where he is seen in such images as a spring of water, a fiery serpent, a burning bush, and many others. We must not be too quick to assume that these are all only metaphors while the personal references are to be taken more literally. We must not forget that *all* ways of speaking about God are metaphorical and partial. I would agree that the personal references are generally more useful to us, because they resonate with our own nature. But it is not insignificant that the Ten Commandments contain a prohibition against "graven images." This prohibition does not refer only to pagan idols but to any representation of the divine. The Hebrew tradition strictly enforces this right up to the present, and even prohibits the uttering of God's name.

This is not only out of respect for the holiness of that name, but also to prevent people from limiting God by thinking and speaking of him in only a few modes when, in fact, his nature is infinite and incomprehensible in its totality.[1]

This brief look at eucharistic symbolism shows that insofar as masculine and feminine are represented at all, they are represented equally. There seems then no good reason why the celebrant, who either represents or mediates the various meanings, could not be a woman as well as a man. The only possible obstacle lies in the fact that one of the priest's roles is to represent the second person of the Trinity, which, while incarnate on earth, was in a male body.

Why is this considered to take precedence over the fact that the priest also represents the whole community of Christian believers, both male and female? Or over the fact that God includes, among his many other attributes, the basic components of femininity as well as masculinity? This question is particularly pressing in view of the fact that in John 1:14 we are told, not that "the Word became male" but that "the Word became flesh." In all theological writing up to the present day it has been the humanity, not the masculinity, of Christ which has been considered the central point of the Incarnation.

Two different Greek words are translated into English as "man," *anthropos* and *aner*. *Anthropos* is generic, and a more accurate translation would be "human," or "person." *Aner* refers to the human male. (A similar distinction exists in Latin, *homo* and *vir*, and what is said here about Greek applies to the old Latin texts as well.) The English language is at a disadvantage in not having clearly separate words for these two meanings, which have become particularly confused in recent times. Many other languages are more fortunate, and to people from those cultures, some of the theological arguments provoked in the English-speaking world by the feminist movement seem incomprehensible or bizarre. Neither in Scripture nor in the original Greek of the creeds formulated in the first few centuries, which have been in continuous use since that time, is the word *aner* used in connection with the Incarnation. The word used is always the generic term *anthropos*, or else *sarx*, which means "flesh."

These facts are not seriously questioned even by the most ardent opponents of women's ordination. We must ask, therefore, why the arguments centering on the maleness of Jesus and his disciples seem, in the minds of those who advance them, so disproportionately persuasive. Considered only logically, this is so puzzling as to arouse in some supporters of women's priesthood the irritating suspicion of hypocritical obstinacy or outright malevolence in their opponents.

Now when this kind of emotional uproar begins to obscure a serious dialogue by shedding more heat than light on it, the solution to the difficulty often lies in the discovery that with respect to some important issue the right question is not being asked. Without realizing it, the participants are actually debating something quite different than would be suggested by exclusive attention to the intellectual content of the arguments up to that point. This is precisely what has happened in this instance. What might the real question be?

For as long as we have any consistent historical records, the entire human family (with possible rare exceptions in small groups usually referred to as "uncivilized") has had a social structure characterized by patriarchy. Unquestionably the ordination of women to the priesthood would be a serious threat to this time-honored patriarchal system. To admit women to priesthood would categorically imply their full social and spiritual equality with men. (Please note that equality does not imply identity!) It would acknowledge that the feminine is no longer to be defined in terms of its relation to the masculine. Instead, women have their own place, co-valent with that of men, before God and all of humanity. The exercise of cultic and ecclesiastical authority would be seen to depend not on a biological accident of birth, but on the spiritual maturity of the individual priest, whether man or woman.

Therefore, the real theological question is whether patriarchy is a humanly originated cultural form, or whether it is a divinely appointed foundation of human society. If it is humanly originated, we are free to alter or abolish it, and doing so would enlarge, but not contradict, our present theological understanding. If it is an essential component of the divine order of creation, then it should not only be retained but strengthened.

This is a truly new question. Until the current wave of the hundred-year-old feminist movement, it has never been raised. Many debates over the role of women in society have raged (or in peaceful times merely simmered) over the centuries, but the underlying concept of patriarchy was never brought into question. The only issue was to decide what the fairest and best way to implement the accepted patriarchy might be. At this time it would be a serious mistake to associate the raising of this new issue exclusively with feminism. As we shall see, it is being raised in sectors of the culture other than the theological one, and for reasons only indirectly associated with the problem of women's rights (or duties!).

Let us now take a look at patriarchy itself.[2] The available anthropological and historical evidence suggests that it is a universal cultural form which arose independently in numerous polytheistic cultures; and it is not, therefore, even in the West, associated with the rise of

monotheism. There is some agreement among scholars that it was pre-
ceded by a matriarchal societal organization. It was well established
long before the time when even the oldest part of the Old Testament
was written. What might this imply for our way of interpreting the
ancient biblical patriarchal tradition?

Even under a conservative interpretation of the process of scriptural inspiration it is evident that God's messages to us must be mediated through the individual consciousness of the human writer.
The living encounter with God does not take place through the intellect, but is always a numinous and archetypally mysterious experience. After the vision or other message from God, rational consciousness comes into play, and is used by the prophets, saints, and
apostles (or perhaps the person-in-the-street) to try to mediate their
experience to the community at large in intellectually comprehensible terms. The baffling but powerful visions of the apocalyptic
writers have been subject to far less of this intellectual filtering and
explicating process than have other portions of the canon. The most
rational and intellectual writers, such as St. Paul, are the ones whose
ideas show the clearest evidence of having gone through their personal cultural filter. Writers who are mainly recounting stories rather
than theologizing about those stories display this characteristic somewhat less prominently. And those who show it the least are those
who are simply reporting their visions with little or no attempt at
interpretation.

This comes about because the human receptor organ for revelation
and inspiration is that part of our psyche which is unconscious and
nonrational. Another way of putting this is to say that it is that part of
our psyche which naturally has the *both/and* rather than the rational
either/or mode of dealing with phenomena and events. It is this
nonrational part which is activated in dreaming, in many different
states of expanded consciousness, in some uses of intuition, and in
artistic and even scientific creativity. It is this part which has the
natural capacity to attend to God in all his many modes and manifestations. (I am, of course, not suggesting that all phenomena associated with this part of the psyche are of divine origin.) The rational
part of the psyche, on the other hand, is characterized by logic, by
conscious intentionality and decision-making, and by what is usually
called "ego-consciousness." Intellectual activity and all those interac-
tions with our cultural milieu of which we are aware and over which
we have some measure of control are essentially rational. Of course
these two modes are not sealed off from one another, but are in a
constant state of dynamic interaction. There are recognized patholo-
gies associated with extreme predominance of either mode. This is

true not only for individuals but for whole cultures, and in fact, serious imbalances of this kind contribute heavily to the collapse of particular civilizations.

How might this understanding of the role of the human cultural filter in the writing of Scripture clarify the issue before us? Questions are never raised about customs which everyone not only accepts but takes for granted. A reading of the biblical narrative makes it clear that the existence of patriarchy was in this category. Many other customs and practices were questioned, and in fact the entire record is one in which, through his chosen prophets and ministers, God urged his people to change, to be renewed, to overthrow that which had degenerated or was simply outworn. Because God's plans for his people are clearly dynamic and evolutionary rather than static, we must seriously consider the idea that the consistently patriarchal consciousness which is taken for granted throughout Scripture may not, as we have hitherto assumed, reflect a necessarily permanent social organization. One could equally well assume that during the period in which the books of the canon were written, the time was not yet ripe for God to lead humanity to a different pattern. In that case, the patriarchal flavor of Scripture would be seen to be due simply to the fact that at the time when the writing was undertaken, patriarchy was prevalent and was therefore unavoidably mediated through the consciousness of the authors.

The argument has been proposed that because patriarchy appears in the Book of Genesis it is part of the divine order of creation, and therefore not to be tampered with. But it is equally true that nearly all of the language of the Bible describes an agricultural society. This is not only clear from the content of the narratives, but also from the most commonly used figures of speech in both the Old and New Testaments. There are descriptions of cities, but most often the city in Scripture is the locus of threat and evil. As our own civilization has evolved, we have felt free to reject quite automatically and unconsciously this underlying biblical bias in favor of agrarian social and economic organization, and we do not perceive this change as having major theological significance. There is no logical reason why the institution of patriarchy should not be viewed in the same way. To cite the order of creation as given in the Genesis accounts is to introduce an immediate inconsistency, since, along with the beginnings of patriarchy, those accounts also presuppose an agricultural society. There can be no justification for insisting that one is mutable while the other is not.

It is easy for us to forget how recent the contemporary understanding of the vastness of space and time really is. The theory of evolution is even more recent; Darwin's *Origin of Species* was first published in 1859 while his *Descent of Man* was not published until 1871. Readers old enough to remember the Scopes trial in 1926 will realize how recently his theories gained general acceptance. They caused, naturally, exceptionally heated controversy in theological circles because it was feared that they cast doubt on the divine authenticity of the biblical narrative. It took a long time for people to realize that what was at issue was not God's actual message to us, but simply the personal cultural filter of the writers through whom we received it. The doctrine of creation was not being attacked, we were merely learning something new about God's technique, which turns out to include the savagely beautiful complexity of the evolutionary process.

Now there is a general evolutionary principle which states that the development of any individual member of a species, from the moment of fertilization to maturity, recapitulates, in more or less accurate miniature, the vast evolution of that entire species since its beginnings billions of years ago. If we are not to fall into the dualist heresy, we must assume that this fact holds true, not only for biological evolution but also for the gradual evolution of consciousness. It follows that if we consider the psychological process through which a human child grows from infancy to maturity, we may learn something about the general growth process for the whole human race.

At first the infant is not aware of the distinction between self and others in the environment, but is locked in a unitive relationship with its mother. This may be seen to correspond with the primitive cultural organizations, which were matriarchal in character, in which the members of the group did not experience themselves as individuals with a unique personal destiny, but as members of a collective. This collective identity was in turn experienced as a unitive, dependent relationship with "Mother Nature." The idea of dominating or controlling nature, or of taking any real initiative with respect to it, had not yet arisen. Nature had to be lived in, with, under, and through—often placated and cajoled. Her storms, droughts, and plagues were perceived as evidence of her capricious dissatisfactions with her children, and sometimes as direct punishments for failure to meet her demands. The sacrifices and fertility rites of primitive religions reflect this condition very clearly.

As human infants continue to develop, there is a gradual process of differentiation in which they come to recognize themselves as separate persons. The person from whom it is most urgent that they become separate is the mother, since it is with her that the original state of unconscious unity is experienced. The most basic step in the long process of this differentiation is the recognition of the father. It is no doubt for this reason that the corresponding period in the development of human consciousness was characterized by the gradual appearance of patriarchal culture. In this view, patriarchy was a beneficent and necessary condition for the emergence of human consciousness from the original archaic identity with "Mother Nature."

After infancy has been successfully negotiated, and the first stages of separation from the mother achieved, comes childhood, the period in which the rules of civilized behavior are learned. The concept of responsibility is gradually inculcated, beginning with the lesson that one is accountable to others for one's actions.

On the larger scale of the development of consciousness, the process thus far described corresponds to that which is illustrated in the early myths of the Old Testament. Abraham was called forth and informed of his uniqueness, of his differentiation from the general group of humanity. It would be too time-consuming to go through the history of his descendants point by point, but suffice it to say that in the story of Moses receiving the tables of the Law we have the culmination of this part of the process. It was through the Law that the idea of individual responsibility was thoroughly inculcated and the process of individual differentiation carried out. Nevertheless, this stage is far from representative of full human maturity. Although individuals are no longer lost in an undifferentiated relationship with nature or the feminine maternal principle, they are still heavily dependent on the community standards of the patriarchal tribe or nation. The exercise of conscience at this stage does not consist in determining for oneself what is right, but in determining whether one has obeyed to the best of one's ability the laws imposed by a higher authority.

When childhood is over, the individual passes into adolescence. The salient indispensable feature of this stage is the physiological development of sexuality and the psychological growth required to assimilate it. With this comes the possibility, but not the absolute necessity, of going on to full psychological and spiritual maturity. It is entirely possible for people to live out their whole lives respectably, even admirably, without going beyond this stage of incorporating the received value system of the patriarchal society. At any time in history the great majority of individuals lead a fundamentally collective existence, conditioned as that may be by the ideals and standards developed by those articulate and relatively well-educated persons, (overwhelmingly male under patriarchy), who are in the effective vanguard of the evolutionary process.

Until the seventeenth century the idea of the supremacy of indi-

vidual conscience over the community's view of "truth" did not begin to take public hold on a large scale. This occurred in the context
of the development of the idea of religious toleration in the wake of
the Reformation, and was assisted by the accelerated progress of
international trade and commerce, which required at least a modi-
cum of acceptance of differing cultural and religious styles. The full
consequences of this change have not yet been appreciated, much
less implemented. Humanity no longer fights religious wars, but the
uncharitable intolerance with which all parties embrace the political
ideologies of our secular wars suggests strongly that the devil has not
given up the ship, but has merely run a different flag up the mast.
We perceive, uneasily, that international conduct is at best imma-
ture, but we do not seem to be able to grow up.

Full personal maturity requires development of conscience
beyond the stage of responsibility to uphold the received standards
of family, tribe, nation—or church. In short, it requires the kind of
development the potential for which was ushered in by the Incarnation. The life and teachings of Jesus make it clear that he was offering to humanity a liberation from the old Law, and a freedom which,
to the rulers of the time, had the appearance of anarchy. What he was
proposing was the full, individual responsibility of each person directly to God. Naturally such a radical transcendent vision could not
take root overnight and give rise immediately to new cultural forms.
Therefore, it is not surprising that patriarchy continued to be the
prevailing cultural pattern within which Christian traditions were
developed, particularly after the mixed blessing of Christianity becoming the state religion following Constantine's conversion. But a
dispassionate examination of the teachings of Jesus does not reveal
any divine ground for perpetuating the human institution of patriarchy beyond such time as it has outlived its usefulness.

All of Jesus' utterances were designed to lead listeners to a richer
and deeper dimension of consciousness than was indicated by the
Mosaic Law. In his terminology the kingdom of God was not to be
described by the social and legal conditions of the heavenly community but by the individual spiritual maturity of the participants.
How else are we to understand the saying that the kingdom is
within? The desperately high standard of self-examination which he
proposed was not designed to increase our burden of guilt, though it
has all too often been used that way over the centuries by Pharisaic
legalists who failed to understand that what he was really trying to
tell us is that the fullest possible extension of individual consciousness is the path to true freedom in God. He was mounting a major
assault on the collective mode of being. He took for granted that

women were to be included as independent participants in the kingdom, and this position made him a radical feminist in the cultural
context of his time (or ours!).[3] It was Milton misinterpreting St. Paul,
not Jesus himself, who said, ". . . he for God, she for God in him."

In a society where, for whatever reasons, one sex is defined even
partially as hierarchically superior to the other, the qualities and
principles of the secondary sex, however valuable and even actually
valued they may be, will be developed only in subsidiary relation to
the values and qualities of the dominant sex. They will therefore
remain largely unconscious and unarticulated, or at best, will only
be developed in a rudimentary and tentative way. It should be obvious that this actually stunts the full personal growth of the subsidiary sex, and therefore deprives the dominant sex of the advantages
which would accrue from having fully mature partners. I use this
sexually unspecific language to make it clear that however much I
believe that patriarchy has outlived its usefulness and should be
replaced by a different principle of social organization, I am under
no circumstances advocating a new matriarchy. That would be
equally harmful to the future development of the human family. It
would not help us in the least to have the qualities and values of
men distorted and driven underground. God forbid!

I should like to suggest a new meaning to Jesus' famous statement
in Matthew 22:30 that in heaven there will be neither marrying nor
giving in marriage. The usual interpretation that sexual relations will
be superfluous in heaven is at least inadequate, if not actually untrue. Since biblical writers were not squeamish in referring to sex,
we may conclude that what Jesus meant was the actual institution of
marriage as it existed at that time. The context describes a woman
given in marriage to each of seven brothers, in order of decreasing
seniority, in hope that she might produce an heir. We read: ". . . de-
ceased, and having no issue, left his wife unto his brother." At that
time the wife was a possession, and was owned by her husband in
exactly the same way in which he owned his ox, his ass, his children,
his slaves, and whatever other worldly goods he had. Under Jewish
law a wife had more protection than in the neighboring pagan societies, but even so, the husband's control was nearly absolute. It is
only now, two thousand years later, that the last of the laws reflecting
that attitude are being changed, and not without struggle in some
quarters. The battle over slavery is still painfully recent, and it is
only in this century that laws against cruelty to children, even by
their parents, have been enacted.

Such change as has been achieved so far has come about very
largely through the gradual unfolding of the Christian principle of

responsible liberty for all. It was St. Paul, much maligned by many modern women, who decreed that far from having the right to be a despotic tyrant in his home, a man must love his wife "as Christ loves the church." This puts the Christian first-century wife in a far better position than that of her pagan sisters. Still, that there will, in heaven, be no marrying or giving in marriage surely means that the old form of patriarchal marriage is to be obsolete. As we look around our culture it is obvious that the original pure form of such marriage hardly exists, having been gradually eroded by the rise of the principle of liberty. The church has quite properly assisted this process in many ways, but there is still more to be done. Naturally, this is not to suggest that there were never any benevolent patriarchs. Many men and women have lived happy, harmonious, and fruitful lives under that system, but not all slave owners were tyrants, either. It is the underlying principle which is at issue, not the question of whether the old system was ever well implemented.

As we look around us, it is very evident that the patriarchal system is in a state of serious disorder. Professor William Thompson, in his book *At the Edge of History,* has written a scathing indictment of the irresponsible and power-hungry ways in which our political and technological establishment is hurtling our civilization in the direction of unimaginable disaster.[4] His own analysis of the reasons is largely based on the premise that the major factor is the one-sided, runaway development of the masculine principle unchecked by any balancing evolution of feminine values. To this I would add that the lack of spiritual values aggravates the problem. The resulting situation is extremely unstable, and if we are very lucky, the worst that will result is a painful period of social chaos. From the other side, patriarchy is being attacked by the women's movement, whose voices are many—ranging from gently reasonable through irritatingly strident all the way to angrily destructive. Unfortunately, the women are not doing significantly better than the men in tempering their viewpoint with spiritual concerns.

These social facts will not go away, and nostalgic glances over our shoulder at the vanished stability of more benevolent times may turn us into so many irrelevant ecclesiastical pillars of salt, but will certainly not contribute to a solution of the problem. By the failures of both nerve and faith, which were involved in the church's misguided and overliteral approaches to the discoveries of physics, biology, and psychology in the last few centuries, its position of leadership in the shaping of cultural values has been almost lost. Not merely out of a naturally optimistic temperament, but much more significantly out of a belief in the power of God to guide us through the Holy Spirit, I believe the present situation gives us one more opportunity through which we may recoup this loss. The time has come for the next responsible step in the development of full human maturity, in which men and women, each fully free, each fully responsible, will be able to do more *together* than the sum of what they have so far been able to do separately. (As we have become aware through our experience with the problems of race relations, the "separate but equal" way not only does not work but is in the long run destructive.)

This essential (and in some form inevitable) change in human social organization should be *led*, rather than merely nervously followed, by the church. Under the church's guidance, informed by the Holy Spirit, the development of new attitudes and social forms can take place in a manner which keeps in view the long-term responsibilities of both men and women. These responsibilities include the care and education of the young, the problems of world population, and all the other questions of social and political justice which are currently so perplexing to us. If, instead, this step in human evolution is shortsightedly abandoned to the spiritually bankrupt secular arm, we will have only the social and moral chaos which always results when attention is principally focused on short-term personal pleasures—the ultimate hideous end-point of the "do your own thing, let's have no hassles" attitude.

The time has come for the church to give up its patriarchal nostalgia. It must now take an active part in the process of bringing into full function the neglected feminine half of human potential. If we continue to permit the present serious distortion of the *imago dei*, we will gravely hamper our progress toward a better implementation of the original divine vision.

NOTES

1. For a more thorough treatment of the points covered thus far, see Barnhouse, Ruth T., "An Examination of the Ordination of Women to the Priesthood in Terms of the Symbolism of the Eucharist," *Anglican Theological Review*, vol. LVI, no. 3, July 1974.

2. For a more extensive treatment of this subject, with references, see Barnhouse, Ruth T., "Patriarchy and the Ordination of Women," *Nashotah Review*, Vol. 15, no. 3 (fall 1975) and *St. Luke's Journal Theology*, Vol. xviii, no. 4 (Sept. 1975), joint issue.

3. For a very illuminating and readable exposition of this point, see Faxon, Alicia Craig, *Women and Jesus* (Philadelphia: United Church Press, 1973).

4. Thompson, William Irwin, *At the Edge of History* (New York: Harper/Colophon, 1972).

chapter 21

THE SACRAMENTALITY OF SEX

John W. Dixon, Jr.

> For I through the law died to the law, that I
> might live to God. I have been crucified with
> Christ; it is no longer I who live, but Christ
> who lives in me; . . .
> Paul the Apostle
> in his Letter to the Galatians, 2:19–20

A PRELIMINARY MEDITATION

This passage is a great puzzle to the mind of the church. It is no
puzzle at all to the devotions of the church. In truth, we do not know
what Paul meant when he said, "it is no longer I who live, but Christ
who lives in me." It might be better to say we cannot *explain* it; we
may, in fact, *know* it by means other than our argumentative reason.

As long as we are not so wholly dependent on the principle of
rational, explanatory thought, Paul's statement could, in ecstatic devotion, be received as an affirmation of union below conscious thought.
Under present definitions of rationality and thought, it can mean
nothing at all. Our gravest temptation is to reject rationality, go back
to a much earlier time and thus make the statement mean things it
was never intended to mean.

Paul's statement is more inclusive than the problem of the sacrament; it would appear to go back to the beginning of the Christian
life and describe the process of "conversion." But the sacrament is
one of the means for carrying forward what was begun in conversion,
and the sacramentals are all those things which fulfill and sustain the
Christian life. Thus, to explain the statement is to explain the sacraments; to know what the sacramentals are is to come closer to understanding Paul's statement. If we can understand them both we might
be able to know them better and participate in them more fully.

PRELIMINARY ASSERTIONS:

1. A sacrament is not a "sign" of anything, including inward or spiritual grace. It is the means for constructing the soul.
2. Sex is always a sacrament. The problem is, how is it a *Christian* sacrament?
3. The true purpose of sexuality is not gratification or fulfillment, which are only enticements and rewards. The true purpose of sexuality is completeness.
4. The dull and dessicated sacramentality of the modern church might be given healing vitality by the working of the sacramentality of sex. Equally, the destructive passion of sex might be disciplined to creativity by its joining to the principle of the sacrament.
5. The most pressing theological problem today is to understand the nature and role of women. This is not because women are more important than men, but because our culture has spent about five thousand years exploring the definition and role of men.

So much having been said, it remains now to fill out the contents of these assertions.

The origins of religion are forever lost to us, since they go back beyond any evidence at all. The oldest evidence is certain works of art which are profound in their consistency. They are representations of naked women—faceless, fat, and pregnant—and representations of the great animals; both in caves, usually deep in the earth.

What these great works meant to their creators we can never know but only guess. We can try to experience them as deeply and seriously as we can, knowing that we can experience them only through sensibilities that are very different from those of the prehistoric people who made them. If we do so, we find that we are in the presence of tremendous energy, the swarming abundance of the life of the animal, the soft abundance of the fertile body of the mother.

We know too little about these works, but what we can know is God's own plenty: that deep in the body of the earth there is the fruitfulness of the earth. In the darkness of the caves, the modern visitor can learn what must be known: that we, too, are part of the fruitful energies of the cave in the earth; that the power of the creatures of the earth and the fertility of the bodies of women are grounds and origins of our own work on the earth.

Among the more painful of the superstitions that beset us is the conviction that we, coming so long after those who made such things, are by nature and education immune from their power or the need for their power. The past is not distant from us but deep within us. We are different people, not as creatures transformed—caterpillar into butterfly or tadpole into frog—but as a tree adds rings. The painters of the caves are within us, the painted animals and the carved women are parts of our very selves.

We will know ourselves only as we can work back through those layers of ourselves, knowing each layer, and knowing its relation to all that went before it. We should not consider ourselves as travelers on a pilgrimage through time. Rather we bring essential parts of our journey with us.

As we sense ourselves so deeply involved with our past, so must we be equally involved with our bodies. Our bodies have, indeed, changed, but they too bring their past with them. Genesis and Darwin agree on the ladder of ascent or descent—both spatial images of value for which I would prefer the tree growing out of the center. We began in the sea, grew to reptiles to mammals to humanoids to humans, and the quality of each remains with us, only barely covered by the subsequent layers. There is the cold, pitiless, subintelligent vitality of the reptile; the passionate energy of the beast using intelligence as a tool and a weapon without moral judgment; and finally the intelligence at the service of moral decision. The tree image is almost literally present, although not quite rendering the anatomical picture. The oldest "reptilian" brain is, in us, the brain stem at the top of the spinal column and controls those bodily functions we conceal behind the terms "automatic" and "instinctive." Folded around this knob and nearly enclosing it is the bulk of the brain, the "mammalian" brain, or rather the "paleomammalian" brain. Enclosing this brain mass is its outer surface, the neocortex.

A lot but not all is known about these brains and their functions. A few examples:

1) All people, in varying degrees have the experience of rage, which may or may not be controlled by will or belief.
2) Old people whose cerebral cortex has ceased to function, and the most pious people under anesthesia, will talk and behave with the grossest sexuality, entirely in conflict with the principles of their responsible lives.
3) In nations, judgment of morality and of greatness are entirely separate. In nations professing morality, the murderous tyrant is idealized as a hero, as Napoleon and Caesar have been.
4) The most reasonable and pious people have dreams of an appalling immorality. Even amateur analysis can easily uncover the powerful sexual and economic base for much of our ordinary acts.

The conclusion: our lives are under the control of distinct bodily systems. They are hierarchically ordered; the cerebral cortex is both physically and figuratively "higher" than the brain stem and the limbic system. The higher levels can partially control the lower, but that control can be weakened or destroyed, temporarily or permanently, by chemistry, by aging, or by culture. The crocodile, the tiger, and Hitler are within us, integral parts of ourselves, ever waiting the opportunity to control the body.

How is power controlled to peace, lust to love? Not alone. Morality is generated in community, developed in community, transmitted by community. No statement I could make goes more counter to the contemporary conviction which holds that the individual is both whole and all, that each individual has an absolute right to control his or her behavior from childhood on, without control by parent, teacher, or any social force. Such a conviction can only be based on the belief that morality and reason are linked within the organism and need only be left alone to develop fully. There is no evidence at all to sustain that conviction, and all evidence is against it. "The kingdom of God is within you" said Jesus, meaning the collective you—the community—or, in other words, "The kingdom of God is in the midst of you."

This conviction is not new at all; it is for us part of the nineteenth-century positivism which was an outgrowth of a primitive stage of science. Too simply put, this view is that of "the ghost in the machine," a spirit or mind which is somehow separate from the body, which receives information from the body, thinks about it, and issues instructions to the body. Curious companions are found agreeing on this view of the nature of man; they differ only concerning the purposes of the instructions given to the body. The purpose may be the indulgence of the body economically or sexually, or the control of the body for some intellectual or spiritual or moral purpose. But, whatever the different purposes, the analysis is the same; the ascetic and the licentious agree, the bank president and the hippie are brothers underneath their stated purpose, because they act on the same image of the human.

Yet we are not at all related to the world in that way. It is now necessary to describe still a third hierarchical structure making up our way of being. The first of these in my account of them was the growth of the human psyche historically, the successive layers of the self's development. The second was the hierarchical ordering of the nervous system from the brain stem (and its attendant nervous system) to the cerebral cortex. The third is the system of relations between these two. The key word now is "pattern" or "paradigm" or "model."

At the lowest, most elementary level, the principle of the paradigm can be illustrated by the simplest form of the reflex arc: what we do when we touch something hot. If the conventional picture of thought were accurate, our nervous system would inform the brain that the hand was against something that was hot. The brain would then think about it, deciding that contact was both painful and dangerous and that, therefore, the hand should be moved away. Then the brain would issue instructions to the hand—but by that time the damage would be done. No, there is a pattern of response built into the nervous system. The heat sets the pattern into action and the hand is immediately snatched away. The word "instinct" is an evasion of the problem because it defines nothing; and instinct is simply a pattern of response in the nervous system.

There are a great many such patterns which we are born with or which early experience forms into our nervous system so thoroughly that they are beyond conscious control. There are others that are clearly learned but that are as deeply implanted; take, for example, simple perception.

Conventional understanding of the human process has it that bits of isolated information arrive at the brain, which then combines them into an identifiable whole. Were this true, simple perception would be exceedingly difficult and perceiving complex objects impossible. Everything in our world is changing, nothing is fixed. A door, for example, can be as small as a doll house door or as large as a cathedral door. It can be many shapes and an infinite range of colors. No organism could ever experience enough doors to build up the definition of "door" by accumulated experience. Rather we develop a paradigm in our nervous system which, when stimulated by one of these endlessly different doors, responds instantly with the sense and, if necessary, the word, "door."

This is learned and is therefore cultural, but it becomes a part of the reflex apparatus. It goes further. We build up a paradigm, "woman" and "wife," "man" and "husband." It is built up over the years by the experience of particular persons, by culture in the form of stories—and indirectly by the stories in that they form the persons who form us.

Two people so formed get married. Their ability to reason out the problems of marriage is a help, but only a small help, against the extraordinary power of the paradigm. And this is precisely the problem of marriage; *nobody*, no specific, cranky, concrete, particular person ever can fit the paradigm. Something has to change. Either one person or the other voluntarily changes or is compelled to change, or the paradigm changes, or there is no marriage.

I am asserting that we do not just have *ideas* about what a woman is or what a man is and, therefore, what a marriage is. What controls us is the pattern, the paradigm, the image, the model, which is as surely fixed into our nervous system as the reflex arc that causes us to snatch our hand away from a hot stove. What we think of as our freedom to choose is remorselessly shaped by the paradigms that have formed in our nervous systems. In fact, such freedom as we have consists mainly of two things; the ability to classify (to decide which paradigm applies to a particular situation), and the ability to choose among the differing and contradictory paradigms that are contending in us.

So far from our culture being something outside ourselves which we, as whole and complete beings, experience, our culture is a part of ourselves as much as our nervous system is. We don't think *about* these images, as though they were ideas. We think *with* them, by means of them.

Another illustration will show how a culture can be controlled by abstract principles of relation and not simply images of persons. American businessmen and politicians unceasingly claim their own place as Christians and extol the role of Christianity. Yet their dominant pattern of relation to the world is not Christian love but competition. Competition is a zero-sum game: what one wins another must lose. Thus, it is the very antithesis of Christian love, which would have two come together to generate something new. Yet no principle is more powerful in American life. Most Americans, including most of the American churches, are controlled by the idea of competition, the compulsive need to be "No. 1," which is a principle of a far older, more primitive religion than Christianity.

For these paradigms, these complex systems of paradigms, are not simply things we have as we have small change. They are more nearly something we *are*, for they shape our world, our feelings about our world, our actions and purposes within our world.

Paul's statement "It is no longer I who live but Christ who lives in me," now becomes intelligible. In the definition of the self I have described, it is literally true. The whole structure of images, the paradigms, that made up Paul's world had been shattered; the old man had died. Christ lived in him by the new ordering of the self in the world.

Being a Christian, then, is not holding to certain opinions or behaving in a certain way. Being a Christian is letting the old structure, the old paradigm, die and being reborn to the new being which is the Christ paradigm.

This symbolic layer of the self is at the top of the self's structure or around the outside. It is not the whole but it is the part that determines the true self. The lowest level or the innermost circle is shared by all living creatures. To go higher or toward the outside is to pass through those levels of the self that we share with increasingly complex creatures. We then arrive at the level of intelligence which is, first of all, the nonmoral intelligence of the animal, and we finally achieve the human level by the paradigm of order and purpose that constitutes the highest or outermost layer. It is this outer layer that secures the uniqueness of the self. It is the truest self, so when it is broken and remade it is truly a new self even though the lower and inner levels or layers remain, in part, undisturbed.

Out of this there begins to emerge a definition of the role of the church. It is not the primary role of the church to soothe and comfort, to support the reigning orders, to advise on morals, or, in fact, to do most of the things the church spends its time actually doing. It is the function of the church to communicate the Christ to people so he can be born in them and thereby make a soul for eternal life. The church rightly uses all the things I have listed and many more besides. But they are the means, not the end, which is the engendering of Christ in the soul.

It is possible now to define a sacrament. A sacrament is one of the things or acts appointed to the church as communicating Christ to the worshipers in the sense of implanting and renewing the image of Christ in the soul, the paradigm which is truly the real presence. A sacramental is one of those things or acts that function the same way without having been appointed as always and everywhere central to the liturgy of the church for all the faithful.

A sacrament is not a sign, neither is it a box containing a sacred power which can be distributed by the keeper of the keys, nor is it a faucet dispensing the sacred power to anyone who turns it. It is one term in a relation, and the nature of a relation is determined by the terms being related as well as by the instrument of the relation. The elements of a sacrament, the ritual act in which the elements are used, have their own character, their own structure and rhythm, which inescapably shapes the sacramental relation. Equally, the use of the elements and the acts shapes the relation, making possible the false use of a sacrament. The sacrament conveys the energy, the power; and in conveying it, defines it. But the reception of it also defines it, and out of the false use of a sacramental proceeds a false religion.

In its appointed sacramentals, variously recognized among the churches, the church has, in detail, accepted the sacramentality of human social and economic life. Of the seven appointed sacraments, six deal wholly with social and economic life and the seventh almost wholly. Baptism sanctifies the entry into life, confirmation the entry into the sacred community, confirming the death of the old and the birth of the new. The Eucharist sustains the life of the sacred community with the fruits of the earth transformed by human labor. Marriage and ordination establish special offices within the sacred community; penance is the pedagogical and restorative punishment. Unction confirms the passage to a new mode of life.

Thus, in magnificent detail, the church takes up human life into its ritual, shapes it, places it in the context of the sacred community. Yet in the sacramental life, human experience is understood almost wholly as social and economic. Sex appears by implication only, and rather grudgingly, as a part of marriage.

The absence of sex from the liturgy is not necessarily caused by fear of the power of sex. At the center of the major sacrament of the church is alcohol, a power nearly as attractive and certainly as destructive as sex. The instinct of the church is correct at this point (and I speak as one who does not use alcohol); an enlivening and terrible power is placed at the center of the church's experience, symbolizing how all of the fruitful aspects of the human experience need be—must be—brought under the holy discipline. These things the church has taken into its sacramental discipline without fear or flinching, and in doing so has shown a profound insight into the human situation.

There must, therefore, be a different reason for the absence of sex from the sacraments than simple timidity or taste. The reason must be located and identified before sex can become formally a sacramental. Sex is not, in itself, a Christian sacrament, a carrier of the image of Christ, the Christ paradigm. It is a sacrament of the ancient religion, the religion of the natural energies and, unknowingly, it is being presented as such to the community today. "Sex is good" say the prophets of this religion, as though the presence of a sacred power is automatically good, as though the ritual act of sex gives access to the good stored up in it. This prophecy is preached in the church, and the church, lacking any sense of its own integrity, blankly shuts it out or fawningly yields before it.

Yet there was reason for the exclusion of sex, whatever terrible price we now pay for the exclusion. There was not only reason, there was necessity for it; however much the necessity has changed.

Sex is a power, an energy beyond imagining. A compelling symptom of our awareness of this power is our language, for there is no true language for sex appropriate to it. The word is hopelessly ambiguous. In itself it simply refers to gender with no relation at all to the

genital interaction of people. The names for the organs and act of sex
are Latin, a hidden language. Popular names are blunt, like exple-
tives, because that is what they are. Even those who claim to be
liberated constantly resort to genteelisms such as "sleep together"
for an act done while awake, "make love" for a relation that does not
in the least require love, "have sex" when sex is something everybody has.

All this is not hypocrisy. It has its own profundity of implication. It
accepts and acknowledges the power. The vulgar term for sexual
relations is a popular curse because words are carriers of the fearful
energies. It is a cruelty to the needs of the psyche to deprive it of
such words by making them respectable, for they are the means to
drain off and use the natural forces in us. Lovers murmur them in the
secret dark when they are in the throes of the natural energies, and
that is as it should be.

But popular evasion also has in it a strangely touching and often
forlorn hope. "To sleep with" is to surrender safety in trust and to
place sex in the hope of trust in the other. "To make love" is to know
that out of the physical act love can be generated. "To have sex" is
to affirm what may be the most important element in the sacramentality of sex, that at the root of it is indifference, a divided whole which
might in the act of union be restored.

It is grievous sentimentality to think that the sexual energies are,
in themselves, part of the Christ paradigm, the Christ-in-us. They
belong to the deeper levels of the self, or the more central. The place
for the Christ paradigm is surrounding the whole, not changing it all.
We remain human in the mode of all humans, always as subject to
the natural human forces. St. Anthony would not have been so terrified of the demons that visited him in the night, nor the pious so torn
by the dreams and fantasies that torment them, if they knew and
could accept their common ordinary humanity.

Yet the presence of the natural energies, desires, even lusts, is not
sanctified by their natural existence but by what we do with them.
The image of the tree is useful; the Christ model is the outer layer.
It is essential to life (destroy the bark and the tree dies), but the bulk
of the tree is quite separate from the bark, unchanged by it. I am
proposing that much of human life is, in fact, like that, subject to
uncontrollable energies, uncontrollable at least in fantasy and desire.
Human life is not quite that clear-cut, for the Christian presence
does change the tonality of the whole. But it does not necessarily
transform the whole. A Christian is not a cleaned plaster copy of a
human being, but a real, complete human being. The Christ paradigm changes that tonality because of what it does in the other direc-

tion; it provides the forms and the processes whereby we live and act in the world. The natural energies, welling up in demonic power from the depths of the self, find the forms for their full and humane expression in the ordering of the sacramental life.

The church tried to treat the Christ model as an iron band around the self, imprisoning the natural energies within moral commandments. The consequence has been a terrible psychic damage. Jesus certainly knew of this sort of thing. He tells the parable of the man who expelled a demon from himself. The demon wandered around, got homesick, and checked his old home. Finding it "empty, swept, and garnished," he moved in with seven of his friends "and the last state of that man was worse than the first." We are in that last state.

Was it necessary to get into that last state? Present scorn would hold it a singular perversity of Christendom that we ever got into this mess. The scorn is probably a good spiritual discipline, for we have, indeed, turned the Christ who promised the abundant life into the stern and joyless jailer of all things ordinarily human. But I hold two things: it was necessary to fix this control on our common life; it is necessary now, not to lift it up, but to transform it. It was, in short, necessary to imprison sexuality in order, finally, to liberate it into its true sacramental role.

I shall introduce my treatment of this claim with several assertions, all controversial, which, unhappily, cannot be fully demonstrated here:

1. There has never anywhere been a matriarchal society in the sense of women holding political power (as distinct from matrilineal and matrilocal societies).
2. There have been many societies whose spiritual, imaginative life was centered on the female rather than the male and so can be called spiritual matriarchies.
3. All the developed "high" civilizations have been strongly patriarchal both in government and the spiritual life, although there are great differences among them in the role of the feminine principle (as indicated by the role of female divinities).
4. All the developed "high" civilizations have been characterized by a significant degree of sexual repression, as symbolized by the postponement of marriage well beyond the onset of puberty.

These assertions are not beyond argument but I believe them to be accurate—and consequential.

They relate to a further observation. There is a large and growing literature on the differences between the sexes. The conclusion

seems, to a layman, to be that there are no discernible differences
along the traditional lines of distinction—rational *vs.* intuitive
thought, and the like. There are only two detectable differences: (1)
men are, on the average, larger and stronger; and (2) men are, on the
average, more aggressive. Small differences but enormously consequential. They suggest that, as long as society is organized around
the image of competition, in almost every case men are going to win.
If the desirable situation for women is defined according to the
model of men, as so many are pressing for, opportunities will be
made for a few aggressive, exploitative women and most will be
condemned to a sense of failure and self-hatred. But that is not the
only option history has provided.

The world of the spiritual matriarchies was dominated by the natural energies, not by the moral personality; by the forces of generation and fertility, not by persons who are generative and fertile. The
prehistoric figures of women are naked, obese, and pregnant—but
faceless. Woman was Woman, Mother, Earth, infinitely desirable,
infinitely terrible. The consequences in social custom and worship
struck the prophets as bizarre, comical, or wicked. From the point of
view of biblical religion they were just that. But the prophets were
great prophets and bad anthropologists. We may not like what we
learn about ourselves by studying Canaanite or Mesopotamian religion, but we do learn something we need to know. Baal and Astarte
are not superstitions of the past but dimensions of ourselves.

India possesses the finest statement of the matriarchal faith, the
cave temples dug into the earth, into the womb of the mother, so that
entry into them is a reentry into the body of the mother. In some of
them, the echo is such that chanted sound has no source but comes
from the whole temple, dissolving the separated self into the abiding
and undifferentiated unity.

Against this the patriarchal cultures worked their way out. The
cycle was changed into a line, the eternal return was changed into
pilgrimage, repetitiveness was changed into possibility. There is no
true personality in the matriarchal faith.

Thus, the dominance of patriarchy was a liberation into greater
possibility. Once the power of sex was brought under control, it was
possible to develop those parts of the personality that are not part of
the cycle of fecund sexuality.

Control of sexuality in a patriarchal society meant the control of
women, for women were "the sex," sex itself, the manifestation of
the natural forces, the embodiment. Women were feared, hence the
demonic images of the destroying female. Women were desired,
hence the images of the complaisant, accessible woman. Women are
still just as feared, just as desired. There is an unpleasant, evil, nasty

side to all this but feelings of revulsion are of little use in understanding the human. Those who feel morally superior to history are going to get trapped in the energies of history.

The power of women, of sexuality, was partly controlled, partly repressed and, as a consequence, the greater aggressiveness of the male was released and the whole principle of the masculine was explored and developed. History and culture became the prerogative of the male.

The possibility of personality was established for women as for men, even if that was not the intention; patriarchy was liberation for everyone, at least in principle, but all human achievements exhaust their own possibility. Patriarchy is no longer creative but destructive, and the record of that destruction is to be seen everywhere. Patriarchy is no longer liberating but imprisoning. Where it once liberated the self into greater possibility it has now become a different kind of imprisonment.

There are two errors of equal importance. One is the conviction that what has always been should always be, and that a stage on the human pilgrimage is a constitution for the eternal order of things. Patriarchy had work to do and the work was worth doing. But the work has been done. The second error is to refuse to accept the need for the work and the results of it because it is now finished. To go back is not to be free; the consequence of promiscuity has often been, not true liberation but simply to make the female more accessible to males at their decision and not hers. What is needed now is not to reject patriarchy as wrong or to attempt a revived matriarchy, but to do now for women what patriarchal culture has done for men.

The purpose of sex, in all its definitions, is not satisfaction or fulfillment but completion. It is well not to underrate the pleasures of sex, so vital to its being or the need for it as a fulfillment. It is well, also, not to be too solemn about matters which often need to be treated lightly in order to be truly serious. A natural good, like the song of birds and the taste of fresh fruit, is a dimension of humanity, and the pleasures of sex give a joy that does not need the solemnities of abstract thought. But a natural good for which we are grateful is not yet a sacrament. And finally what we need to know is how maleness and femaleness implant in us the image of God.

And to know, too, the gymnastic, sweaty, moaning struggle that is the genital interaction of the sexes. The model is not the hermaphrodite, for the hermaphrodite is not both sexes but no sex. If sex is a sacramental, it is so in its maleness and femaleness, in the fulfillment of maleness and femaleness, and in the passionate conjunction of the two.

All human institutions and all rituals that shape institutions are more than the things that comprise them. They are the units that are related in the working of the institutions and they *are the relations that relate the units.* All forms of the verb "to be" are exceedingly difficult, complex words, words which ought not to be used lightly. But I mean the "are." That is, the relations that hold together the units are as real as the units themselves. Until we know, truly, that reality is not exhausted in tangibility, we can make no progress in understanding matters such as these. The Christ paradigm is not a metaphor or an idea but reality. The real presence is real.

If we do not understand the sacrament as the means to a relation, a relation embodying the paradigm, we will use the sacrament as magic—which is the attempt to exploit the sacred for some private purpose. This tendency to magic and its emphasis on technique is merely enhanced by a technological society, and not created by it. Much "primitive" religion is precisely the development of an appropriate technique for controlling the power of the sacred. Modern technology may owe more to the religion of magic than it does to science. Certainly there is the same emphasis on knowledge as a thing which is the object of a search and which gives its possessor control over nature. Equally, sex is understood as a technique, as if happiness can be achieved by knowing how to stimulate various orifices and appendages of the body.

Yet identifying and avoiding the technological bias that obstructs a fruitful sexuality cannot, of itself, lead to a sense of sex as a *Christian* sacrament. The magical sensibility has to be respected, even in rejecting it, for it tells us something of major importance about ourselves and our world: things and acts *do* transmit the sacred power. We live in an iconic, sacramental world. The magical mentality fails only in thinking of the power as existing apart from the order of relation, in thinking of sacrality as a neutral and abstract power like electricity which, with indifference, will operate an electric chair or the incubator for a premature baby.

The sacraments and the sacramentals do transmit the sacred power. That power, turned loose, is as dangerous as electricity in the form of a broken high tension power line or of lightning. It is the function of ritual, emerging from the whole life of an institution, to provide the controlling shape (the transmission lines, if the analogy of electricity is retained) that prevents the power from being uncontrolled, from running loose; that directs the power to good and constructive ends. But the sacramental liturgy does a great deal more than the analogy suggests. It determines what religion the sacrament communicates.

Sacred power is not an impersonal force to be plugged into. It appears *only* in the forms of particular religions because a religion is the whole system of relations that shapes the world we live in. Thus a sacrament communicates *some* religion to us.

The new sexuality is a collection of all the old motifs of the religious role of sex. One of the most ancient of all these sacramental motifs is the desperate desire for unity, the obliteration of the self in the natural passions.

Paradoxically, sex also serves an opposite purpose, the enhancement of a completely separated and isolated individuality. It can do this in two ways; first by an affirmation of dualism, which turns the other person into an object of use for domination and exploitation; then by a hedonism that defines human purpose in terms of self-satisfaction.

Another of the ancient motifs—fertility—is powerfully present in our own consciousness by way of its denial, its frightened, passionate, deadly denial. The ancient sculptured figures suggest that fertility was the primary, and perhaps the only, consciously religious use of sex. Modern eroticism makes the anatomy of fertility an obsessive concern within the context of a denial of its function; abortion is extolled as a positive good rather than a tragic necessity, and homosexuality is called a valid mode of sexuality rather than a tragic maiming.

The language of sex could not function as it does—as curse, as magical incantation, as an incitement to passion—were the power of sex not so great as it actually is. These sacramental forces are present. They are neither to be ignored safely nor worshiped idolatrously. They can be sacraments of life or sacraments of death.

The church tried to control and repress the power of sex for centuries. But sex cannot be repressed or controlled by power, for it takes its deadly revenge in lives destroyed by neuroses, nations destroyed by sadistic power, whole aspects of human existence cut out of consciousness.

It is significant that the church could undertake to control sex only by denying the female element in its own life. But the female element will not be restored by the false use of sex. To bring sex wrongly into the public imagination of Christianity is to change Christianity into something else.

Only by the patriarchal enterprise could a great many things, including sex, be understood in ways that are inaccessible to matriarchy. But patriarchy is as partial and a great deal more deadly than matriarchy. We have learned what needed to be learned through the patriarchal enterprise. It is now necessary to learn something else before the idolatry of masculine power and authority kills us all.

To "learn," to "know," is the difficult word here, for the sense of knowing that is generally communicated by the word is characteristically "masculine" in that it is external, analytical, objective, aggressive, it is sought, secured, "conquered" by aggressiveness, all traits which have been assigned to men by culture.

This assignment is justified by the physiological fact that men are, by virtue of their hormonal structure, more aggressive on the average than women and, by this greater aggressiveness combined with greater average size, men will presumably remain the physically dominant sex. There are great uses to this circumstance; since aggressive power will continue to be a dimension of the human experience, there will always be a need for soldiers, police, and middle linebackers. There are great uses to it in the realm of knowing, but where war and police work are, for better or worse, definable as "masculine" activities, it does not follow that government is, and it certainly does not follow that knowing is. Much of what we already understand as knowing is already "feminine" in the same physiological-sociological sense: passive, receptive, engendering, nurturing. A great deal more of it needs to be, must be.

Yet it cannot "be" simply by adding the knowledge of the feminine to the knowledge of the masculine, still in the masculine mode of knowledge. The masculine mode of knowing may be the instrument by which we have learned to know this vital, central role of the feminine mode of knowing, but we will have defeated the very thing we have come to know as central if we think we know in the feminine mode simply because we have come to know that the feminine mode of knowing is centrally important. Whether enacted by men or women, the feminine mode of knowing must permeate and shape the structure of the imagination rather than functioning as another external tool.

Yet the primary task of the sacramentals is the shaping of the imagination or, reversed, a sacramental is precisely those things that shape the imagination and thus generate the true person. Therefore, the sacramentality of sex now becomes truly central.

It is always both temptation and event that Christianity has been used as a means to something else. To use Christianity in these ways, however good the cause, to accept or reject Christianity according to standards of use in good causes, is to make Christianity itself into a sacrament of another religion. It is necessary to take seriously the injunction "seek ye first the kingdom of God and his righteousness, and all these things shall be added unto you." There are things which are falsified when sought directly, but come true only when they are in relation to something else. "Liberation" is not a proper goal but it is a proper measure.

Thus, sex cannot be extolled as a Christian sacrament in itself but only as a part of the wholeness of Christian sacramentality. And yet that wholeness is not truly whole without the sacramentality of sex. This fateful paradox is now a major problem of Christian liturgics.

If the liturgy, if the sacraments, are defined by the construction of the person, the engendering of a living soul, we cannot avoid, finally, a sense of what a Christian is, what kind of person a Christian is.

The first thing needful is negative, for there are definitions of personality now widely accepted that cannot be permitted in Christian sacramentality. The leading example of this is the extravagant and fanatical individualism that denies all claims of others on the self, all restrictions of obligation and responsibility.

But, as John Wesley said, "The Bible knows nothing of solitary religion." The kingdom of God is the whole body of the faithful, living and dead. To be in Christ is to be in the body of Christ which is the whole body of the faithful. We are born of the flesh of others, sustained by that flesh and by the work of the bodies of others. We exist in the simplest sense only in the common work, and we grow and develop only by using the work of others. Extreme individualism is sustainable only in enmity; it is not accidental that those who advocate it do so normally with an extravagance, even a violence, of language.

In sexuality, such individualism leads to a kind of dualism which turns intercourse into mutual masturbation, or to a domination which makes sex an exploitation of one by the other.

To escape from this form of the dilemma, many are reverting to the most ancient mode of sexuality, which is the search for unity either by submergence of the self in the neutral passions or by the idolatry of undifferentiations—sex syllables that refer to the denial of difference or distinction, expressed theologically by the principle of the hermaphrodite god.

The denial of difference, the idolatry of difference, are equally distant from the Christian sense of the person, which is grounded in an absolute realism about the quality of human experience.

I am absolutely dependent on others, related to others. My very flesh came from others; my knowledge, my language came from others; my food, my work, my security are inextricably bound up in my relation to others. I work out my destiny in the tragic contradictions of this paradox.

Even in my sexuality I cannot escape the paradox. It is not so simple to say that as male I hunger for the female. That is, in itself, no more than dualism. Rather, the female is inescapably a part of my experience. Psychologically, this is described by the Jungians as the *animus* (the male in the female) and the *anima* (the female in the

male). Physiologically, it is found in the construction of the brain and
the hormonal system. Nevertheless, there is no way I can be female
or even, in any true sense, feminine. There are wide variations of
temperament and of need that are legitimate in personality. Society
does, indeed, cruelly lock people into far too restricted a definition
of roles, of expression of taste. But, whatever the range of variation,
there is an absolute and impassable gulf.

Whatever my longing for wholeness, to be a unity within myself, I
can never achieve it in myself. Only others, another, can do that for
me. As a man I am only partially human. That other part of me has
to be enacted by someone else.

The aim of Christian sexuality is not satisfaction but completeness.
Not knowing the principle of sexual completeness, our ecclesiastical
forefathers denied the use of the satisfaction. They were right to do
so because by doing so they protected the sense of the person as
more than sexual. But it was right, too, that millions of Christians
ignored the denial and enacted the ceremonial of sexual sacramentality in the joys of their beds.

It is, fortunately, not true that the Christian church lacks resources
for the development of an understanding of sexuality. It is, rather, a
matter of the kind of document to look for. Christian theologians are
of no use, since they subsume sexuality under ethics and mostly miss
the point. But Christian architecture is often a glorious essay in
sexuality.

While the theological theory and the power of ecclesiastical admin-
istration so often denied sexuality and, therefore, condemned the
feminine in all but a limited mode of its expression (the Virgin
Mother), Christian architects went right on building gloriously sexual buildings. In its wisdom, the Eastern church made wisdom feminine, and the great church of Hagia Sophia is a fulfillment of the
feminine beyond most other buildings. It would be hard to account
for the perennial appeal of Gothic architecture. It may be precisely
because of its triumphant sexuality, all masculine with its thrusting
phallic towers on the outside, framing the labial doors leading to the
enclosing womb of the interior.

Thus does the church affirm and embody, against past theory, the
principle that we can now articulate in the theory. By the enactments
of our sexuality we affirm our completeness, and by the affirmation,
more nearly achieve it. To affirm even the possibility of wholeness
or unity within myself is to make myself or claim for myself the right
and the possibility of being a god. As I humble my pride under the
burden of my limitations and seek my fulfillment in the other, I learn
a dimension of the Christ.

It is not sentimental that marriage is seen in the model of Christ and his church and that the model of Christ is understandable only on the model of marriage. The other is necessarily other than myself. I am never complete in myself but only with my wife, as we can never be completely walled off in ourselves but only as we jointly turn outward to the whole in an act which finds both its reality and its symbol in the family.

I have neither the wisdom, the right, nor the authority to judge or decide for others. Celibacy can be a high calling within the community, for it is true that the celibate can attend to important things without external distraction. Those who are unwilling celibates can be sustained within the wholeness of community and are not cut off from fruitfulness by the deprivations of their bodies. Childless marriages still are part of the corporate order, and limitation on the size of families is a psychological and sociological necessity.

The distortions of sexuality are more difficult. Human life is so complex, our problems so great, our resources so limited, and the accommodations we make so often bizarre, that we cannot judge the failures of our brothers and sisters. It is obviously true that being homosexual is not a bar to creativity. But it is not a valid mode or model of sexuality, for it affirms the incompleteness. I cannot affirm my wholeness except in the other who is truly other. It is probably true that any love is better than no love in a loveless world. But love is not a single, lone act isolated from other acts. It is part of a whole, the ordering of relation. It communicates a sense of the structure, of the forming of paradigms. The affirmation of the validity of homosexuality is based on the assumption, the unexamined assumption, that the character of any individual is automatically good and to be respected, that the desires of any person are automatically good and should be fulfilled.

This whole defense is a part of and a specification of a pervasive passion in modern life whose quality is perhaps best indicated by the mechanical impersonality of the language—"maximize self-actualization," "realize one's fullest potential." The goal of the person is here found inward and private. All this denies one of the fundamental truths of Christianity. The last thing a Christian has any business worrying about is "self-actualization" and the like, for that way lies the deadliest defeat. "He who finds his life will lose it, he who loses his life for my sake will find it." Fulfillment is found outside the self if it is to affect the self. But in sexual matters fulfillment is completeness, the coming together of differences.

Paralleling this self-centeredness that finds its fulfillment in the addition of like parts is the denial of difference or the denial that difference is important. It is not accidental, although very sad, that part of the women's liberation movement should make common cause with "gay" liberation. With different emphases and different purposes, each denies the use of difference or even, in any fundamental sense, its existence. Some even make use of Paul's statement "In Christ we are one," giving it a Hindu definition—completion by the combination of differences.

Many of these polemicists are neither particularly consistent nor particularly alert to the shapes of the imagination. They waver between the blurring of difference in the fertility cults and a kind of heresy that advocates a transcendence of the natural, a liberation from the natural. But the Gospel does not teach freedom from the natural; it teaches the fulfillment of the natural in its completeness; that is what the Incarnation is all about.

The hermaphrodite is not the proper model of the Christ; marriage is. It is not possible in Christianity to seek rightly the image of the hermaphrodite god despite the fact that the church in its representations of Christ has tried to do exactly that. Images are useful tools, not descriptions of reality, and the image of Christ that matters is marriage, for the true body of Christ is the faithful people, and the true Christ is the relation that exists among them.

It would be gross to say that only marriage completes the humanity of people. We are much too social beings for that, and the body of Christ draws its imagery from the reality of the whole order of our relations. But marriage is the norm for sexuality and the paradigm of our relation, for it is the best way to complete our incompletion. If the demons now loose among us should wreck it temporarily it would be restored, for it is a central relation of sexuality, not one among equal options.

In this is the reality of the sacramentality of sex. We are not whole persons and cannot be. Our sexuality is not only a paradigm of our completion but a paradigm of our humanity as well. Nowhere in our life are we so remorselessly taught our creaturehood, the earthiness of our origin. Nowhere are we so subject to the powers of nature, to the terrible passions of our flesh. The passions are temptations, not as an enemy attacking from the outside but as a dimension of ourselves, permeating dream and fantasy, compelling the intelligence to the servitude of rationalization. Nowhere is failure so abjectly humiliating or power so personal and destructive. Nowhere is pleasure so joyful, delight so satisfying. Nowhere are the possibilities so endless: for charity and forgiveness, for patience and understanding, for an infinite range of patterns of dominations and submissions, for exorcising evil by turning it into a game, for balancing ecstasy with the sweaty reality of the flesh, for power and gentleness, for giving and receiving, for glory and patience.

Once we have learned that we can be complete only in another, then we have learned how to be open to the infinite and sustaining web of relation. And then we learn that being human even in this common wholeness is incomplete, and we might then learn the openness that can be directed toward the source of all wholeness which, in his grace and mercy, can make us all whole.

Thus, the end is in the beginning; sex is a sacramental only if it is taken up into the whole sacramental life. Equally, the sacramental life need not any longer be repressive and, since the need is gone, the right to repression is gone as well; the sacramental life can be whole only if it includes sexuality in both its terror and its wonder, not with the technological sentimentality of the sensual fundamentalist. This requires the utmost care in the introduction of it into the words of the liturgy, into the liturgical forms that people can carry with them for enactment in the privacies of their own life.

Equally, care is required in the sexualizing of the liturgical celebrants. It should be evident that women must now be priests, not because it is just to do so but because it is necessary for the wholeness of the church's soul. The care is required to ensure that women are priests as women, not simply because being priests makes them equal to men. But, as women, it is essential that their priestly role not be confined to the ancient female images—the earth mother, the bearer of fertility, the carrier of the power of sensual passion—for that would tend to turn the church into a fertility cult. Rather they are priests as women in the fullness of their womanly personality which, indeed, includes those roles both physically and imaginatively but much more besides.

Thus conceived, a female priesthood would complete the wholeness of the priesthood and make it possible for men to be priests in the fullness of manhood, avoiding both the image of the androgyne and the image of the patriarchal father. If the image of the wholeness of the human is placed so centrally in the liturgy at the point of communication between the human and divine; if the priesthood is understood not as the image of divine authority but as the image of human relation offered to God in sacrifice, received, blessed, from God as sacrament; then the church will provide the paradigm in shape and sacramental action which can form the souls of communicants, whose responsibility is to enact the image in the complexities, the privacies, and the passions of their life together and thus give the full depth and image of incarnate humanity to transcendent purpose.

Because we are incomplete, we long for completion. The sacramen-

tal function of sex is to ensure that we know we are incomplete and
that we can never be complete in ourselves or in our likeness but
only in and with the other. Only as we know the other as truly other,
only as we love and sustain the otherness of the other can we know
the otherness of the earth and that to find my life in myself is to lose
it. Thus we can learn that the Christ is not mine nor in me, not yours
nor in you, but that the hope for the real presence of the Christ is
what takes place between us. Our sexuality is not all we are, nor is
the sexual relation the only relation between people. But it is model,
paradigm, symbol, and, in showing forth the nature of the Christ, it
is one of the true sacramentals to call the Christ to us.

Thus, as a sacrament communicating the Christ, re-calling the
Christ, sex (sex as gender, sex as intercourse) must be in union. It is
not in the fulfillment of the self or in the fulfillment of the other but
in the union of the self and the other.

We can now know that no human can stand or act as the image of
God or the image of the Christ. To identify that image with men or
with a man, or to use it to justify the monopoly of the priesthood by
men is blasphemous. But it is worse than blasphemous; it is danger-
ously foolish. We have not heretofore understood the structure of
ourselves well enough to anticipate that foolishness, but we do now
understand. The Christ is within us, in the midst of us, and the only
image of Christ now sacramental to us is neither male nor female nor
the denial of maleness and femaleness, but the true relation between
them. The actuality of sex compels us to look outside ourselves, and
sex becomes sacramental when it is the means to true completion.

Marriage, true marriage, is paradigm, symbol, and sacrament. Sexuality so defined can find proper liturgical statement in a complete
priesthood which would, itself, be symbol, instrument, and celebration.

chapter 22

THE SEXUALITY OF GOD

Urban T. Holmes

There is something which appears ludicrous in the very idea of the *sexuality* of God. It seems obvious that God is above sex, which only a crude anthropomorphic religion can fail to see. God is a spirit (Jn. 4:24). The sacred is everywhere and cannot be located in that body, which identifies and incarnates our sexuality. To be male is to have a penis, and to be female is to have a vagina. God has neither. Therefore, the divine is beyond sexuality.

At this time in the history of Western culture, when there is a growing discomfort and even protest in the face of the masculine names of God—Father, Husband, King, Lord—not to mention the masculine gender of pronouns referring to God, to say that God is not a sexual being has been found very helpful. The suggestion is that we must find ways of talking about the divine that overcome such identification. One by-product of the desexualization of God would be the removal of any justification for an exclusively male priesthood on the grounds that it represents a masculine God.

There are difficulties with this line of argument which may surprise some. For the moment, however, it is important to acknowledge the truth, in the assertion that God is not a sexual being. To reduce God to any finite, relative category such as sexuality is to make the sacred less than the infinite, absolute being we believe the divine to be. All images we use to describe God suffer from our own finite limitations. Anything we predicate of God—whenever we say: "God is . . ."—necessarily carries with it the contrary assertion that God is at the same time *not* this which we predicate. For example, if I say that God is good, at the same time I need to say that God is not reducible to the goodness you or I have known in this finite world in our own limited, relative existence. The sacred is far more than this.

It is possible and in some sense necessary, to approach theology from the viewpoint, then, of saying what God is *not*, which is called the *via negativa*, "the negative way." This is the only way we can avoid reducing the divine to our own limited categories.

The *via negativa* is particularly strong in a tradition of Christian spirituality which advocates the "forgetting" of the temporal world in which we live and moving into a mystical experience, which is beyond knowing itself. It seeks an immersion in the ineffability of God. The argument is that we live on the lovableness of the unknown lover. Man's empty quest is met across the abyss between creator and creature by the indescribable compassion of the divine. It is an approach which is found classically in the English church in the fourteenth-century anonymous treatise, *The Cloud of Unknowing*.

It is also true, on the other hand, that something cannot be loved unless we have some sort of prior knowledge of that which we love, no matter how little or formless.[1] If I say, for example, that I love my wife, if that statement is anything more than nonsense, it is necessary that I have some kind of particular referent that has meaning to me in mind. It may only be a feeling that I have in her presence, but feeling is a kind of knowing. Furthermore, if the presence of God is to have any moral significance, the object of our love must be even more clearly known. What follows from this is that the *via negativa* is fine, as long as we balance it to some degree with the *via positiva*, which means a positive predication about God which bears some relationship to the divine self. What that relationship is between predication (the word "good," for example) and the being of God has been argued—generally over the nature of analogy—since the thirteenth century.[2] The point I am making here is that at least within the Christian community we can make predications about God which have meaning, even if that meaning has less than a univocal relationship to the actual nature of God.

Once this is admitted we have reason to question the simple dismissal of the attribution of sexuality to God. Any positive predication of the nature of God involves embodiment or the incarnation of value into that which can be sensed and described. Ask yourself what goodness is and you answer with what you have seen or heard. You describe objects of your experience that point to a value called "goodness," which is what we attribute to God even while knowing that the sacred is infinitely more than this. Sexuality refers to a value, which we experience as embodied but which is not reducible to its embodiment—that is, male or female persons, either perceived separately or in relationship.

This is clearly evident in the common predication of personality to God. The Christian God is usually thought of as personal, even if we avoid thinking of the sacred as a person (which would appear to make God less than ultimate).[3] By this we mean that we enter into a relationship with the divine that has all the characteristics of an "I-thou" encounter.[4] I would argue, however, that we do not experience any personal relationships which are not sexual. In saying this I understand that this statement is easily misunderstood, since our tendency is to think of sexual relationships as either involving or intending genital contact. It is also true that this statement evokes the fear of a kind of anatomical tyranny that accompanies the sexual stereotyping of a given culture (for example, that women exist to be sexual playmates or housekeepers). My intention is to avoid either implication.

What I am saying is that there is no such thing as a *neuter* person. This is not just a trick of language, where we always refer to persons as "she" or "he." Every person possesses both a feminine and a masculine configuration, which belies any attempt to engage others in an asexual manner.[5] Whereas what we frequently describe as feminine and masculine are cultural stereotypes, there is a core meaning to femininity and masculinity that underlies any social conditioning of the human person and is an identifiable constant value in everyone. Since masculinity and femininity describe an essential structure which one encounters in oneself and in the world and which inevitably comes into play in interpersonal relationships, it is a very denial of that relationship to cast it into a neuter category.

It is entirely possible, however, that when a male person encounters another person, the feminine rather than the masculine configuration of self dominates that given relationship. This is certainly true for a male priest, for example, who does effective work as a hospital chaplain. The presence of a certain mode of sexuality in a given relationship is not determined, therefore, by the anatomical definition of that person's sex, although there is an expectation elicited in relationships by maleness or femaleness of masculinity or femininity, respectively.

It should not surprise us, therefore, that if we say *God is personal*, it also follows in the *via positiva* that God is sexual. In fact, Genesis said it long ago. "So God created man in his own image; in the image of God he created him; male and female he created them." (Gen. 1:27). Somehow the very sexuality of man relates to the icon ("image") or "name" (the term the medieval scholastics used for analogy or likeness) of God. The meaning of the experience of God is embodied or incarnated in the interpersonal meeting, which is an inevitable interplay of the feminine and masculine configurations of every self.

I would carry this a step further to make the point that the intrapersonal, as well as interpersonal, differentiation of the self into masculine and feminine is a primary issue in the unfolding of the person. In the evolutionary process, after the gift of life itself there is sexual or gender differentiation. To be is to be in relationship at the very heart of the self, which calls us into a sexual encounter. We cannot realize our being until we plumb the depths of the interpersonal, which demands that we render the very heart of ourselves vulnerable: our masculinity and femininity.

This is why the issue of sexuality is fundamental and why religion, which seeks to bring man to his ultimate resolution, is both threatened by and necessarily involved in the matter of sexuality. It is very risky because it requires us to be more than the structures of society wish us to be.[6] Christianity has struggled for most of its history to repress or withdraw from this issue, and the results can only be described as disastrous. Obligatory celibacy, the suppression of women, the identification of sexual passion with sin; these are cases in point where we have sought to avoid the most potent symbol of man's oneness with the creation and its creator.

I believe there is an identifiable movement now in Christian theology to recognize that not only must we not suppress or avoid the fundamental reality of human sexuality, but we need also to assert that in speaking of God as personal we must acknowledge the sexuality either implicit or explicit in that predication. Even the people who choose to evoke the *via negativa*, on the one hand, find themselves, on the other hand, incapable of simply speaking of God as "it," but necessarily referring to God as "him." The reader may have noticed that up to this point I have deliberately avoided any reference to God with a noun or pronoun necessarily implying gender. Aside from God, I have spoken of the "sacred" and the "divine." My feeling about this, aside from the awkward nature of the exercise, is that it has made God less personal and more a metaphysical abstraction. We need to acknowledge that the attribution of sexuality to God is necessary if the interrelationship between God and man is to carry the power of the "I-thou."

Having said this, however, the next step is to point out that sexuality in its wholeness is not the choice between the masculine or the feminine, but the affirmation and the interaction of both the feminine and masculine. They are of equal value. The whole person and the whole relationship between persons is only realized when the feminine and the masculine are both free in the developing self.

The feminine configuration of the human person is that manner of engaging life which emphasizes, among others, the communal, the intuitive, the creative, the aesthetic, the symbolic, the receptive, the mysterious. The masculine configuration of the human person is that manner of engaging life which emphasizes, among others, the individual, the logical, the structural, the practical, the signative or univocal, the assertive, the self-evident. We sometimes speak of the feminine as "thinking with the left hand" and the masculine as "thinking with the right hand."[7] It might help to remember that the sacred identified with the earth is more often than not feminine and the divine associated with the sky is masculine, which relates to the sense of the former as a source of fecundity and the latter as ruler.[8]

Whereas I think it has to be said that the female sex evokes in personal interaction a sense of the feminine and the male sex a sense of the masculine, it needs to be emphasized again—because it is so often lost in the heat of the argument—that *every person possesses both masculinity and femininity.* The individual who allowed herself or himself only to be one or the other would be insufferable. What we are describing in using the terms "masculine" and "feminine" are two intrinsically interrelated modes of being-in-the-world which are essential to the wholeness of self and community.

Therefore, if we are to think of God as sexual, we have to think of the divine as both feminine and masculine *if this symbolization of God is to convey a personal wholeness.* God becomes he/she. Otherwise the attribution of personality to God would be skewed or out of balance. A purely masculine God would be as intolerable as a purely masculine human, and the same could be said for the purely feminine. I think there is no doubt that the legitimate protest within liberation theology at the suppression of women by the church throughout our history is ultimately a rejection of the enormity of a hypermasculine God. To suggest that such a protest is merely a contemporary fad is to be blind to history. The whole sweep of civilization can be seen as a struggle over this issue.[9]

When we look about us at other world religions to see what they do with the predication of sexuality to God, the doctrine of nonduality or monism in Hinduism strikes our attention. There is a whole tradition there in which the nonduality of ultimate reality (*advaita*) is expressed in the union of the masculine and the feminine, which apart from one another bespeaks the nonreality of life (*maya*).[10] The purpose of life is to recover the oneness of everything; but that is not, as is sometimes presumed in the West, a simple absorption into an impersonal reality, but rather the realization of the coincidence of oppositions to the achievement of a higher synthesis: the sacred or divine, embodying both the feminine and the masculine, the true androgyne (God as symbolic he/she).[11]

In the Tantric tradition of Hinduism the mating of man and woman becomes, therefore, a "sacrament" of the oneness of reality. Obviously, this notion presents Hinduism and other religious traditions with all kinds of problems as it conjures up images of religious orgies and temple prostitution, which much of Christianity has handled by reducing coitus to subhuman behavior, regrettably necessary for the procreation of the race. My suggestion is that we need to retrace our thinking—certainly in a careful manner—concerning the sacramentality of coitus, and if we do we will find ourselves with a new appreciation of the Tantric tradition that affirms the androgynous nature of God.

As a matter of fact, as Professor Terrien argues in another essay in this volume, the excessively masculine predication of God is not universal in the Bible. Feminine characteristics creep into the description of the divine person (Hos. 11:1–4, Is. 1:2, Prov. 9:1–6). These recur from time to time in Christian thought, although they always play a very secondary role. God is almost a crypto-he/she. It is only now that we seem to be willing to face the issue squarely.

One way some scholars are struggling with the androgynous nature of God's personality is to attribute to the persons of the Trinity differing sexual identities. There is a resurgence of the notion that the Holy Spirit is "she," in spite of the explicit male function in the account of the virginal conception of Jesus (Lk. 1:34). Wisdom in the Scriptures, which is traditionally interpreted as a type of the Christian definition of the Holy Spirit, is feminine. The Spirit as feminine is then set over against the masculinity of the Father and the Son. Although I find no explicit statement of this, it seems possible that, as the Holy Spirit proceeds from the Father and, possibly, the Son— just as woman was taken from man (Genesis 2:22–24)—there is a danger of subordinationism of the Spirit in this concept. This would be particularly true were the attribution of femininity to the Holy Spirit present in a hypermasculine culture.[12]

I think that the effort to affirm the androgynous nature of God, as possessing both masculine and feminine configurations of the divine person, by identifying a person of the Trinity as feminine is not helpful. This is equally true of Carl Jung's identification of the feminine in God with the Blessed Virgin and his desire to "round out" the Godhead by making it a quaternity.[13] If for no other reason, it makes more of the fourth- and fifth-century notion of "person" than the Fathers of the Church ever intended. It leans heavily in the direction of polytheism.

This is important. In the development of the doctrine of the Trinity there was the growing understanding that God sees as one, but is seen by man as three. The being (*ousia*) of God is an indissoluble unity, but God is worshipped as three objects or expressions of that oneness. The term for these three in the Eastern church is "hypostases" (independent objects as viewed externally), and in the Western church "persons." The word person is what has gotten us into trouble, because for contemporary man "person" often means a discrete being, sometimes identified with consciousness. It has considerably expanded over the Greek *prosopon*, meaning "face," and its Latin translation, *persona*, meaning "mask." This means that the three in the Godhead exist in the thinnest possible relationship. If we accept the contemporary meaning of person, however, we end up with three distinct beings, internally independent, seeing as three.

In taking the concept of sexuality and dividing it among the persons of the Trinity, if we understand sexuality as this deep configuration of the self, we do two things which are erroneous.

In the first place, we make more of the nature of the three persons than the ecumenical councils intended. Sexuality is a basic component of personal intentionality: the structure of meaning with which we engage the world. If we separate the person sexually we divide the intentionality and consequently the action of God, which leads to polytheism. There is a single power, will, energy, and intentionality to the Godhead, which, if we take sexual symbol seriously, is violated by dividing the persons of the Trinity into male and female. I would emphasize, however, that this is quite different from discussing the function of the masculine and feminine symbols within the unity of the Godhead.

Second, the attempt to differentiate the sex of the persons of the Trinity isolates masculinity from femininity, and fails to recognize that one or the other only has meaning as it interacts *within* the self, as in Jesus. Every person is potentially androgynous, and to the extent that we are thinking of Jesus as the proleptic of the whole person and fulfilling the potentiality of every man, Jesus is androgynous. This is not, however, the same thing as discussing the sexuality of the second person of the Trinity.[14]

Of course, the argument that the Father and the Son are masculine has for its proponents the value of building a basis for the necessity of the exclusively male priesthood. The Orthodox scholar, Alexander Schmemann, has expressed this in a very succinct, if rather typically Eastern, manner. Speaking of the priest as conveying the priesthood of Christ, he writes:

If the bearer, the icon, and the fulfiller of that unique priesthood is *man* and not woman, it is because Christ is *man* and not woman.[15]

Schmemann shows little evidence in his discussion of an understanding of the difference between the physiological realities of
maleness and femaleness and the qualities of consciousness of masculinity and feminity; nor does he apparently grasp the essentially
androgynous nature of the person.

It seems altogether more appropriate, in pursuing the *via positiva*
and the sexual symbolization of the experience of God, to begin with
the unity of the Godhead and ask the question: How in the experience of God do we become aware of those fundamental and interrelated symbols of femininity and masculinity?

The answer to this question might begin with Paul Tillich's observation concerning the symbolic value of saying God is the ground of
being. "It points," he says, "to the mother-quality of giving birth,
carrying, and embracing, and, at the same time, of calling back, resist-
ing independence of the created, swallowing it."[16] God as the under-
girding mystery, the primal creativity of which some process theologians speak, is grasped in terms of the feminine symbol.

To carry this a step further: if we presume the persons of the
Trinity in their original fourth- and fifth-century form—objects as
seen by us, the external expressions of the unity of the Godhead—
then in some sense we can posit an interior *inter*personal life within
the Godhead. Traditionally this interpersonal life of the community
of the Godhead is called *perichoresis*. It means that the persons of
the Trinity reciprocate in every way with one another, or to put it
another way, exist eternally in each other. The three persons of the
Godhead co-inhere, therefore, while not being confused. Theirs is a
perfection of interaction and community as seen by us. It appears to
me that this notion of *perichoresis* has, just as the ground of being,
the symbolic power of the feminine. This means that when we engage God in the fullness of the divine being, without differentiation,
we encounter God as "she."

The doctrine of the three persons of God, however, also catches up
the experience of the sacred as perceived by us in different expressions or objects (*hypostaseis* is the Greek word, *personae* the Latin).
This is a differentiation of the Godhead, an assertion of the divine in
a more explicit and actively present form. This notion is a masculine
symbolization of God. What I am suggesting, therefore, is that to
speak of the persons of God, is to express the masculine symbolization of the divine, not in the sense of being male, but in the meaning
of the masculine configuration of the single being (*ousia*) of God.
(We should be careful not to impose our contemporary definitions of
"person," which gives God three "beings.")

Creation, redemption, and sanctification—three functions traditionally assigned to the Father, Son, and Holy Spirit, respectively—are purposeful actions in a masculine mode. Their assignment to the particular persons of the Trinity is an univocal act on man's part, even while we recognize that the single divine being, by virtue or *perichoresis*, shares in all three functions. This univocal definition is an attribution of masculinity to our perception of God. Therefore, it is utterly appropriate to refer to the particular persons of the God-head in all cases as "he."

What I am suggesting, therefore, is that in attributing sexuality to the personality of God in an androgynous form we are *symbolizing* in fact the mystery of the divine Trinity. God as he/she is God with one nature or being, possessing three persons or objects as seen by us. This being is not known apart from the persons, nor can persons be considered to possess anything but a single being.

It is not within the compass of this paper to discuss at length the explicit implications of this for liberation theology and its relation to women. Some should appear obvious. I might only note that if the task of the priesthood is to mediate the presence of God in any sense, it needs to embody both the feminine and the masculine. Further-more, that male and female physiology are related to such symboliza-tion, but not in some absolute sense. (A male can symbolize the feminine and a female the masculine, although the difficulty in do-ing this is not merely cultural.) Certainly, however, a willingness to acknowledge the androgynous symbolization of God does free us from making claims for the traditions of the church that run counter to some of the most compassionate movements of the contemporary Christian community, without lapsing into a sentimental or superfi-cial notion of the priesthood.

NOTES

1. Bernard J. F. Lonergan, S.J., *Method in Theology* (New York: Herder and Herder, 1972), pp. 277–278, says that the formula *nihil amatum nisi praecognitum* ("nothing may be loved unless it is foreknown") does not hold in the case of God. He is inclined to accept the approach of the author of *The Cloud of Unknowing* and speaks of the transcendence of lovableness. Per-haps he has too narrow a definition of "knowing."

2. I am referring to the dispute over the analogy of being. The issue is whether or not any predication of God has a univocal relationship to divine being. Paul Tillich, *Systematic Theology* (London: James Bisket & Co., 1957), vol. II, p. 132, speaks of the difference between the analogy of being, which argues for such a univocal knowing, and the analogy of imagination, which sums up the position that all predications of God are, at best, ways of speaking about God that may be helpful in that they point to God and invite

our participation in God. In this paper my discussion follows from the analogy of imagination.

3. In referring to God as "personal" and not as a "person," I want to avoid opening up the argument of this paper to the objections of Paul Tillich, *op. cit.*, p. 271, to the use of the term "person" to refer to God. At the same time, I do not necessarily imply that Tillich was correct.

4. This reference to "I-thou" is dependent, of course, upon the work of the great Jewish philosopher, Martin Buber, who opposed the intimate meeting described in this phrase to "I-it" and "I-you" encounters. His belief was that the transcendent became manifest in the midst of the "I-thou" encounter.

5. Two patterns of psychological research suggest themselves in this statement. One is to be found in the work of Carl Jung, the founder of analytical psychology, who speaks of the *animus* (masculine) and the *anima* (feminine) archetypes within the self, which contain elements that transcend our culture. C. G. Jung, *Two Essays on Analytical Psychology*, trans. by R. F. C. Hull, Bollinger Series XX (New York: Pantheon Books, 1953), pp. 186–209. The other is the research of Robert Ornstein, who describes the distinctive functions of the two hemispheres of the brain: the right hemisphere controlling the left side of the body and the feminine functions of the person, and the left hemisphere controlling the right side of the body and the masculine functions. Obviously this relates to man's entire evolutionary history and not just a given culture. Robert E. Ornstein, *The Psychology of Consciousness* (New York: Viking Press, 1972), pp. 50–72.

6. In generally accepted social theory, society is made up of a series of institutions (government, family, school, church, military, industry), in which persons are socialized into prescribed status sets and role sets. Robert K. Merton, *Social Theory and Social Structure* (rev. ed., New York: The Free Press, 1968), pp. 41–45. The persistent tendency is to reduce the self's understanding and action to patterns rendered predictable by the institution. Deviant behavior is frowned upon, if not repressed by various sanctions. The effect is to render the self one-dimensional or univocal in character. Contact with our sexuality in any depth opens the self to aspects of our inner life which have not been conditioned by the social structures, since institutional control of sexuality is notoriously superficial. Hence, the person in touch with this runs the risk of living out of a self-understanding that is not predictable in terms of the society as a whole. This is risky and threatening.

7. Jerome S. Bruner, *On Knowing: Essays for the Left Hand* (New York: Atheneum, 1971), first introduced me to this image.

8. Mircea Eliade, *Patterns in Comparative Religion*, trans. Rosemary Sheed (New York: World Publishing Company, 1963), pp. 240–242. Eliade describes the primeval pair, the sky and the earth. The earth is our mother and the sky is our father.

9. Herbert W. Richardson, *Nun, Witch, Playmate: The Americanization of Sex* (New York: Harper & Row, 1971), argues that the evolving self-consciousness of man is directly related to his understanding of himself as a sexual being. Whereas I think there are excesses in his book, Richardson's

thesis is sound and it puts to rest all the glib comments of some theologians who complain that liberation theology and its concern for a new examination of the relationship between male and female, masculinity and femininity, is simply the passing fancy of Western culture.

10. Benjamin Walker, *The Hindu World: An Encyclopedic Survey of Hinduism* (New York: Frederick A. Praeger, 1968), vol. II, pp. 390–393, offers a succinct discussion of "sex mysticism" in Hinduism. As he describes it, the Tantric tradition provides a sophisticated philosophical explanation of an intuitive insight common to many religious traditions. It should not be dismissed, for example, because this philosophy has been popularized to appeal to the prurient interests of the patrons of pornography.

11. The term "androgyne" (meaning "man-woman") is *not* synonymous with the word "hermaphrodite." It refers to the joining of the personality configurations of the masculine and feminine, not to the abnormal mixture of physiological characteristics of male and female.

12. The subordination of the Holy Spirit to the Son is traceable to Origen, who argued that all things come through the Logos, including the Holy Spirit. This subordinationism tends to reappear in subsequent centuries, particularly in the East, where the word *hypostasis* makes more of the objective independence of the three than the Latin *persona*. G. L. Prestige, *God in Patristic Thought* (London: SPCK, 1952), p. 251, says that subordinationism and polytheism are related. I think the effect of distributing sexual differentiation among the persons of the Trinity does lead to both subordinationism and polytheism. It is in Eastern Gnosticism of the late ancient world that femininity is attributed to the Holy Spirit. The tendency of Gnosticism for subordinationism and polytheism is well known.

13. C. G. Jung, The *Archetypes and the Collective Unconscious,* trans. R. F. C. Hull, Bollinger Series XX (2nd ed., Princeton University Press, 1969), pp. 107–110, 366–367.

14. Human nature is androgynous, and if the Christ is both human and divine in his human aspect he is androgynous, but in his divinity he partakes of whatever pertains to the second person of the Trinity.

15. Alexander Schmemann, "Concerning Women's Ordination," *St. Vladimir's Theological Quarterly,* XVII, 3 (1973), 242. The easy identification of the ministerial priesthood with Christ's has been called into question. For example, J. M. R. Tillard, O. P., "What Priesthood Has The Ministry?" *One in Christ,* IX (1973), 237–269.

16. Paul Tillich, *Systematic Theology* (Chicago: University of Chicago Press, 1963), vol. III, pp. 293–294.

contributors

RUTH TIFFANY BARNHOUSE, M.D., has been a practicing psychiatrist for twenty-three years. She has a Th.M. in Spiritual Direction from Weston Seminary and is a member of the psychiatry department of Harvard University. Her most recent articles have appeared in *Anglican Theological Review* and *Counseling and Values*.

ALAN BELL is the Senior Research Psychologist at the Institute for Sex Research at Indiana University. Since receiving his doctorate, he has been engaged in research on the subject of homosexuality.

ROBERT M. COOPER is Professor of Christian Ethics and Moral Theology at Nashotah House, Nashotah, Wisc. He is a frequent contributor to theological journals both here and abroad, and is also a poet of note.

JOHN W. DIXON, JR., lecturer and author, is Professor of Religion and Art in the School of Religion of the University of North Carolina at Chapel Hill. His articles have appeared in the *Anglican Theological Review* and other professional journals.

ROBERT S. ELLWOOD, JR., is Professor of Religion in the School of Religion of the University of Southern California. An Episcopal priest, he lectures and writes on current religious movements in America.

ROSEMARY HAUGHTON is a Roman Catholic theologian. She is the author of a number of books, including *Theology of Marriage, The Mystery of Sexuality*, and most recently, *The Drama of Salvation*.

URBAN T. HOLMES, III, is the Dean of the School of Theology at the University of the South. His most recent books include The *Future Shape of Ministry, To Speak of God*, and *Confirmation: The Celebration of Maturity in Christ*.

ELEANOR L. McLAUGHLIN is Associate Professor of Church History at Andover-Newton Theological School. She is Episcopal representative at the Faith and Order Commission of the National Council of

268

Churches, and Chairwoman of the Commission on Women and Ministry of the Diocese of Massachusetts.

W. WALTER MENNINGER, M.D., is Director of Residency Training at the Topeka State Hospital in Kansas and Adjunct Faculty Member in Advanced Pastoral Studies at the San Francisco Theological Seminary. He is also an instructor in Human Sexuality at the Menninger School of Psychiatry and the author of the nationally syndicated column, "Insights."

WILLIAM MUEHL, an Anglican layman, is trained as a lawyer and teaches homiletics at the Yale Divinity School. He has written a number of books on Christian social responsibility.

FRANK PATTON, JR., is a member of a New York City law firm. He has contributed articles to *Worldview* magazine and Christianity and Crisis.

NORMAN PITTENGER is on the divinity faculty of the University of Cambridge and is senior resident at King's College, Cambridge. He is the author of more than sixty books in the areas of theology and sexuality.

JOHN SNOW is Professor of Pastoral Theology at the Episcopal Divinity School in Cambridge, Mass. He is the author of *On Pilgrimage: Marriage in the 70s.*

CHARLES Socarides, M.D., is an Associate Clinical Professor of Psychiatry at the Albert Einstein College of Medicine in New York City and a Collaborating Psychoanalyst at The Columbia Institute. He has published over forty psychoanalytic papers and two books, *The Overt Homosexual* and *Beyond Sexual Freedom.*

ROBERT M. STEIN, M.D., is an Associate Professor at the University of Southern California. A graduate of the C. G. Jung Institute in Zurich, he has a private practice in Beverly Hills and is the author of *Incest and Human Love.*

SAMUEL TERRIEN, Professor of Hebrew and Cognate Languages at Union Theological Seminary in New York, is considered the Dean of Old Testament Theologians.

ANN BELFORD ULANOV is Professor of Psychiatry and Religion at Union Theological Seminary. She is a graduate of the C. G. Jung

Institute in Zurich and a member of the International Association of Analytical Psychologists.

ELSA P. WALBERG is Director of the Ecumenical Ministry to Older Persons, Inc. in Melrose, Mass. She was a schoolteacher for many years before being ordained to the diaconate in 1972.

PENELOPE WASHBOURN teaches at St. Johns College, the University of Manitoba, Canada.

DONALD F. WINSLOW is Professor of Historical Theology at the Episcopal Divinity School in Cambridge, Mass.

RAYMOND C. YERKES, M.D., a child psychiatrist, is consultant to the Greater Lawrence Mental Health Center in Lawrence, Mass.

ROBIN B. YERKES is on the staff of the Adolescent Unit at the Greater Lawrence Mental Health Center. She is engaged in therapeutic work with adolescents and their families.

bibliography

Bailey, Derrick Sherwin. *The Mystery of Love and Marriage: A Study in the Theology of the Sexual Relation* (London: SCM Press, 1952).

An invaluable book, which needs to be reprinted. There is no single study that duplicates this ground-breaking book. The author explains the meaning of "one flesh" in a way that speaks most effectively to our times.

Bailey, Derrick Sherwin. *Sexual Relation and Christian Thought* (New York: Harper & Row, 1959).

This book is a basic history of the evolving understanding of sexuality in two thousand years of Christian history. The story is honestly and dispassionately told.

Barnhouse, Ruth Tiffany. "An Examination of the Ordination of Women to the Priesthood in Terms of the Symbolism of the Eucharist" in *Anglican Theological Review* LVI (1974): 279–291.

This article relates the whole symbolic role of the priest in the Eucharistic setting to the feminine symbol. It is a companion piece to the article by Urban T. Holmes, III, listed below.

Barnhouse, Ruth Tiffany. "Sexism in Counseling: Some Theoretical Aspects" in *Counseling and Values* vol. 19, no. 3 (April, 1975).

This short article compares Freudian and Jungian approaches to woman, and also discusses some dangers in denying the differences between men and women.

de Castillejo, Irene Claremont. *Knowing Woman: A Feminine Psychology* (New York: Harper/Colophon, 1974).

This book is an excellent introduction for the general reader to the Jungian perspective on women (and therefore also men!). It is full of common sense, easy to read, and very worthwhile.

Dixon, John W., Jr. "The Erotics of Knowing" in *Anglican Theological Review* LVI (1974): 13–16; and "Paradigms of Sexuality" in *Anglican Theological Review* LVI (1974): 151–170.

This is an imaginative and insightful analysis of the role of sexuality in our whole consciousness of coming to being. It is excellent background reading for Dixon's article in this collection.

Edwards, O.C., Jr., and Holmes, Urban T., III. "Marriage and Mating: Creation, Society, and Jesus" in *Anglican Theological Review*, Supplementary Series II (1973): 4–27.

This article attempts to separate the issues of mating and human sexuality from related, but not necessarily congruent, questions of the socialization of children in the family. The author's belief is that if we do this there will be some clarity in much of the debate over sexual roles and their interaction.

Greeley, Andrew M. *Sexual Intimacy* (New York: Seabury Press, 1973).

An excellent book for the general reader by a priest who is also a sociologist. Contains an excellent refutation of the current trends in much secular literature to view sex purely from the behaviorist standpoint. His perspective is both human and Christian.

Holmes, Urban T., III. "The Feminine Priestly Symbol and the Meaning of God" in *St. Luke's Journal of Theology* XVII, no. 4 (September 1974): 3–22.

This is an analysis of the possible implications of the ordination of women to the priesthood based on symbolic action theory in anthropology. It is a companion piece with the co-editor's article, listed above.

Johnson, Robert. *He!* (King of Prussia, Pa.: Religious Publishing House, 1974).

Jungian in perspective, this little book is beautifully illustrated and describes well the special maturation problem involved in leaving boyhood and becoming a man. This is done in terms of the Parsifal legend. A good companion piece to de Castillejo's *Knowing Woman*.

Karlen, Arno. *Sexuality and Homosexuality* (New York: Norton, 1971).

Anyone wishing to be informed about this topic without having to submit to the rhetoric often resorted to by partisans of one opinion or another should read this book. Mr. Karlen spent several years with a team of research assistants ferreting out all that was known on this topic from the earliest times to the present. In addition to solid information about all aspects of it, there is also an excellent bibliography.

May, Rollo. *Love and Will* (New York: Norton, 1969).

This is perhaps the most important work of this outstanding American existential psychologist. Basically it is a phenomenological analysis of the role of Eros in the interpersonal lives of people.

Mead, Margaret. *Male and Female: A Study of Sexes in a Changing World* (New York: Morrow, 1949).

This classic study needs to be included in any bibliography that is concerned with sexuality and changing sex patterns.

Money, John and Patricia Tucker. *Sexual Signatures: On Being a Man or a Woman* (Boston: Little, Brown, 1975).

This is a popular work by a well-known biological analyst of gender identity. His approach is genetic and chemical.

"The Redbook Report: A Study of Female Sexuality" in *Redbook* Magazine (June, September, October 1975).

A year ago the editors of *Redbook* published a questionnaire competently designed by sociologists in which they invited women to report on their sexual life. To their astonishment 100,000 women replied, making this the largest sample ever taken on this issue. There are some surprising findings, most notably that women who describe themselves as strongly religious enjoy sex more than others.

Richardson, Herbert W. *Nun, Witch, Playmate: The Americanization of Sex* (New York: Harper & Row, 1971).

An unfortunate title and some loose generalizations have obscured what is basically an excellent introduction to the relationship between man's emerging self-consciousness and his understanding of his sexuality.

Sayers, Dorothy L. *Are Women Human?* (Grand Rapids, Michigan: Eerdmans, 1971).

Originally published in 1947, the two essays in this small book contain the best and wittiest arguments for the inclusion of women as first-class citizens, while also answering in advance the arguments of super-militant feminists.

Snow, John H. *On Pilgrimage: Marriage in the '70s* (New York: Seabury Press, 1971).

A balanced theological discussion of marriage as a continual process of renegotiation between persons seeking self-understanding and a creative life. It is neither conservative nor radical, but thoughtful.

Ulanov, Ann Belford. *The Feminine in Jungian Psychology and in Christian Theology* (Evanston: Northwestern University Press, 1971).

This book should be read by every Christian who is seriously interested in a creative transformation of the "battle of the sexes" into redeeming Christian action in the world. It is original and brilliant, well worth the effort to understand its complexity. The most difficult material is presented clearly, and as simply as possible. No one active in ministry can afford to miss this book.

(Additional suggestions for further reading will be found at the end of individual articles.)